Marzano Research Development Team

Director of Publications
Julia A. Simms

Production Editors
Katie Rogers
Laurel Hecker

Editorial Assistant/Staff Writer
Ming Lee Newcomb

Marzano Research Associates

Tina Boogren
Bev Clemens
Jane Doty Fischer
Jeff Flygare
Tammy Heflebower
Mitzi Hoback
Jan K. Hoegh
Russell Jenson
Jessica Kanold-McIntyre
David Livingston
Pam Livingston

Sonny Magaña
Margaret McInteer
Diane E. Paynter
Debra J. Pickering
Kristin Poage
Salle Quackenboss
Ainsley B. Rose
Tom Roy
Gerry Varty
Phil Warrick
Kenneth C. Williams

Visit **marzanoresearch.com/activitiesandgames**
to download reproducibles from this book.

Table of Contents

Italicized entries indicate reproducible forms.

About the Authors

 **Katie Rogers** is the production editor for Marzano Research in Denver, Colorado, where she writes and edits books and research reports. She has experience teaching at the middle school level, mentoring students at the college level, and writing in a variety of areas, including main-page copy for university websites, marketing materials, and a contribution to TEDxMileHigh. She holds a bachelor of arts degree in sociology from Colorado College, where she developed a strong interest in social theory and education research.

 **Julia A. Simms** is director of publications for Marzano Research in Denver, Colorado. She has worked in K–12 education as a classroom teacher, gifted education specialist, teacher leader, and coach, and her books include *Coaching Classroom Instruction, Using Common Core Standards to Enhance Classroom Instruction and Assessment, Vocabulary for the Common Core, Questioning Sequences in the Classroom*, and *A Handbook for High Reliability Schools*. She has led school- and district-level professional development on a variety of topics, including literacy instruction and intervention, classroom and schoolwide differentiation, and instructional technology. She received her bachelor's degree from Wheaton College in Wheaton, Illinois, and her master's degrees in educational administration and K–12 literacy from Colorado State University and the University of Northern Colorado, respectively.

About Marzano Research

Marzano Research is a joint venture between Solution Tree and Dr. Robert J. Marzano. Marzano Research combines Dr. Marzano's forty years of educational research with continuous action research in all major areas of schooling in order to provide effective and accessible instructional strategies, leadership strategies, and classroom assessment strategies that are always at the forefront of best practice. By providing such an all-inclusive research-into-practice resource center, Marzano Research provides teachers and principals with the tools they need to effect profound and immediate improvement in student achievement.

Foreword

In 1984, I attended an invitational conference at the Wingspread Conference Center in Racine, Wisconsin. The purpose of the gathering was to ask interested educators how to best contribute to the burgeoning interest in teaching thinking skills. Although many possibilities were suggested (and many came to fruition), six other educators and I were particularly involved in the development of a framework and curriculum designed to enhance students' thinking and reasoning skills.

The centerpiece of both our framework and the curriculum materials was argumentation. Skills such as observing, formulating questions, comparing, classifying, analyzing, identifying errors, inferring, and drawing conclusions formed the backbone of our work. Throughout the 1980s and 1990s we interacted with thousands of teachers and students in hundreds of schools, helping them to better understand the complex processes associated with argumentation and other thinking processes and skills.

One memory from this time is particularly powerful for me. While studying World War II, a teacher asked his students to make inferences regarding how the Nazis could have justified the killing of millions of Jewish people simply because of their race and ancestry. Students compiled a vast amount of information and observations: quotes from *Mein Kampf*, excerpts from letters, examples of Nazi propaganda, and so on. Observations and information covered the walls of the classroom. As the teacher guided his students through the process of classifying, comparing, analyzing, and examining their collected information, students generated a particularly powerful conclusion: the heart of prejudicial thinking is sound reasoning from untrue premises. This conclusion expressed what had happened in Nazi Germany during World War II so eloquently and so clearly that I have remembered it ever since.

This story was not an isolated incident. During the two decades I spent training teachers and leaders to implement direct instruction in thinking, reasoning, and argumentation skills, I was consistently astounded by the effects of this type of instruction on students. Free, critical, and creative thought is a bedrock of our society, and it made perfect sense to provide direct instruction in this kind of thinking in our schools. Unfortunately, as often happens in education, the thinking skills movement eventually waned as other topics and issues came to the forefront of research and policy. Such a powerful movement seemed to have been cut short before its time.

Not surprisingly, then, I was delighted to see the renewed emphasis on argumentation and thinking skills in the Common Core State Standards (CCSS). Throughout the college and career readiness, mathematical practice, and English language arts and mathematics content standards, students are asked to analyze arguments, present claims, construct support, explain relationships between argument elements, identify errors in reasoning, evaluate rhetoric, and so on. These foundational skills were powerful twenty years ago and are still powerful today.

With this renewed awareness of the importance of argumentation comes a need for teachers to seriously consider how best to teach and support argumentation in the classroom. Although various programs are rapidly becoming available, teachers who are already pressed for time may not be able to carve out the additional hours these types of curricula require. For this reason, I strongly support the authors' efforts in this book to provide clear, concise, concrete guidance to teachers about specific argumentation skills from the CCSS, how to teach them in concert with the content students are already required to learn, and how to reinforce them through fun, engaging activities and games.

Rogers and Simms have created an accessible, research-based resource that teachers can use on a daily basis in their classrooms. They've prepared everything teachers will need: a wealth of examples, items, templates, and other resources so that each skill is ready to teach and every game is ready to play. Busy teachers will appreciate the authors' attention to detail and their awareness of the bigger context of the classroom, the CCSS, and the unique needs and situations of teachers, students, and schools. I highly recommend this book to all K–12 educators and look forward to seeing educators take direct instruction in argumentation to new levels of implementation.

—Robert J. Marzano

Introduction

In 1644, John Milton presented a speech to the English parliament condemning government censorship. In it, he defended the right of citizens to argue with each other, asserting that people must argue in order to learn. "Where there is much desire to learn," he wrote, "there of necessity will be much arguing, much writing, many opinions; for opinion in good men is but knowledge in the making." Argument has always been central to learning and life in society. However, the 21st century has created opportunities for controversial discussion and debate in more places and in more ways than Milton probably could have ever imagined.

With the growth of the Internet, opportunities to engage in argumentation have increased considerably. Online forums, social networks, and the comment sections of news websites provide space for debate and discussion about a variety of topics (Anderson, Brossard, Scheufele, Xenos, & Ladwig, 2013; Gil de Zúñiga & Valenzuela, 2011; Mossberger, Tolbert, & McNeal, 2007; Papacharissi, 2004). Political discussions on the Internet attract participants who are often underrepresented in politics, such as people of color, women, and young adults (Correa & Jeong, 2010; McCaughey & Ayers, 2003; Mossberger et al., 2007). This finding is particularly salient when one considers the importance of discussion within the democratic process: when people discuss political issues, they are more likely to take political action in elections and other political events (Huckfeldt & Sprague, 1995; Shah, Cho, Eveland, & Kwak, 2005; Wyatt, Katz, & Kim, 2000).

Although online debate may encourage individuals to participate in argumentation, it does not inherently prepare them to do so effectively. Internet discussions are notorious for eliciting heated, irrational, and even uncivil interactions (Papacharissi, 2004; Shils, 1992). As is similarly the case in offline discussions, individuals sometimes interpret challenges to their online claims as personal attacks, which can lead them to react defensively or even lash out at others. The tendency of users to take online arguments personally has been repeatedly satirized on humor websites such as Cracked.com (2010; Christina H, 2012) and xkcd (2008a; 2008b). Some have speculated that the option to post anonymously does not hold users accountable for rudeness or insensitivity in their comments (Hlavach & Freivogel, 2011; Kling, Lee, Teich, & Frankel, 1999). In fact, the prevalence of offensive and irrational comments in online forums has prompted some websites—such as *Popular Science*—to close their comment sections entirely (LaBarre, 2013).

In addition to being unsavory, the sometimes hostile nature of online debate may have implications for the democratic process. Bill Reader (2012) pointed out that "with online forums, the gatekeeping has largely disappeared—anybody can post a comment in any manner and on any topic, often without any prescreening by editors" (p. 496). In some ways, the absence of "gatekeeping" can be good for democratic discussion. However, research suggests that online incivility can actually influence the way people think about issues. A study from the University of Wisconsin–Madison indicated that people's perceptions and opinions about the subject matter of an article became more ingrained after they read uncivil comments, even if they did not have much knowledge or an opinion about the topic beforehand (Anderson et al., 2013).

Furthermore, despite their apparent interest in online politics, eighteen- to twenty-nine-year-old citizens in the U.S. demonstrate "shockingly low levels of political knowledge and information" (Kaid, McKinney, & Tedesco, 2007, p. 1094). Results from the 2010 National Assessment of Educational Progress (NAEP) indicated that only one-quarter of high school seniors showed at least a proficient level of civics knowledge, even though many of them were old enough to vote (National Center for Education Statistics, 2010). Tony Wagner (2008), the Innovation Education Fellow at the Technology and Entrepreneurship Center at Harvard, put it this way:

> Students can always look up when the Battle of Gettysburg took place, or who General Sherman was, but they can't just Google the causes of the Civil War and make sense of what comes up on the screen. To understand such an issue, you have to know how to think critically, and you need a broader conceptual understanding of American history, economics, and more. (p. 263)

Fortunately, students do not need to rely on Internet message boards to learn to think critically, debate constructively, or become informed citizens. Teachers can help students develop argumentation skills through direct, comprehensive, and ongoing instruction in argumentation. Such instruction prepares students to meet the cognitive and interpersonal demands of life in a democratic society (such as the United States) and is a crucial requirement of the Common Core State Standards (CCSS; NGA & CCSSO, 2010a, 2010b, 2010c, 2010d).

Argumentation and Democratic Life

In the 1980s, education researcher Carole Hahn explored the relationship between classroom climate, controversial discussions, and the resulting political attitudes of students. In her study of adolescents in five different nations (England, Denmark, Germany, the Netherlands, and the United States), Hahn (1998) found that students who discussed controversial public policy issues in safe, open, and respectful environments were more likely to develop the skills needed for life in a democracy. Specifically, students who were encouraged to express opinions and explore alternate perspectives in school were more likely to:

◆ Expect political leaders to act in the best interests of their constituents

◆ Believe that citizens can affect or influence policy decisions

◆ Express interest and general awareness of politics and policy issues

◆ Have confidence in their own ability to influence decisions made in groups

◆ Intend to participate in politics in the future

Spencer Foundation Vice President Diana Hess (2011) has insisted that educators have a responsibility to prepare students for respectful, authentic discussions about public policy. "A democracy without controversial issues," she wrote, "is like an ocean without fish or a symphony without sound" (p. 69). Paula Cowan and

Henry Maitles (2012) agreed, adding that "there must be space in the classroom to discuss socially or politically sensitive issues, whether they be local issues relating to bullying, racism, homophobia and animal welfare, or such international events as the 2003 Iraq War, terrorism or globalization" (p. 5). Given the pervasiveness of controversy and debate in democratic life, it seems obvious that argumentation should be a central feature of 21st century schools.

However, some individuals have warned against the inclusion of controversial issues in the classroom, particularly among younger students (Norwood, 1943; Scruton, Ellis-Jones, & O'Keefe, 1985; Totten, 1999). Classroom discussions about controversial public issues are scarce (Hahn, 1991; Kahne, Rodriguez, Smith, & Thiede, 2000; Shaver, Davis, & Helburn, 1978), and controversial discussions of any kind rarely occur in social studies classrooms (Nystrand, Gamoran, & Carbonaro, 1998). This may be because some teachers feel uncomfortable or unprepared to facilitate them (Torney-Purta, Lehmann, Oswald, & Shulz, 2001). Hess (2011) pointed out:

> Many teachers want to create environments in which students feel safe, valued, and respected. Controversial issues, by their very nature, can create passionate responses. This passion often degenerates into silence, anger, disrespect, and name-calling—the very opposite of the interactions teachers hope to promote. . . . Faced with this choice, many opt for respect over passion and avoid heated discussions. But teachers don't have to make this choice. It *is* possible to talk about controversial issues in civil and productive ways so that students bring a healthy amount of passion to the classroom without treating one another harshly. (p. 70)

We agree that avoiding controversy in the classroom is not an effective way to prepare students for democratic life. Although avoiding disagreements may be easier in some cases, such practices fail to train students to participate effectively in society. Moreover, they neglect to equip students with the college and career readiness skills outlined in the CCSS.

Argumentation and the Common Core

Argumentation in the classroom has experienced a renewed emphasis with the advent of the CCSS, which defined *argument* as "a reasoned, logical way of demonstrating that the writer's position, belief, or conclusion is valid" (NGA & CCSSO, 2010b, p. 23). The CCSS "put particular emphasis on students' ability to write sound arguments on substantive topics and issues" (NGA & CCSSO, 2010b, p. 24) and cited a number of sources to support this emphasis (ACT, 2009; Graff, 2004; Milewski, Johnson, Glazer, & Kubota, 2005; Postman, 1997). To be college and career ready, the CCSS stated that students should be able to:

> Construct effective arguments and convey intricate or multifaceted information. . . . They comprehend as well as critique. . . . They work diligently to understand precisely what an author or speaker is saying, but they also question an author's or speaker's assumptions and premises and assess the veracity of claims and the soundness of reasoning. . . . Students cite specific evidence when offering an oral or written interpretation of a text. They use relevant evidence when supporting their own points in writing and speaking, making their reasoning clear to the reader or listener, and they constructively evaluate others' use of evidence. (NGA & CCSSO, 2010a, p. 7)

As with many standards statements, the one quoted here and others in the CCSS contain many different elements of knowledge and skill that students are expected to master. To identify specific argumentation skills that could be the subject of direct instruction and practice, we conducted an analysis of the CCSS.

In our analysis, we first identified those CCSS that relate to argumentation. In addition to the college and career readiness standards quoted previously, a number of English language arts (ELA) content standards and one standard for mathematical practice address argumentation. Second, we examined each standard to identify the components of argumentation within it. For example, in the previous quote (page 3) from the college and career readiness standards, students are expected to construct effective arguments, convey intricate or multifaceted information, comprehend arguments, critique arguments, understand precisely what an author or speaker is saying, question an author or speaker's assumptions, and so on. After identifying these components, we grouped them into thirteen overarching argumentation skills, each of which is robust enough to be the subject of direct instruction and student practice. These thirteen overarching skills are listed and described in table I.1.

Table I.1: Argumentation Skills From the CCSS

Distinguishing fact from opinion involves discriminating between statements that are observably true and statements that express personal beliefs.
Presenting and supporting claims involves generating an assertion and providing evidence to back it up.
Explaining the relationship between claims, grounds, and backing involves clarifying exactly how a piece of evidence supports a claim.
Organizing an argument involves arranging claims, grounds, and backing in a logical order.
Citing textual evidence involves using specific quotations or information from a text to support a claim.
Distinguishing a claim from alternate or opposing claims involves using precise language to refine the meaning of a claim or to make it more specific.
Making inductive inferences involves forming reasonable guesses based on observations and background knowledge.
Distinguishing connotation from denotation involves recognizing different implications or nuances among words with similar definitions (such as *aroma* and *stench*).
Evaluating persuasive rhetoric involves determining a writer or speaker's motive based on connotation, emphasis, tone, and figurative language, as well as judging whether these elements were used to mislead.
Identifying errors in reasoning involves analyzing a claim or evidence to decide whether it is logical.
Identifying insufficient or irrelevant evidence involves analyzing evidence to decide whether it adequately supports a claim.
Perspective taking involves recognizing the reasoning behind various (and sometimes conflicting) viewpoints on an issue.
Communicating responsibly involves taking the initiative to create and maintain a positive interaction through constructive words, actions, and behaviors.

Table I.2 (pages 5–13) shows the argumentation-related CCSS we identified and the overarching skill(s) associated with each standard.

Table I.2: Argumentation-Related Standards and Associated Overarching Skills

Grade	CCSS	Distinguishing fact from opinion	Presenting and supporting claims	Explaining the relationship between claims, grounds, and backing	Organizing an argument	Citing textual evidence	Distinguishing a claim from alternate or opposing claims	Making inductive inferences	Distinguishing connotation from denotation	Evaluating persuasive rhetoric	Identifying errors in reasoning	Identifying insufficient or irrelevant evidence	Perspective taking	Communicating responsibly
K	Use a combination of drawing, dictating, and writing to compose opinion pieces in which they tell a reader the topic or the name of the book they are writing about and state an opinion or preference about the topic or book. (W.K.1)	x	x											
	Participate in collaborative conversations with diverse partners about kindergarten topics and texts with peers and adults in small and larger groups. (SL.K.1)													x
	Construct viable arguments and critique the reasoning of others. (Practice. MP3)		x		x						x	x		
1	Write opinion pieces in which they introduce the topic or name the book they are writing about, state an opinion, supply a reason for the opinion, and provide some sense of closure. (W.1.1)	x	x											
	Participate in collaborative conversations with diverse partners about grade 1 topics and texts with peers and adults in small and larger groups. (SL.1.1)													x
	Construct viable arguments and critique the reasoning of others. (Practice. MP3)		x		x						x	x		
2	Write opinion pieces in which they introduce the topic or book they are writing about, state an opinion, supply reasons that support the opinion, use linking words (e.g., because, and, also) to connect opinion and reasons, and provide a concluding statement or section. (W.2.1)	x	x											
	Participate in collaborative conversations with diverse partners about grade 2 topics and texts with peers and adults in small and larger groups. (SL.2.1)													x
	Construct viable arguments and critique the reasoning of others. (Practice. MP3)		x		x						x	x		

Continued on next page →

Grade	CCSS	Distinguishing fact from opinion	Presenting and supporting claims	Explaining the relationship between claims, grounds, and backing	Organizing an argument	Citing textual evidence	Distinguishing a claim from alternate or opposing claims	Making inductive inferences	Distinguishing connotation from denotation	Evaluating persuasive rhetoric	Identifying errors in reasoning	Identifying insufficient or irrelevant evidence	Perspective taking	Communicating responsibly
3	Write opinion pieces on topics or texts, supporting a point of view with reasons.													
	a. Introduce the topic or text they are writing about, state an opinion, and create an organizational structure that lists reasons.	X	X		X									
	b. Provide reasons that support the opinion.													
	c. Use linking words and phrases (e.g., *because, therefore, since, for example*) to connect opinion and reasons.													
	d. Provide a concluding statement or section. (W.3.1)													
	Engage effectively in a range of collaborative discussions (one-on-one, in groups, and teacher-led) with diverse partners on grade 3 topics and texts, building on others' ideas and expressing their own clearly. (SL.3.1)												X	X
	Construct viable arguments and critique the reasoning of others. (Practice.MP3)										X	X		
4	Refer to details and examples in a text when explaining what the text says explicitly and when drawing inferences from the text. (RL.4.1, RI.4.1)					X		X						
	Write opinion pieces on topics or texts, supporting a point of view with reasons and information.													
	a. Introduce a topic or text clearly, state an opinion, and create an organizational structure in which related ideas are grouped to support the writer's purpose.	X	X		X									
	b. Provide reasons that are supported by facts and details.													
	c. Link opinion and reasons using words and phrases (e.g., *for instance, in order to, in addition*).													
	d. Provide a concluding statement or section related to the opinion presented. (W.4.1)													

Continued on next page →

Grade	CCSS	Distinguishing fact from opinion	Presenting and supporting claims	Explaining the relationship between claims, grounds, and backing	Organizing an argument	Citing textual evidence	Distinguishing a claim from alternate or opposing claims	Making inductive inferences	Distinguishing connotation from denotation	Evaluating persuasive rhetoric	Identifying errors in reasoning	Identifying insufficient or irrelevant evidence	Perspective taking	Communicating responsibly
4	Engage effectively in a range of collaborative discussions (one-on-one, in groups, and teacher-led) with diverse partners on grade 4 topics and texts, building on others' ideas and expressing their own clearly. (SL.4.1)												X	X
	Construct viable arguments and critique the reasoning of others. (Practice. MP3)		X		X						X	X		
5	Quote accurately from a text when explaining what the text says explicitly and when drawing inferences from the text. (RL.5.1, RI.5.1)					X		X						
	Write opinion pieces on topics or texts, supporting a point of view with reasons and information.	X												
	a. Introduce a topic or text clearly, state an opinion, and create an organizational structure in which ideas are logically grouped to support the writer's purpose.		X		X									
	b. Provide logically ordered reasons that are supported by facts and details.													
	c. Link opinion and reasons using words, phrases, and clauses (e.g., consequently, specifically).													
	d. Provide a concluding statement or section related to the opinion presented. (W.5.1)													
	Engage effectively in a range of collaborative discussions (one-on-one, in groups, and teacher-led) with diverse partners on grade 5 topics and texts, building on others' ideas and expressing their own clearly. (SL.5.1)												X	X
	Construct viable arguments and critique the reasoning of others. (Practice. MP3)		X		X						X	X		

Grade	CCSS	Distinguishing fact from opinion	Presenting and supporting claims	Explaining the relationship between claims, grounds, and backing	Organizing an argument	Citing textual evidence	Distinguishing a claim from alternate or opposing claims	Making inductive inferences	Distinguishing connotation from denotation	Evaluating persuasive rhetoric	Identifying errors in reasoning	Identifying insufficient or irrelevant evidence	Perspective taking	Communicating responsibly
6	Cite textual evidence to support analysis of what the text says explicitly as well as inferences drawn from the text. (RL.6.1, RI.6.1)	X				X		X						
	Write arguments to support claims with clear reasons and relevant evidence.		X	X	X							X		
	a. Introduce claim(s) and organize the reasons and evidence clearly.													
	b. Support claim(s) with clear reasons and relevant evidence, using credible sources and demonstrating an understanding of the topic or text.													
	c. Use words, phrases, and clauses to clarify the relationships among claim(s) and reasons.													
	d. Establish and maintain a formal style.													
	e. Provide a concluding statement or section that follows from the argument presented. (W.6.1)													
	Engage effectively in a range of collaborative discussions (one-on-one, in groups, and teacher-led) with diverse partners on grade 6 topics, texts, and issues, building on others' ideas and expressing their own clearly. (SL.6.1)												X	X
	Delineate a speaker's argument and specific claims, distinguishing claims that are supported by reasons and evidence from claims that are not. (SL.6.3)										X	X		
	Distinguish among the connotations (associations) of words with similar denotations (definitions) (e.g., *stingy, scrimping, economical, unwasteful, thrifty*). (L.6.5c)								X					
	Construct viable arguments and critique the reasoning of others. (Practice. MP3)		X		X						X	X		

Continued on next page →

Grade	CCSS	Distinguishing fact from opinion	Presenting and supporting claims	Explaining the relationship between claims, grounds, and backing	Organizing an argument	Citing textual evidence	Distinguishing a claim from alternate or opposing claims	Making inductive inferences	Distinguishing connotation from denotation	Evaluating persuasive rhetoric	Identifying errors in reasoning	Identifying insufficient or irrelevant evidence	Perspective taking	Communicating responsibly
7	Cite several pieces of textual evidence to support analysis of what the text says explicitly as well as inferences drawn from the text. (RL.7.1, RI.7.1)					X		X						
	Write arguments to support claims with clear reasons and relevant evidence.													
	a. Introduce claim(s), acknowledge alternate or opposing claims, and organize the reasons and evidence logically.	X	X											
	b. Support claim(s) with logical reasoning and relevant evidence, using accurate, credible sources and demonstrating an understanding of the topic or text.		X	X								X		
	c. Use words, phrases, and clauses to create cohesion and clarify the relationships among claim(s), reasons, and evidence.				X									
	d. Establish and maintain a formal style.													
	e. Provide a concluding statement or section that follows from and supports the argument presented. (W.7.1)													
	Engage effectively in a range of collaborative discussions (one-on-one, in groups, and teacher-led) with diverse partners on grade 7 topics, texts, and issues, building on others' ideas and expressing their own clearly. (SL.7.1)												X	X
	Delineate a speaker's argument and specific claims, evaluating the soundness of the reasoning and the relevance and sufficiency of the evidence. (SL.7.3)										X	X		
	Distinguish among the connotations (associations) of words with similar denotations (definitions) (e.g., *refined, respectful, polite, diplomatic, condescending*). (L.7.5c)								X					
	Construct viable arguments and critique the reasoning of others. (Practice. MP3)		X		X						X	X		

Grade	CCSS	Distinguishing fact from opinion	Presenting and supporting claims	Explaining the relationship between claims, grounds, and backing	Organizing an argument	Citing textual evidence	Distinguishing a claim from alternate or opposing claims	Making inductive inferences	Distinguishing connotation from denotation	Evaluating persuasive rhetoric	Identifying errors in reasoning	Identifying insufficient or irrelevant evidence	Perspective taking	Communicating responsibly
8	Cite the textual evidence that most strongly supports an analysis of what the text says explicitly as well as inferences drawn from the text. (RL.8.1, RI.8.1)					×		×						
	Write arguments to support claims with clear reasons and relevant evidence.	×	×	×	×		×					×		
	a. Introduce claim(s), acknowledge and distinguish the claim(s) from alternate or opposing claims, and organize the reasons and evidence logically.													
	b. Support claim(s) with logical reasoning and relevant evidence, using accurate, credible sources and demonstrating an understanding of the topic or text.													
	c. Use words, phrases, and clauses to create cohesion and clarify the relationships among claim(s), counterclaims, reasons, and evidence.													
	d. Establish and maintain a formal style.													
	e. Provide a concluding statement or section that follows from and supports the argument presented. (W.8.1)													
	Engage effectively in a range of collaborative discussions (one-on-one, in groups, and teacher-led) with diverse partners on grade 8 topics, texts, and issues, building on others' ideas and expressing their own clearly. (SL.8.1)												×	×
	Analyze the purpose of information presented in diverse media and formats (e.g., visually, quantitatively, orally) and evaluate the motives (e.g., social, commercial, political) behind its presentation. (SL.8.2)									×				
	Delineate a speaker's argument and specific claims, evaluating the soundness of the reasoning and relevance and sufficiency of the evidence and identifying when irrelevant evidence is introduced. (SL.8.3)										×	×		
	Distinguish among the connotations (associations) of words with similar denotations (definitions) (e.g., bullheaded, willful, firm, persistent, resolute). (L.8.5c)								×					
	Construct viable arguments and critique the reasoning of others. (Practice.MP3)		×		×						×	×		

Continued on next page →

Grade	CCSS	Distinguishing fact from opinion	Presenting and supporting claims	Explaining the relationship between claims, grounds, and backing	Organizing an argument	Citing textual evidence	Distinguishing a claim from alternate or opposing claims	Making inductive inferences	Distinguishing connotation from denotation	Evaluating persuasive rhetoric	Identifying errors in reasoning	Identifying insufficient or irrelevant evidence	Perspective taking	Communicating responsibly
9–10	Cite strong and thorough textual evidence to support analysis of what the text says explicitly as well as inferences drawn from the text. (RL.9-10.1, RI.9-10.1)					X		X						
	Write arguments to support claims in an analysis of substantive topics or texts, using valid reasoning and relevant and sufficient evidence.													
	a. Introduce precise claim(s), distinguish the claim(s) from alternate or opposing claims, and create an organization that establishes clear relationships among claim(s), counterclaims, reasons, and evidence.	X	X	X			X							
	b. Develop claim(s) and counterclaims fairly, supplying evidence for each while pointing out the strengths and limitations of both in a manner that anticipates the audience's knowledge level and concerns.											X		
	c. Use words, phrases, and clauses to link the major sections of the text, create cohesion, and clarify the relationships between claim(s) and reasons, between reasons and evidence, and between claim(s) and counterclaims.													
	d. Establish and maintain a formal style and objective tone while attending to the norms and conventions of the discipline in which they are writing.													
	e. Provide a concluding statement or section that follows from and supports the argument presented. (W.9-10.1)		X		X									
	Initiate and participate effectively in a range of collaborative discussions (one-on-one, in groups, and teacher-led) with diverse partners on grades 9–10 topics, texts, and issues, building on others' ideas and expressing their own clearly and persuasively. (SL.9-10.1)												X	X
	Evaluate a speaker's point of view, reasoning, and use of evidence and rhetoric, identifying any fallacious reasoning or exaggerated or distorted evidence. (SL.9-10.3)									X	X	X		
	Analyze nuances in the meaning of words with similar denotations. (L.9-10.5b)								X					
	Construct viable arguments and critique the reasoning of others. (Practice. MP3)										X	X		

Grade	CCSS	Distinguishing fact from opinion	Presenting and supporting claims	Explaining the relationship between claims, grounds, and backing	Organizing an argument	Citing textual evidence	Distinguishing a claim from alternate or opposing claims	Making inductive inferences	Distinguishing connotation from denotation	Evaluating persuasive rhetoric	Identifying errors in reasoning	Identifying insufficient or irrelevant evidence	Perspective taking	Communicating responsibly
11–12	Cite strong and thorough textual evidence to support analysis of what the text says explicitly as well as inferences drawn from the text, including determining where the text leaves matters uncertain. (RL.11–12.1, RI.11–12.1)					×		×						
	Write arguments to support claims in an analysis of substantive topics or texts, using valid reasoning and relevant and sufficient evidence. a. Introduce precise, knowledgeable claim(s), establish the significance of the claim(s), distinguish the claim(s) from alternate or opposing claims, and create an organization that logically sequences claim(s), counterclaims, reasons, and evidence. b. Develop claim(s) and counterclaims fairly and thoroughly, supplying the most relevant evidence for each while pointing out the strengths and limitations of both in a manner that anticipates the audience's knowledge level, concerns, values, and possible biases. c. Use words, phrases, and clauses as well as varied syntax to link the major sections of the text, create cohesion, and clarify the relationships between claim(s) and reasons, between reasons and evidence, and between claim(s) and counterclaims. d. Establish and maintain a formal style and objective tone while attending to the norms and conventions of the discipline in which they are writing. e. Provide a concluding statement or section that follows from and supports the argument presented. (W.11–12.1)	×	×	×	×		×					×		

Grade	CCSS	Distinguishing fact from opinion	Presenting and supporting claims	Explaining the relationship between claims, grounds, and backing	Organizing an argument	Citing textual evidence	Distinguishing a claim from alternate or opposing claims	Making inductive inferences	Distinguishing connotation from denotation	Evaluating persuasive rhetoric	Identifying errors in reasoning	Identifying insufficient or irrelevant evidence	Perspective taking	Communicating responsibly
11-12	Initiate and participate effectively in a range of collaborative discussions (one-on-one, in groups, and teacher-led) with diverse partners on grades 11-12 topics, texts, and issues, building on others' ideas and expressing their own clearly and persuasively. (SL.11-12.1)												X	X
	Evaluate a speaker's point of view, reasoning, and use of evidence and rhetoric, assessing the stance, premises, links among ideas, word choice, points of emphasis, and tone used. (SL.11-12.3)									X	X	X		
	Analyze nuances in the meaning of words with similar denotations. (L.11-12.5b)								X					
	Construct viable arguments and critique the reasoning of others. (Practice. MP3)		X		X						X	X		

In table I.2 (page 5), we use the dot notation system to identify standards from the CCSS. In ELA, dot notation indicates a standard using letters for its strand (Reading Literary Text [RL], Reading Informational Text [RI], Writing [W], Speaking and Listening [SL], or Language [L]), a number for its grade level (K–12), and a number for the specific standard to which it refers. For example, consider the notation *W.3.1*. The letter *W* indicates Writing, the number *3* indicates grade 3, and the number *1* indicates the first standard in the strand. Therefore, the notation refers to the first standard in the third-grade Writing strand. The mathematical practice standard related to argumentation referenced in table I.2 is denoted by *Practice.MP3* (that is, the third standard for mathematical practice). Since the college and career readiness standards are not grade specific, they are not included in table I.2, although they were included in our analysis.

As illustrated by table I.2, the concept of argumentation spirals and builds through grades K–12. Some standards involve only one skill while others involve several. Furthermore, the skills associated with each standard develop from grade to grade, becoming more complex as students advance. For example, the skill of presenting and supporting claims looks different at each grade level. Kindergartners are expected to present opinions without any evidence, whereas first graders must give reasons—basic evidence—to support their claims. By third grade, students are expected to organize claims and evidence using linking words and phrases such as *because* or *for example*.

While we acknowledge that the process of identifying overarching argumentation skills is not an exact science, we strove to identify those argumentation skills from the CCSS that could be directly taught to students and practiced through games and activities in the classroom. This book presents strategies for teaching each argumentation skill and includes games that teachers can use to reinforce and help students practice each skill.

Direct Instruction in Argumentation

As shown previously, each of the skills in table I.1 (page 4) come directly from the CCSS, and teachers can use the games in this book to help students practice those skills. Note, however, that the games are designed for practicing argumentation skills. Before playing a game, students will need direct instruction in the skills associated with that game. Table I.3 (page 15) shows the argumentation skills associated with each game. Here, we provide guidelines and suggest instructional activities for teachers to use to teach each of the thirteen overarching argumentation skills.

Distinguishing Fact From Opinion

To understand the basic concept of an argument, students have to tell the difference between facts, which are statements that can be verified, and opinions, which express personal beliefs and may be accompanied by reasons for those beliefs. Teachers can use the following process to teach students to distinguish fact from opinion:

1. Explain what facts are.

2. Explain what opinions are.

3. Give examples of facts, opinions, and statements that do not clearly fall into either category.

This process is based on strategies described by Robert Marzano and Debra Pickering (1997). Here, we briefly describe each step of the process.

Table I.3: Argumentation Skills Associated With Games

Game	Grades	Distinguishing fact from opinion	Presenting and supporting claims	Explaining the relationship between claims, grounds, and backing	Organizing an argument	Citing textual evidence	Distinguishing a claim from alternate or opposing claims	Making inductive inferences	Distinguishing connotation from denotation	Evaluating persuasive rhetoric	Identifying errors in reasoning	Identifying insufficient or irrelevant evidence	Perspective taking	Communicating responsibly
I Think, I Like, I Believe	Lower elementary	X	X										X	
Opinion Scoot	Middle elementary		X		X									
Fishing for Facts	Upper elementary	X												
Argument Relay	Upper elementary, middle school, and high school		X		X						X			
Rapid Fire	Upper elementary, middle school, and high school	X	X	X									X	
Which One Doesn't Belong?	Upper elementary, middle school, and high school			X					X	X	X	X		
Text Evidence Bingo	Upper elementary, middle school, and high school		X	X		X		X						
Rhetoric Memory	Middle school and high school								X	X			X	
Claim Capers	Middle school and high school		X	X		X		X						
Convince the Crowd	High school		X	X	X		X		X	X	X	X	X	X

Explain Facts

As stated previously, a fact is a statement that can be verified. For example, the statement "December is generally colder than August in the United States" is a fact. It can be confirmed or disproved by checking data on temperatures in the United States during each month. When teaching students about facts, explain that a fact is a statement that is verifiable and can be confirmed. If a fact is disproven, it is no longer a fact, but an incorrect statement. Emphasize that not all statements can be classified as either facts or opinions. For example, "Barack Obama was born in Kenya" is not a fact or an opinion because it can be disproven. Since there is evidence—a birth certificate specifying that he was born in Hawaii—to invalidate it, the statement is not a fact or opinion, but a false or incorrect statement. Finally, students need to understand what facts are and be able to confirm or disprove them so they can use facts to support their opinions.

Explain Opinions

Opinions are statements with which others may agree or disagree. They cannot be verified, but they can be supported with evidence. For example, the statement "Ronald Reagan was the best president" is an opinion. There are two points to emphasize when teaching students about opinions. First, opinions are often (although not always) accompanied by support or evidence; the person expressing an opinion can usually explain why he or she holds that opinion or belief. Second, statements do not always fit neatly into one category (opinion) or another (fact). Instead, they fall along a continuum, with facts that can be empirically verified at one end (for example, "Eight convicted felons were executed last year") and statements that are pure opinion at the other (for example, "Capital punishment is wrong"). If students are having trouble classifying a statement as fact or opinion, it is likely because it is close to the middle of the continuum (for example, "Capital punishment deters crime").

Give Examples

After teaching students the difference between facts and opinions, give them clear examples of each and discuss why they are facts or opinions. We present several examples of each in table I.4.

Table I.4: Examples of Fact and Opinion

Term	Definition	Examples
Fact	A statement that can be verified and confirmed	Colorado became the thirty-eighth state in the United States on August 1, 1876.
		At sea level on Earth, water boils at 212 degrees Fahrenheit.
		Abraham Lincoln delivered the Gettysburg Address on Thursday, November 19, 1863.
		In 2013, the film *Argo* won the Academy Award for Best Picture.
Opinion	A statement with which others may agree or disagree	Colorado is the best place to live in the United States.
		Hot water is never pleasant to drink.
		Abraham Lincoln was the most eloquent of all the U.S. presidents.
		Argo did not deserve the 2013 Academy Award for Best Picture.

To reinforce the idea that facts and opinions fall along a continuum—with pure facts at one end, pure opinions at the other, and some statements in between—also give students examples of statements that fall closer to the middle of the continuum. Students will likely find these statements more difficult to classify as facts or opinions. Examples of such statements include:

◆ There is intelligent life elsewhere in the universe.

◆ I think it's going to rain this afternoon.

◆ Increased taxation stifles economic growth.

After presenting a number of examples of facts, opinions, and statements that fall in between, ask students to make statements or find them in the media. Discuss as a class where each statement falls on the continuum from fact to opinion or whether it belongs on the continuum at all.

Presenting and Supporting Claims

Presenting and supporting claims involves stating opinions and providing evidence to support them. To teach students how to present and support claims, we recommend the following process:

1. Present an example claim to students and model how to support it with evidence.

2. Explain the concepts of claims, grounds, backing, and qualifiers to students.

3. Explain that certain words and phrases can signal different parts of an argument.

This process is based on a number of sources (Marzano & Heflebower, 2012; Marzano & Pickering, 1997). The following sections describe each step of the process in detail.

Present and Support an Example Claim

Introduce the idea of presenting and supporting claims by modeling it for students. State a claim about an issue that will be of interest to students (for example, "Students should attend school year-round"). Explain that you are going to try to convince them to agree with your claim. Ask them to notice the strategies that you use to persuade them. Then present evidence for your claim. For example, you might say, "Students should attend school year-round because they often forget what they learned in school over the summer. A 2007 study by three researchers named Alexander, Entwisle, and Olson found that during the school year, the academic growth of low-income students was comparable to that of other students but during the summer, low-income students forgot more information than other students. It's true that year-round schooling may not be the only solution to this problem of forgetting information, but it would prevent achievement gaps that are created by summer breaks."

After presenting a claim and support for it, ask students to explain the strategies they observed you using. You can prompt them to notice specific parts of your argument using the following questions:

◆ What opinion was I trying to persuade you to agree with?

◆ What reason did I give you to agree with me?

◆ What evidence did I give to support that reason?

◆ Which potential objection did I address?

The first question is designed to help students identify the claim, the second prompts them to identify grounds for the claim, the third highlights backing, and the fourth concerns qualifiers. Once students have answered questions like these, you can introduce the formal terms for each part of an argument.

Explain Claims, Grounds, Backing, and Qualifiers

Robert Marzano and Tammy Heflebower (2012) described four elements of an effective argument, which are based on Stephen Toulmin's (2003) model of argumentation: claim, grounds, backing, and qualifiers. Table I.5 describes and exemplifies each element.

Table I.5: Four Elements of an Argument

Element	Definition	Example
Claim	A new idea or opinion. A claim may simply present information or suggest that certain action is needed.	Students should attend school year-round.
Grounds	The initial evidence—or reasoning—for a claim. Grounds are answers to the question, "Why do you think your claim is true?"	Over the summer, students forget what they learned in school.
Backing	Information or facts about grounds that help establish their validity. In some cases, backing is simply a more in-depth discussion of the grounds.	Alexander, Entwisle, and Olson (2007) found that during the school year, the academic growth of low-income students was comparable to that of other students. They reported that gaps in achievement actually occurred over the summer.
Qualifiers	Exceptions to claims that indicate the degree of certainty for the claim.	Year-round schooling may not be the only solution to this opportunity deficit for low-income students.

As shown in table I.5, an effective argument usually presents a claim and provides support in the form of grounds, backing, and qualifiers.

Teachers can explain each element in more depth. For claims, point out that there are different types of claims: value claims assert that something is good, bad, right, or wrong, and action claims assert that something should or should not be done. There are also different types of backing: expert opinion, research results, and factual information. The type of backing that students use in their own arguments and encounter in others' arguments will vary, as different grounds call for different types of backing. Table I.6 defines and exemplifies each of these types of backing.

Signal Words and Phrases

Signal words (such as describing words or transition words) can help students identify each element of an argument. For example, the words *because* and *reason* often signal grounds. Phrases such as *according to*, *reported in*, and *found by* frequently indicate backing. Concession words and phrases like *despite*, *although*, *granted that*, and *in spite of* usually precede qualifiers. Table I.7 lists signal words and phrases for each element of an argument.

Table I.6: Different Types of Backing

Type of Backing	Definition	Examples
Expert Opinion	A statement made by an individual who is recognized as an expert in his or her field.	Someone with a doctorate in climatology and years of field-research experience offers an opinion on the severity of global warming. An experienced and successful director of Broadway plays offers an opinion on the quality of an acting performance. An official at the U.S. Federal Reserve offers an opinion on the state of the economy.
Research Results	Data collected through methodical investigation or through scientific experiments that are designed to test a hypothesis. Conclusions based on research results are not as unanimous and definitive as facts, but they come closer as more studies yield the same findings.	The U.S. Census Bureau reports working women's full-time earnings to be 75.7 percent of working men's earnings (DeNavas-Walt, Proctor, & Smith, 2012). The use of academic games in the classroom is associated with a gain of 20 percentile points in student achievement (Haystead & Marzano, 2009). About 20 percent of youth in grades 9–12 report being bullied at school (National Center for Injury Prevention and Control, 2012).
Factual Information	Information that has evidential support and is generally acknowledged to be proven or true.	The state flower of Montana is the bitterroot. The American Civil War began in 1861 and ended in 1865. Ladybugs help plants by eating pests such as aphids.

Source: Adapted from Marzano & Heflebower, 2012.

Table I.7: Signal Words and Phrases for Argument Elements

Element	Signal Words and Phrases
Claim	Describing words (such as *awful, amazing, beautiful, disgusting, miserable,* and *favorite*), modal verbs (such as *should, must,* and *ought to*), and superlatives (such as *best, worst, most,* and *smartest*)
Grounds	Cause and effect words (such as *because, as a result, due to, since,* and *for that reason*) and temporal transition words (such as *first, next,* and *finally*)
Backing	Illustrating transition words (such as *for example, for instance, to explain, to elaborate, specifically, in particular, such as, according to, as reported in,* and *as found by*)
Qualifiers	Concession words (such as *even if, despite the fact, albeit, admitting, granting, although, at any rate, at least, still, even though, granted that, while it may be true, in spite of, of course, just because . . . doesn't mean, necessarily,* and *whereas*)

Signal words and phrases can also alert students to the various types of backing being used to support grounds and claims. Table I.8 (page 20) lists the different types of backing and the signal words and phrases usually associated with each type.

Table I.8: Words and Phrases That Signal Different Types of Backing

	Signal Words and Phrases
Expert Opinion	*According to, as* [so-and-so] *stated, in keeping with, expert, endorsed, believed, recommended, accomplished, foremost, leading, master, pre-eminent*
Research Results	*As reported in, studies show, according to, data, findings, found, percent, percentile, average number of, reports, statistics, participants*
Factual Information	*True, certain, absolute, objective, proven, unquestionable, infallible,* and any form of the verb *to be* (including *is, was, are,* and *were*)

Note that certain signal words and phrases overlap. For example, the phrase *according to* is listed as a signal phrase for both expert opinion and research results. As with all signal words and phrases, those associated with each element of an argument and with the various types of backing should be evaluated in context. To illustrate, a statement that contains the modal verb *should* is likely to be an action claim (as in "Kids should be allowed to stay up past 9 p.m."), but there are also instances when it simply indicates a question (as in "Should we go outside?"). Students should use signal words and phrases as clues to alert them to the various elements of an argument and the various types of backing.

Explaining the Relationship Between Claims, Grounds, and Backing

Explaining the relationship between claims, grounds, and backing involves explicitly stating how each piece of evidence presented supports the original claim. It forces students to think more deeply about the relationships between the various elements of an argument. To help students learn this skill, teachers can:

1. Ask students to make a claim and provide grounds, backing, and qualifiers for it.

2. Ask students to explain relationships within their own claim.

3. Ask students to explain relationships in other claims.

Here, we provide detail about each step of the process.

Make a Claim

To understand the relationship between claims, grounds, and backing, students first need to make a claim and provide grounds, backing, and qualifiers for it. You might ask individual students to each design a claim with grounds, backing, and qualifiers, or students could collaborate in small groups to design group claims and support. For example, a group of students might claim that people should not smoke. As grounds for the claim, they say, "Because many medical organizations have found that smoking causes lung cancer." Their backing might include research results and expert opinions from the American Association for Cancer Research, the American Lung Association, the National Cancer Institute, and the U.S. Department of Health and Human Services illustrating that smoking causes lung cancer. They might qualify their argument by saying that there are cases of lung cancer that are not caused by smoking.

Explain Relationships Within Their Own Claim

To explain the relationship between claims, grounds, and backing, students should clearly articulate how their backing supports their claim. To do this, students must make explicit relationships that might be implicit.

For example, the small group that claimed people should not smoke because smoking causes lung cancer (grounds and backing) might explain that getting lung cancer is undesirable. Their grounds and backing provide support for the idea that smoking causes lung cancer, but the premise or general rule that links their evidence to their claim is that no one wants lung cancer. Explicitly stating the connection between a claim, grounds, and backing simply involves connecting the backing back to the original claim. It can be useful to think of this process in a circular fashion, as depicted in figure I.1.

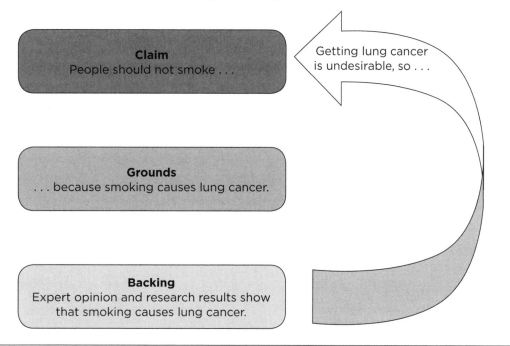

Figure I.1: Explicitly stating the connection between a claim, grounds, and backing involves connecting the backing back to the original claim.

Of course, this particular connection—that lung cancer is undesirable—is rather self-evident. Sometimes people automatically connect evidence to a claim without consciously acknowledging or explaining the general rule. However, giving students practice in explaining simple relationships between claims, grounds, and backing in familiar arguments helps prepare them to explain more complex relationships in other arguments.

When students explain the connection between claims, grounds, and backing, it helps them understand that claims are not always the first step in an argument. Often, claims are the result of evidence, or information that leads someone to a conclusion. For example, if you notice that five crimes were committed within two blocks of one another, it might lead you to claim that a particular neighborhood is unsafe. As grounds, you might say, "Because a high number of crimes are committed there." Backing might include statistics about the average number of crimes per block in the city that year. To explain the connection between claims, grounds, and backing, you could say, "Lots of crime makes a neighborhood unsafe [premise or rule], and this neighborhood has lots of crime [grounds and backing]; therefore, this neighborhood is unsafe [claim]."

Explain Relationships in Other Claims

When students are analyzing their own claims or others' claims, explaining the relationship between claims, grounds, and backing can help them identify erroneous or illogical reasoning. For example, a student might claim that a woman would make an irrational president because women cry more easily than men (claim and grounds), and give as backing the results of a study showing that women cried more often than men during tragic or sad movies. Another student explaining the connection between claims, grounds, and backing in this claim might point out that this claim is equating "being irrational" with "crying during tragic or sad movies," two things that are not necessarily equal. This allows students to identify errors in reasoning or claims based on general rules that are not necessarily valid.

Organizing an Argument

Organizing an argument involves arranging claims, grounds, and backing in a logical order. Marzano and his colleagues (1988) defined organizing skills as those used to "arrange information so it can be understood or presented more effectively" (p. 80). Students typically find support for a claim by collecting relatively unorganized information from many sources. To present their argument, they need to organize the information. Teachers can use the following process to help students organize arguments:

1. Help students understand the structure of an effective argument.

2. Have students classify information according to whether or not it supports a claim.

3. Have students organize supporting information into grounds and backing for the claim.

4. Have students use nonsupporting information to write qualifiers for the claim.

Here, we detail how teachers can help students accomplish each step in the process.

Structure of an Argument

Fundamentally, an argument is a claim supported by evidence (grounds and backing). Qualifiers state exceptions to a claim. Based on the CCSS and Toulmin's (2003) model, we recommend the argument organization template depicted in figure I.2.

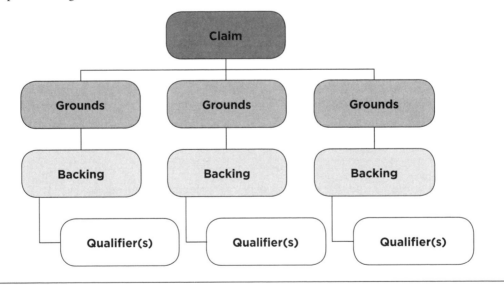

Figure I.2: The organization of an effective argument.

Adapted from Toulmin, 2003.

As shown in figure I.2, a well-organized argument is typically centered on one main claim. This claim can be supported by as many grounds (young students might call these reasons) as necessary, but it usually has at least two or three, each of which is supported by backing. Students can then use qualifiers to modify or clarify any of these three elements.

To help students understand the structure of an argument, teachers might show them how it works with a simple example claim, such as the one in figure I.3.

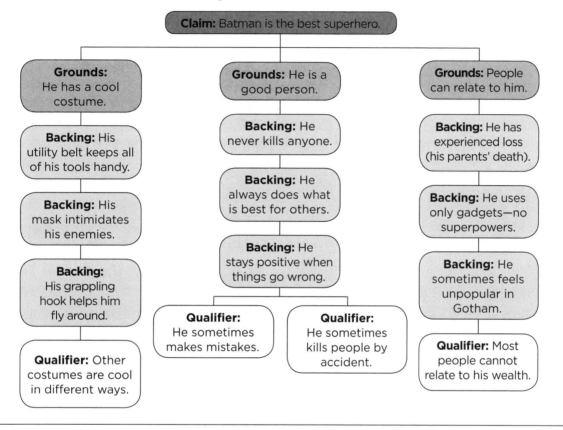

Figure I.3: A well-organized argument for the claim that Batman is the best superhero.

In a persuasive essay, the claim—often called a thesis statement—is introduced in the first paragraph or section. Grounds are then presented one by one in the body of the essay, each supported by backing—factual information, expert opinion, or research results.

Classifying Information

As students collect information to support their claims, they will probably also find information that does not support their claims. Each type of information is important and can strengthen an argument if properly organized and then used appropriately. As students collect information, they should classify it according to whether or not it supports the claim. For example, a student collecting information to support the claim "Electric cars reduce pollution and environmental damage" might classify the information she finds as shown in table I.9 (page 24).

Table I.9: Information Related to the Claim "Electric Cars Reduce Pollution and Environmental Damage"

Supports the Claim	Does Not Support the Claim
According to a 2012 study, emissions from electric cars compare equally or favorably to gasoline-powered cars. In countries where electricity is mainly generated by burning coal, electric cars produce about the same emissions as gasoline-powered cars. In countries where electricity is generated in cleaner ways without coal, electric cars produce less than half the emissions of gasoline-powered cars (Wilson, 2013).	Building an electric car produces about thirty thousand pounds of carbon-dioxide emission, compared to fourteen thousand pounds for a conventional car. Unless the car is driven for a long time, an electric car can actually create more carbon-dioxide emissions over its lifetime than a gasoline-powered car, because its manufacture releases so much pollution (Lomborg, 2013).
Elon Musk, CEO of electric car manufacturer Tesla, stated, "In a stationary power plant, you can afford to have something that weighs a lot more, is voluminous, and you can take the waste heat and run a steam turbine and generate a secondary power source. . . . Even using the same source fuel, you're at least twice as better off" (as quoted in Davies, 2013).	The electricity used to recharge electric cars is often produced by burning fossil fuels (such as coal), which produces carbon-dioxide emissions (Zehner, 2013).
The U.S. Energy Information Administration (EIA, 2013) projected that the share of national electricity from renewable resources would increase from 11 percent in 2009 to 15 percent in 2025. The EIA also projected that the share of national electricity from coal would decrease from 44 percent in 2009 to about 28 percent in 2025.	The mining of compounds used in electric car batteries, such as lithium, copper, and nickel, requires high amounts of energy. These compounds can release toxic wastes if improperly handled (Zehner, 2013).
The Union of Concerned Scientists reported that when "electricity used to power the vehicle comes from resources such as wind and solar power, EVs [electric vehicles] can operate nearly emissions-free" (Anair & Mahmassani, 2012, p. 2).	

Acknowledging and classifying information that does not support the claim, rather than ignoring it, allows students to construct qualifiers that ultimately strengthen their arguments. However, students should first organize the information that supports their claim into grounds and backing.

Organize Grounds and Backing

To review, grounds are overarching reasons to agree with a claim. They often begin with the word *because.* The claim "Dogs are better than cats," for example, might be supported by the following grounds: because they are smarter, because they are friendlier, because they are less picky about what they eat, and so on. Backing, on the other hand, is specific evidence (such as expert opinions, research results, or factual information) that shows the grounds are valid. To support the grounds that dogs are smarter than cats, one might cite a quote from an expert animal trainer or research that shows dogs are smarter.

The information that students collect to support their claim is backing. They can organize the backing they collect into related categories and then write grounds for each category. Table I.10 shows how the student who collected supporting information for the claim "Electric cars reduce pollution and environmental damage" might sort supporting information into categories and create grounds for each category.

Table I.10: Supporting Information Sorted Into Grounds and Backing

Grounds	Backing
Electric cars emit less carbon dioxide than gasoline-powered cars.	According to a 2012 study, emissions from electric cars compare equally or favorably to gasoline-powered cars. In countries where electricity is mainly generated by burning coal, electric cars produce about the same emissions as gasoline-powered cars. In countries where electricity is generated in cleaner ways without coal, electric cars produce less than half the emissions of gasoline-powered cars (Wilson, 2013).
	The U.S. Energy Information Administration (EIA; 2013) projected that the share of national electricity from renewable resources would increase from 11 percent in 2009 to 15 percent in 2025. The EIA also projected that the share of national electricity from coal would decrease from 44 percent in 2009 to about 28 percent in 2025.
Burning fossil fuels in large plants to create electricity that powers electric cars is more efficient and produces less pollution than burning fossil fuels in the engines of individual cars.	Elon Musk, CEO of electric car manufacturer Tesla, stated, "In a stationary power plant, you can afford to have something that weighs a lot more, is voluminous, and you can take the waste heat and run a steam turbine and generate a secondary power source. . . . Even using the same source fuel, you're at least twice as better off" (as quoted in Davies, 2013).
Clean energy sources, such as solar and wind energy, can be used to charge electric cars.	The Union of Concerned Scientists reported that when "electricity used to power the vehicle comes from resources such as wind and solar power, EVs [electric vehicles] can operate nearly emissions-free" (Anair & Mahmassani, 2012, p. 2).

As shown in table I.10, the student sorted the expert opinions, research results, and factual information she had collected into three related categories. She then created three grounds or reasons for the claim, each of which describes one of the categories of backing.

Write Qualifiers

Finally, students can use nonsupporting information they find to construct qualifiers for their claim. That is, they can specify situations in which their claim might not apply or address potential objections to their claim as part of their argument. For example, the student who claimed that electric cars reduce pollution and environmental damage found three pieces of information that did not support that claim (see the right column of table I.9). She might construct the following qualifiers using that information:

◆ While it is true that building an electric car uses more energy and emits more carbon dioxide than building a gasoline-powered car, electric cars emit zero carbon dioxide while being driven, offsetting the initial emissions from their manufacture.

◆ Although generating electricity to power electric cars produces carbon-dioxide emissions, many countries in the world are switching to cleaner, renewable energy sources for electricity. This means that electric cars will simply get cleaner and cleaner as power grids around the world become cleaner.

◆ Despite the fact that electric car batteries require lots of energy to produce, when recycled properly, they do not emit toxic wastes. Moreover, compared to the batteries in gasoline-powered cars, the components of electric car batteries are very valuable and therefore more likely to be properly handled and recycled.

Once qualifiers have been constructed, the student can present his or her argument using the organizational structure shown in figure I.2 (page 22).

Citing Textual Evidence

Citing textual evidence involves using specific quotations or information from a text to support a claim. The CCSS require students to "defend their interpretations or judgments with evidence from the text(s) they are writing about" (NGA & CCSSO, 2010b, p. 23). Here, we present two ways that teachers can help students use textual evidence to support and defend their arguments:

1. Ask students to find textual evidence to support an existing claim.

2. Ask students to use textual evidence to construct a claim.

Here, we provide detail about each method.

Support an Existing Claim

At times, students need to support an existing claim with textual evidence. When this is the case, first ask students to annotate the text, marking any evidence that might support the claim. Consider, for example, a student who needs textual evidence to back up the following claim: "In the poem 'Because I could not stop for Death,' Emily Dickinson personifies death to show that we should not fear it." The student begins by highlighting all words or phrases in the poem that use personification, a device that attributes human characteristics to nonhuman entities, as shown in table I.11.

Table I.11: Personification in "Because I could not stop for Death" by Emily Dickinson (1890/1960)

Because I could not stop for Death— He kindly stopped for me— The Carriage held but just Ourselves— And Immortality.	Or rather—He passed us— The Dews drew quivering and chill— For only Gossamer, my Gown— My Tippet—only Tulle—
We slowly drove—He knew no haste And I had put away My labor and my leisure too, For His Civility—	We paused before a House that seemed A Swelling of the Ground— The Roof was scarcely visible— The Cornice—in the Ground—
We passed the School, where Children strove At Recess—in the Ring— We passed the Fields of Grazing Grain— We passed the Setting Sun—	Since then—'tis Centuries—and yet Feels shorter than the Day I first surmised the Horses' Heads Were toward Eternity—

After highlighting all instances of personification, the student arranges the textual evidence into categories, which become the grounds for the claim. The textual evidence itself is the backing for each of these grounds. Table I.12 illustrates how the student might sort his textual evidence.

Table I.12: Textual Evidence From "Because I could not stop for Death" by Emily Dickinson (1890/1960)

Grounds	Backing
Dickinson portrays Death as a kind person.	"Death" (line 1) is capitalized like a person's name.
	The speaker refers to Death with the pronoun "He" (line 2) instead of the pronoun "it."
	The line "He kindly stopped for me" (line 2) makes Death seem courteous and thoughtful—the speaker could not stop for herself, so he does it for her.
The speaker embraces Death as she would a suitor.	Death picks up the speaker in a "Carriage" (line 3) as if he is courting her.
	The carriage held "but just Ourselves" (line 3), which makes the two seem like lovers.
	The phrase "His Civility" (line 8) portrays Death as gallant or chivalrous; he is taking care of the speaker.
	From the repeated use of the pronoun "We" (lines 5, 9, 11, 12, 17), we can infer that the speaker has accepted her union with Death.
The speaker seems relaxed by the fact that death is out of her control.	The line "We slowly drove" (line 5)—as well as the repeated use of the phrase "We passed" (lines 9–12)—makes the journey to death seem painless and relaxing. The speaker is able to look one last time at the world she is leaving behind.
	The setting sun is also personified as a man: "He [the sun] passed us" (line 13). Because the only other inhuman thing personified in the poem is Death, it could be that the gradual beauty of a sunset also symbolizes death.

Highlighting potential evidence, narrowing it down, and sorting it into grounds is an excellent way for students to support a pre-existing claim with textual evidence. Sometimes, however, students must collect textual evidence and use it to construct a claim.

Construct a Claim

When students need to construct a claim based on textual evidence, they must first find textual evidence that seems interesting or important. One of the best ways to do this is to annotate the text by marking important or interesting quotes with pencil, highlighter, or sticky notes and then organize the quotes in a double-entry journal, as shown in table I.13.

Table I.13: Double-Entry Journal for Textual Evidence From "Casey at the Bat" by Ernest Lawrence Thayer (1888)

Quotations	Why the Quotation Seemed Important
Clung to that hope which springs eternal in the human breast (line 6)	This seems like a really big, noble idea.
Upon that stricken multitude grim melancholy sat (line 11)	This seems like something really important and bad has happened, like somebody died.
When the dust had lifted (line 15)	This is what people say after horrible fights or wars.

Continued on next page →

Quotations	Why the Quotation Seemed Important
Then from 5,000 throats and more there rose a lusty yell; / It rumbled through the valley, it rattled in the dell; / It knocked upon the mountain and recoiled upon the flat (lines 17–19)	This is exaggerating how the audience acts when Casey heads to bat. It makes it sound like a tall tale (like Paul Bunyan or something).
There went up a muffled roar, / Like the beating of the storm-waves on a stern and distant shore (lines 33–34)	This seems really important too because it makes it sound like the audience is as powerful as the ocean.
"Kill him! Kill the umpire!" shouted some one on the stand; / And it's likely they'd have killed him had not Casey raised his hand (lines 35–36)	Did Casey really keep them from killing the umpire? Killing is pretty serious. Could one person really stop thousands of people?
With a smile of Christian charity great Casey's visage shone (line 37)	This makes me think of God.
Close by the sturdy batsman the ball unheeded sped — / "That ain't my style," said Casey. "Strike one," the umpire said (lines 31–32) But Casey still ignored it, and the umpire said, "Strike two" (line 40)	Casey has ignored two pitches which means he is being cocky.
Oh, somewhere in this favored land the sun is shining bright; / The band is playing somewhere, and somewhere hearts are light, / And somewhere men are laughing, and somewhere children shout; / But there is no joy in Mudville—mighty Casey has struck out (lines 49–52)	This sounds like something really bad has happened, a lot worse than someone just striking out in a baseball game. It is kind of funny that everyone is so depressed about a baseball game. It's also funny that Casey struck out because he was so sure he was going to win.

In the double-entry journal in table I.13, the student first filled in the left column with phrases from the poem that seemed important or interesting. Then the student explained why each quote seemed important or interesting in the right column. Once students have identified textual evidence that seems important and articulated why it is important, they can look for connections or patterns in the quotations they have found. For example, the student who identified the textual evidence in table I.13 might notice three patterns: (1) some of the textual evidence compares the baseball game to a war, (2) some textual evidence compares the power of the audience to natural forces, and (3) other textual evidence makes Casey seem almost godlike. These patterns together make the events of the poem seem exaggerated. Finally, students should make a general statement that explains the connections or patterns they observed. The student who read "Casey at the Bat" might make the claim "The author of 'Casey at the Bat' uses exaggerations to make fun of how seriously some people take sports games." The student would then arrange the textual evidence into grounds and backing to support the claim, as shown in figure I.4.

After organizing the grounds and backing in their double-entry journals, students should skim or reread the text to search for more textual evidence to use as backing in support of their claim. As shown in figure I.4, the student has added some new quotes from the text that were not included in her double-entry journal. At this point, students should also search for contradictory or conflicting evidence and use it to refine their claims or grounds.

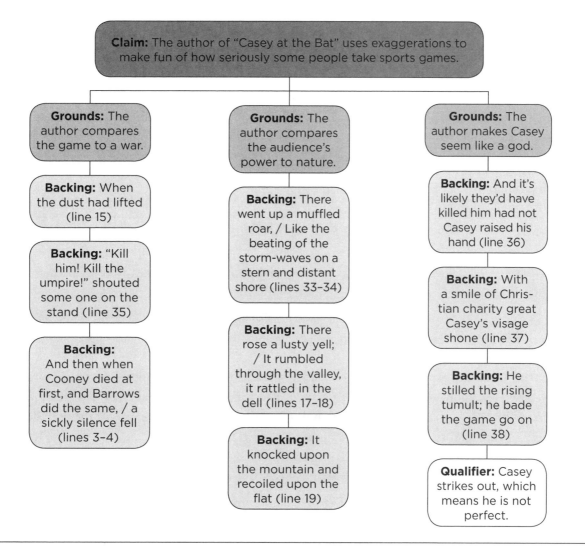

Figure I.4: Organization of an argument using textual evidence from "Casey at the Bat."

Distinguishing a Claim From Alternate or Opposing Claims

Distinguishing a claim from alternate or opposing claims involves using precise language to refine the meaning of a claim or make it more specific. For example, in the previous example claim, "Batman is the best superhero" (page 23), the term *best* does not precisely distinguish the claim from alternate or opposing claims. This claim might mean that Batman is the most handsome superhero, or that he is the smartest superhero, or that he is the most resourceful superhero, or that he is the kindest superhero, and so on. These are alternate claims. A villain might define the best superhero as one who doesn't catch many bad guys (an opposing claim). Depending on how *best* is defined, "Batman is the best superhero" can mean many different things. Therefore, students need to be able to use precise language to distinguish a claim from alternate or opposing claims. To help students do this, teachers can:

1. Ask students to examine the words used in the claim, grounds, backing, and qualifiers to identify and revise subjective or imprecise terms.

2. Ask students to use words and phrases that signal basic relationships to express meaning more clearly.

Here, we explain and exemplify each strategy.

Revise Subjective or Imprecise Terms

Once students have articulated a claim, given grounds for the claim, provided backing for the grounds, and specified qualifiers, they can examine the wording of the claim to eliminate subjective or imprecise terms. For example, figure I.3 (page 23) illustrated the structure of an argument using the simple claim "Batman is the best superhero." One of the grounds for that claim is "He has a cool costume." The term *cool* is a subjective term: what is cool to one person might not be considered cool by someone else. Table I.14 lists other examples of subjective or imprecise terms that might be used in claims.

Table I.14: Examples of Subjective or Imprecise Language

all	cool	fun/funny	lots/a lot	quality
always	every	great	never	some
amazing	everyone	I think that	nobody	something
anything	everything	important	none	stuff
awful	excellent	in my opinion	often	things
best	fantastic			

The list in table I.14 is not exhaustive. Teachers could have students generate additional words and phrases that might be considered imprecise and discuss better alternatives. For example, in the Batman claim, replacing the word *cool* with the word *useful* makes the grounds much more defensible; one can list the distinctive tools and features of Batman's costume that highlight its unique practicality when compared to others. Similarly, the backing "He never kills anyone" is imprecise because villains sometimes do die as a result of their interactions with Batman. A more precise way of stating that particular backing might be "He never kills anyone on purpose."

Another example can be found in figure I.4 (page 29), which organizes text evidence to support the claim "The author of 'Casey at the Bat' uses exaggerations to make fun of how seriously some people take sports games." The student originally chooses to use "The author makes Casey seem like a god" as grounds for the claim, but then she notices that Casey's strikeout at the end of the poem does not support these grounds very well. This realization causes the student to read the poem more closely. Based on more text evidence, she concludes that while the author does not consistently depict Casey as flawless, the audience reveres Casey throughout the poem. Therefore, the student might revise the grounds statement to read "The audience worships Casey like a god," which supports her claim more accurately and more precisely.

Use Words and Phrases That Signal Basic Relationships

Robert Marzano, Patricia Hagerty, Sheila Valencia, and Philip DiStefano (1987) identified four types of basic relationships that students can use to refine their claims and distinguish them from alternate or opposing claims. Those relationships are:

- **Addition**—One idea is similar to or adds to another idea.

- **Contrast**—One idea is different from or subtracts from another idea.

- **Time**—One idea occurs before, during, or after another idea.

- **Cause**—One idea is the cause or condition for another idea.

Each of these relationships has specific subtypes, and each subtype has signal words and phrases associated with it, as shown in table I.15.

Table I.15: Subtypes and Signal Words and Phrases for Basic Relationships

Basic Relationship	Subtypes	Signal Words and Phrases
Addition	**Equality:** He is tall, *and* he is handsome.	*and, moreover, equally, too, besides, furthermore, what is more, likewise, similarly, as well, in addition, besides, at the same time*
	Restatement: I am tired. *In fact*, I am exhausted.	*indeed, actually, in actuality, in fact, namely, that is, that is to say, another way of saying this*
	Example: She does many things well. *For example*, she is excellent at cards.	*for example, first, second, third, one, two, three . . . , for a start, to begin with, next, then, finally, last but not least, for one thing, for another thing, another example would be*
	Summation: He does many things well. He cooks. He sews. *In all*, he is an excellent homemaker.	*altogether, overall, then, thus, in all, therefore, all in all, in conclusion, in sum, in a word, in brief, briefly, in short, to sum up, to summarize*
Contrast	**Antithesis:** I will be there, *but* I won't be happy.	*but, yet, or rather, what is better, what is worse, contrariwise, conversely, oppositely, on the contrary, else, otherwise, on the other hand*
	Alternative: *Either* it will rain, *or* it will snow.	*alternatively, either . . . or, neither . . . nor, rather than, sooner than*
	Comparison: Kyana is tall. *In comparison*, her brother is short.	*in comparison, in contrast, like*
	Concession: I don't like violence. *Nonetheless*, I'll meet you at the fights.	*however, anyhow, besides, else, nevertheless, nonetheless, only, still, though, in any case, in any event, for all that, in spite of that, all the same, anyway, though, at any rate, in any case, regardless of this*
Cause	**Direct Cause:** She won the race *by* maintaining her concentration.	*by, due to, owing to, through*
	Result: Aakash went home. *Consequently*, the party ended.	*consequently, hence, now, so, therefore, thus, as a consequence, for all that, as a result, whereupon, accordingly, the result was, this is the reason*
	Reason: He went to the store *because* he needed food.	*because, because of, in that, so that, since, so on account of, for the fact that*
	Inference: Isabel is going on a long trip. *In that case*, she should plan well.	*else, otherwise, in that case, then*
	Condition: *Unless* you stop, I will leave.	*now that, providing that, supposing that, considering that, granted that, admitting that, assuming that, presuming that, seeing that, unless . . . then, as long as, in so far as, if, where . . . there, when . . . then, no sooner . . .*

Continued on next page →

Basic Relationship	Subtypes	Signal Words and Phrases
Time	**Subsequent Action:** They went to the game. *Afterward*, they went to the dance.	*afterward, next, since, then, after that, later, in the end, shortly, subsequently, so far, as yet, before, until, finally*
	Prior Action: They went to the game *before* they went to the dance.	*after, earlier, initially, in the beginning, originally, at first, previously, beforehand, formerly, before that, before now, until then, up to now, by now, by then*
	Concurrent Action: David thought about Pratha *while* Pratha thought about David.	*simultaneously, while, meanwhile, meantime, at this point, at the same time*

Source: Adapted from Marzano & Heflebower, 2012.

A student might use the signal words and phrases in table I.15 to refine and distinguish a claim such as "Miguel de Cervantes's *Don Quixote* is a funny book." First, the student might ask herself, "Which of the four basic relationships is represented in my claim?" She decides that her claim is one of contrast; she is asserting that *Don Quixote* is a funny book in contrast to other, more serious books of its time on the same subject. Then, the student considers the subtypes of contrast relationships: antithesis, alternative, comparison, and concession. After she determines that her claim is essentially one of comparison, she uses the signal words and phrases associated with that subtype to restate her claim in a way that distinguishes it from alternative or opposing claims: "In contrast to other romances of its time, *Don Quixote* explores chivalry from a humorous perspective." Notice that the student also refined the imprecise term *funny* and clarified the genre and subject of her claim.

Making Inductive Inferences

Making inductive inferences involves forming reasonable guesses based on observations and background knowledge. Marzano and Pickering (1997) highlighted the process of inductive reasoning and presented three strategies teachers can use to introduce students to that process:

1. Help students understand the mental process of making inductive inferences.

2. Give students a model for the process of making inductive inferences.

3. Help students focus on critical steps and difficult aspects of the process.

Here, we describe each strategy in detail.

Understand the Mental Process

To introduce students to the process of making inductive inferences, use a concrete example. Walk into the classroom, slam the door, throw a pile of books and papers on your desk, frown, sigh, and cross your arms in front of your chest. Ask students what conclusions they reached as they observed these actions (for example, they might say, "You're angry"). Explain that when they make specific observations and draw conclusions from them, they are performing a mental process called making inferences. To help them understand that inferences are not necessarily true, ask them to identify other possible causes of your behavior, such as being in a hurry or being tired.

A Model for Making Inductive Inferences

Although making inductive inferences is a mental process, a concrete model can help students make high-quality inferences. Marzano and Pickering (1997) recommended the following process:

1. Without assuming anything, focus on specific pieces of information or observations.

2. Look for patterns or connections in the information and observations.

3. Make a general statement to explain the patterns or connections.

4. Gather more information and observations to see if your statement holds up; if not, adjust it accordingly.

To provide opportunities for students to practice the process, go on an inference walk around the school building or grounds. Model the process using a think-aloud. For example, in the cafeteria, you might say, "I'm looking around, and I notice that mayonnaise and pickles are set out at the condiment table. I'm also noticing that there isn't any silverware set out by the trays today. I smell chicken cooking, and I can see hamburger buns stacked up in the lunch line. Let me put all of this information together. It could be that chicken sandwiches are today's entrée. What else do I see or know that would support or refute that inference?" Once students are familiar with the process, have them practice in small groups or pairs as the class moves to different locations.

Critical Steps and Difficult Aspects

As students practice making inductive inferences, it is important to make sure they are aware of particular complexities that accompany the process. First, when students are learning to make inductive inferences, they may state conclusions that are not the result of seeing patterns or connections in information; that is, they may state ideas that are not actually inferences. For example:

◆ **Restating original information**—"I conclude that the man is happy because he said he was glad."

◆ **Describing an observation**—"I conclude that the boiling water turned into steam."

◆ **Offering opinions**—"I conclude that she should not have hit her sister."

These are not inferences. Students need many opportunities to practice generating conclusions that represent patterns or connections among observations or pieces of information.

Second, students need to base their inferences on observation and information rather than assumptions and biases. For example, concluding that Edgar Allan Poe was obsessed with death because "Poe's poems are weird" is not an inference because it is based on opinion, not observation. To help students understand what constitutes objective information or observations and what is considered a subjective opinion, assumption, or bias, give examples of each (as shown in table I.16) and discuss what makes each distinctive.

Table I.16: Examples of Objective and Subjective Information

Objective Information or Observations	Subjective Opinions, Assumptions, or Biases
Samantha has her head down on her desk.	Samantha is pouting.
The little boy ran away from the woman.	The little boy is naughty.
He walked quickly to the door.	He wanted to see what was outside.
There is a lot of salt in this food.	This food is terrible.
She has a temperature of 101 degrees.	She has the flu.

Finally, inferences should be based on as many observations or pieces of information as possible. Inferences cannot be proven to be true, but they become more likely as more information is found to support them.

Distinguishing Connotation From Denotation

Distinguishing connotation from denotation involves recognizing different implications or nuances among words with similar definitions (such as *aroma* and *stench*). Teachers can use the following process to help students understand the difference between the two:

1. Explain connotations and denotations.

2. Ask students to generate examples of terms that have the same denotation but different connotations.

3. Ask students to think of multiple denotations for a particular term.

Here, we provide detail about each step of the process.

Explain Connotations and Denotations

Denotations are definitions or literal meanings of words. Connotations are more nuanced—they are different shades of meaning associated with a particular term or phrase. To illustrate, the words *aroma* and *stench* are similar in denotation; both refer to strong smells. However, the word *aroma* has positive connotations (it usually describes a good smell) while the word *stench* has negative connotations (it usually describes a bad smell). Additionally, the same word can have multiple denotations. For example, the word *run* can mean to move quickly, to drip or leak, to use a running play in football, and so on.

Examples of Connotations

To help students understand connotation, ask them to list a number of terms that refer to the same concept (that is, synonyms for the concept). For example, given the concept *smart*, students might come up with a variety of synonyms such as *clever, intelligent, brainy, shrewd, nerdy, bright, brilliant*, and so on. Ask them to then classify the terms they generate into those with positive, negative, or neutral connotations. Once the terms have been sorted into categories, have students discuss the defining characteristics of each category.

Examples of Multiple Denotations

To help students understand denotation, ask them to list all the denotations of simple words that have multiple meanings (for example, *play, blow, break, split, run, fly, fall, light*, and *space*). Students might explain that *play* can refer to a theatrical production, to something children do, to participating in sports, and so on. The overall goal of this activity is for students to understand that one word can have multiple different denotations. Students can engage in making these lists by creating videos that highlight the various denotations of particular words (see an example of such a video by NPR's Radiolab [Radiolab, 2010] at www.radiolab.org /story/91974-bonus-video-words).

Evaluating Persuasive Rhetoric

Evaluating persuasive rhetoric involves determining a writer or speaker's motive based on connotation, emphasis, tone, and figurative language, as well as judging whether these elements were used to mislead. To help students evaluate persuasive rhetoric, teachers can use the following process:

1. Identify and clearly articulate the speaker's perspective.

2. Identify biased language in the speaker's argument.

3. Understand appeals the speaker may be using.

4. Examine the motives behind the speaker's perspective.

Here, we briefly describe each step of the process.

Articulate the Speaker's Perspective

The best way for students to identify and articulate a speaker's perspective is to try to restate the claim a speaker is presenting and list the grounds, or reasons, the speaker is using to defend his or her claim. For example, a speaker might say, "Smoking should not be banned in the United States because individuals should have the right to choose whether or not they smoke. Banning smoking violates the Constitution because it takes away that right. Measures have already been taken to protect populations that are hurt by smoking, such as children or nonsmokers who are exposed to secondhand smoke. Additionally, the government depends on taxes from cigarette sales for revenue, so banning cigarettes would actually hurt the country's finances."

Students might diagram the speaker's perspective as shown in figure I.5.

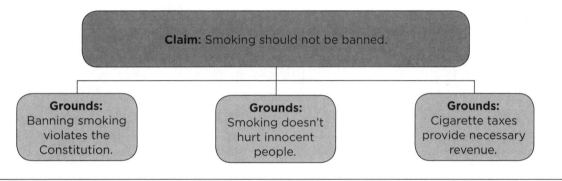

Figure I.5: Diagramming a speaker's perspective.

Identifying and articulating the speaker's perspective by diagramming his or her claim and grounds allows students to then identify biased language in each element of the argument.

Identify Biased Language

Once students have deconstructed an argument into its component parts, they can look more closely at the words themselves. When a speaker uses biased language, he or she strategically uses words with connotations that convey a hidden message or claim. This technique can make a claim seem innocuous or agreeable to an audience, even if the audience would otherwise disagree with it. Consider, for example, the excerpts from political speeches made by Barack Obama and Mitt Romney in table I.17 (page 36).

As shown, the student has highlighted words in each excerpt that have strong connotations, many of which are metaphorical, emotional, or grandiose. These include adjectives (such as *worst*, *unequal*, and *American*), nouns (such as *crisis*, *opportunity*, and *corruption*), and verbs (such as *recover*, *collapsed*, and *inspire*). Such words can be considered biased because they subtly express the opinion of each speaker.

Table I.17: Speeches by Barack Obama and Mitt Romney

Obama	Romney
Some of our most urgent challenges have revolved around an increasingly integrated global economy, and our efforts to recover from the worst economic crisis of our lifetime. Now, five years after the global economy collapsed, thanks to coordinated efforts by the countries here today, jobs are being created, global financial systems have stabilized, and people are being lifted out of poverty. But this progress is fragile and unequal, and we still have work to do together to assure that our citizens can access the opportunity they need to thrive in the 21st century.	An opportunity society produces pioneers and inventors; it inspires its citizens to build and create. And these people exert effort and take risks, and when they do so, they employ and lift others and create prosperity. . . . Even if we could afford the ever-expanding payments of an "entitlement society," it is a fundamental corruption of the American spirit. The battle we face today is more than a fight over our budget, it's a battle for America's soul.

Source: "Text of Obama's Speech at the U.N." (2013) and "Anatomy of a Stump Speech" (2012).

For example, both speakers discussed the need for employment rates to rise and for Americans to have jobs. On its own, this sentiment is generally unobjectionable; most people would agree with it. However, each speaker used words that aligned with his personal views about government. Obama used the phrases *lifted out of poverty* and *work to do together*, which imply that government aid and cooperation among citizens improve the economy. He also used the words *fragile* and *unequal* to describe the economy, suggesting that it ought to be more regulated. Romney, on the other hand, used words like *pioneers*, *inventors*, *effort*, and *risks*, which imply that individual success and limited government produce economic growth.

Understand Appeals

Students can evaluate the biased language they have identified to understand another persuasive device that speakers use to communicate with audiences: appeals. Appeals are ways in which a speaker connects with his or her audience. Students need to know what appeals are so they do not confuse them with evidence. There are three types of appeals, as described by Marzano and Pickering (1997):

◆ **Personality**—In this type of appeal, the speaker or writer tries to convince you to like him. He might use personal stories, act very interested in you, or be very congenial.

◆ **Tradition or accepted belief**—In this type of appeal, the speaker or writer tries to convince you to "do the right thing." Appealing to tradition involves referring to generally accepted beliefs or values to convince you to do something.

◆ **Rhetoric**—In this type of appeal, the speaker or writer tries to convince you by using beautiful language, impressive phrases, clever idioms, and well-crafted gestures. Appealing through rhetoric attempts to impress the listener through powerfully constructed communication.

By making students aware of these types of appeals, teachers can help them understand that speakers and writers sometimes use techniques to convince that do not involve presenting evidence. In the previous example, Obama and Romney both used the pronoun *we* to appeal to personality; Obama said "we still have work to do together," and Romney spoke of a "battle we face." Each wanted the members of his audience to feel like he was on their side. They also appealed to tradition or accepted belief: Romney said that Obama's economic views contributed to a "corruption of the American spirit." Because the phrase *American spirit* typically refers to a shared set of beliefs among U.S. citizens, Romney's statement implied that Obama is anti-American.

Finally, the two speakers used beautiful or impressive phrases to appeal rhetorically to the audience. Romney likened the presidential election to a "battle for America's soul," and Obama called the recession "the worst economic crisis of our lifetime."

Students should watch for these appeals and recognize that, while appeals can strengthen an argument, they are not the same as evidence for the argument. After students understand a speaker's perspective, biased language, and appeals, they can consider the speaker's motives for making the argument.

Examine Motives

The final step in evaluating persuasive rhetoric is to examine the speaker's motives. Students can do this by asking the question, "What principles underlie the speaker's logic?" To determine the logic behind a speaker's perspective, students can make generalizations that highlight how the speaker is moving from his or her claim to grounds. For example, in the previous claim about banning smoking (see figure I.5, page 35), students might observe that the speaker is using logic such as the following to generate grounds for his or her claim:

◆ People have the right to do certain things, even if those things might hurt them.

◆ People should be allowed to do things that hurt themselves, but not other people.

◆ It is okay for the government to make money off something that hurts people.

If a speaker's logic was that people have the right to do certain things, even if those things might hurt them, students could infer that the principle of personal freedom is a primary consideration for the speaker. If a speaker's logic involved the idea that people should not be allowed to do things that hurt other people, students might infer that while personal freedom is important to the speaker, it does not extend to situations where others might be hurt. Finally, from the speaker's logic that it is okay for the government to make money off something that hurts people, students might conclude that the speaker is motivated by economic motives, rather than altruistic ones.

Identifying Errors in Reasoning

Students can analyze a claim or evidence and decide whether it is logical by identifying errors in reasoning. To guide students in identifying errors in reasoning, teachers can use the following process:

1. Explain the different types of errors.

2. Give students practice exercises for identifying errors.

The following sections expand on these steps.

Explain the Different Types of Errors

Over time, 20th century philosophers (Johnson-Laird, 1983; Johnson-Laird & Byrne, 1991; Toulmin, Rieke, & Janik, 1981) have identified a number of common—yet fallacious—lines of thinking and arguing. Marzano (2007) classified them into four main categories:

1. Faulty logic

2. Attack

3. Weak reference

4. Misinformation

Errors of faulty logic occur when someone uses incorrect premises or unsound reasoning to make claims or draw conclusions. To illustrate, consider the following claim: "Mark will probably want to watch the football game because he is a boy." The underlying premise of this claim—that all boys enjoy watching sports—is incorrect. Some boys enjoy sports; others do not. Therefore, the claim makes an error of faulty logic. Attack refers to the use of irrelevant and often personal information to undermine an argument. For example, claiming that every argument a specific politician makes is necessarily flawed because he once had an affair is committing an error of attack. Using weak reference simply means that unreliable or untrustworthy sources were used, and misinformation means that information was incorrect or used incorrectly. Table I.18 lists specific logical errors and organizes them into the aforementioned four categories.

Table I.18: Four Categories of Errors in Reasoning

Type of Error	How the Error Can Occur
Faulty Logic	**Contradiction:** Presenting conflicting information
	Accident: Failing to recognize that an argument is based on an exception to a rule
	False Cause: Confusing a temporal (time) order of events with causality or oversimplifying the reasons behind an occurrence
	Begging the Question: Making a claim and then arguing for the claim by using statements that are simply the equivalent of the original claim
	Evading the Issue: Changing the topic to avoid addressing the issue
	Arguing From Ignorance: Arguing that a claim is justified simply because its opposite has not been proven true
	Composition: Asserting something about a whole that is really only true of its parts
	Division: Asserting something about all of the parts that is generally, but not always, true of the whole
Attack	**Poisoning the Well:** Being so completely committed to a position that you explain away absolutely everything that is offered in opposition to your position
	Arguing Against the Person: Rejecting a claim using derogatory facts (real or alleged) about the person who is making the claim
	Appealing to Force: Using threats to establish the validity of a claim
Weak Reference	**Sources That Reflect Biases:** Consistently accepting information that supports what we already believe to be true or consistently rejecting information that goes against what we believe to be true
	Sources That Lack Credibility: Using a source that is not reputable for a given topic
	Appealing to Authority: Invoking authority as the last word on an issue
	Appealing to the People: Attempting to justify a claim based on its popularity
	Appealing to Emotion: Using a sob story as proof for a claim
Misinformation	**Confusing the Facts:** Using information that seems to be factual but that has been changed in such a way that it is no longer accurate
	Misapplying a Concept or Generalization: Misunderstanding or wrongly applying a concept or generalization to support a claim

Source: Adapted from Marzano, 2007.

As Marzano and Heflebower (2012) pointed out, students will frequently encounter errors in reasoning on television, on the Internet, and in other forms of media. To argue effectively, students must be aware of various reasoning errors in order to evaluate their own thinking, as well as the claims of others. To develop this awareness, students can practice identifying the different kinds of errors.

Practice Exercises for Identifying Errors

To help students practice identifying errors of faulty logic, attack, weak reference, and misinformation, teachers can use exercises like those in figure I.6.

---

1. Lila says that cell phones cause cancer. Vinodh asks why she believes that, and she says that no one has been able to prove that they don't, so they do.

2. Bao says that students don't have to do what the principal says because she once heard the principal yell at a student.

3. Greg and Mario are talking about global warming. After a heated discussion, Mario says, "Listen, my dad is a climatologist for the government, and he says that global warming is real. So it is. End of story."

4. Henok's dad grounds him for the weekend because he didn't do his homework or study for a test and therefore got a bad grade on the test. Henok tells his friends, "My dad is so unfair. He grounded me because the test was difficult."

Answers: 1–faulty logic (arguing from ignorance); 2–attack (arguing against the person); 3–weak reference (appealing to authority); 4–misinformation (confusing the facts)

Figure I.6: Sample exercises for identifying errors in reasoning.

Teachers can ask students to identify items such as those in figure I.6 as errors of faulty logic, attack, weak reference, and misinformation. For a finer level of detail, students can identify the specific subtype of error (for example, contradiction, poisoning the well, appealing to authority, or confusing the facts).

Identifying Insufficient or Irrelevant Evidence

Identifying insufficient or irrelevant evidence involves analyzing evidence to decide whether it adequately supports a claim. Teachers can use three strategies to help students identify insufficient or irrelevant evidence:

1. Diagram backing.

2. Determine whether evidence is sufficient.

3. Determine whether evidence is relevant.

Here, we review each of these strategies.

Diagram Backing

Identifying which grounds each piece of evidence (backing) supports can help students identify whether the evidence is sufficient or relevant. For example, a speaker might state, "Schools should hire more teachers so that classes can be smaller. Smaller classes will allow teachers to know each student better and allow them to provide more individual instruction. Teachers would also have more energy and be able to design more engaging lessons, which would improve student achievement. Three studies have found that the achievement of students in smaller classes is higher than the achievement of students in larger classes. Also, a study found that teachers with fewer students were more confident, were more relaxed, and had better relationships with students. Finally, another study showed that the quality of teaching is higher in classrooms with fewer students."

Students might diagram the speaker's backing as shown in figure I.7.

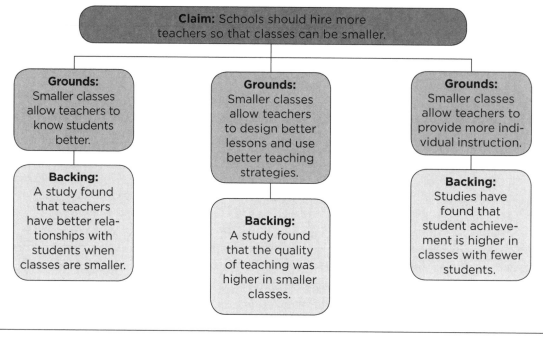

Figure I.7: Diagramming backing.

Diagramming backing in this way allows students to deconstruct an argument into its component parts and develop a clearer understanding of the argument itself. Students can see how each element of the argument is connected to another element. This makes it easier for them to verify that all evidence is sufficient and relevant.

Determine Whether Evidence Is Sufficient

Evidence is sufficient when there is enough of it to provide ample support for a claim or grounds. If a person cannot reasonably agree with a claim given the evidence provided, then the evidence is probably insufficient. For instance, given the claim "Alaska is a more enjoyable place to live than Colorado," a student might present the following grounds: "Because the state of Alaska is warmer on average than the state of Colorado." To back up the grounds, the student says, "The average temperature of Juneau, Alaska, is 41.5 degrees, but the average temperature of Alamosa, Colorado, is only 40.8 degrees." This backing is insufficient evidence for the grounds that Alaska is warmer than Colorado for a few reasons. For one, the student has only compared the average temperatures of two cities, one from each state, and one city may not be indicative of the climate of an entire state. Juneau is located in the southern part of Alaska and is one of the warmest places in the state. Compared to the average temperature of Barrow, Alaska, a northern city on the coast of the Arctic Ocean, Juneau's average is a full thirty degrees warmer. In addition, Juneau's average temperature of 41.5 degrees is only 1.5 degrees warmer than Alamosa's average of 40.8. The difference seems too small to support a claim that one state is decidedly warmer than the other.

In the example diagrammed in figure I.7, a student might question whether the evidence provided is sufficient. In two cases, backing is represented by only one study. Also, citation information is not provided for any of the studies mentioned in the argument. This should lead students to investigate further into the validity of the evidence provided.

Determine Whether Evidence Is Relevant

Evidence is relevant when it directly relates to proving or disproving an element of the claim. When it does not, it can be considered irrelevant. Consider, for example, a criminal case in which someone is tried for murder. To convict a defendant of first-degree murder (as opposed to second-degree murder or manslaughter), a prosecutor must prove that the act was premeditated; in other words, she must prove that the defendant had planned the murder beforehand. In such a circumstance, pointing out that the defendant once stole a pack of gum from a drugstore is irrelevant evidence because it does not directly relate to proving that the murder was premeditated. On the other hand, eyewitness testimonies of the defendant making threats on the victim's life would be considered relevant. These testimonies could contribute to proving that the murder was premeditated.

Perspective Taking

Students must learn to take multiple perspectives in order to argue effectively. In *The Big Sort*, journalist Bill Bishop (2008) explained that throughout the past half-century, Americans have gradually become more and more divided, increasingly socializing in communities filled with people who share their views:

> The second half of the [twentieth] century brought social specialization, the displacement of mass culture by media, organizations, and associations that were both more segmented and more homogeneous. We now worship in churches among like-minded parishioners, or we change churches, maybe even denominations, to find such persons. We join volunteer groups with like-minded companions. We read and watch news that confirms our existing opinions. . . . Media, advertising, city economies—they've all segmented, specialized, and segregated. (pp. 37–38)

As a result of the "big sort," diverse viewpoints rarely coalesce in one physical location. However, as Hess (2011) pointed out, this circumstance makes schools uniquely suited for controversial discussions. Classrooms in the United States "feature ideological, religious, and social class diversity among students" (Hess, 2011, p. 70) and therefore represent various perspectives on social issues. Walter Humes (2012) went one step further, asserting that schools have a duty "to extend, not simply confirm, experience, and this involves exposing youngsters to alternative ways of life and values different from those encountered at home" (p. 19).

In addition, the CCSS require that students be able to take multiple perspectives. The authors asserted that a college- and career-ready student will "actively seek to understand other perspectives and cultures through reading and listening" and is able to "communicate effectively with people of varied backgrounds" (NGA & CCSSO, 2010a, p. 7). Consequently, we have included perspective taking as a critical skill needed for effective argumentation.

Marzano and Heflebower (2012) stated that "in order to be able to see an issue from multiple perspectives, students must first be aware that different perspectives can and do exist" (p. 153). Thus, an important aspect of teaching students the skill of perspective taking is helping them understand that people can see the same thing in very different ways. We propose two ways to teach perspective taking:

1. Give examples of situations that demonstrate different perspectives.

2. Engage students in hands-on activities that highlight various perspectives of students in the class.

The following sections provide more information about each method.

Examples of Different Perspectives

The first way to introduce the concept of multiple perspectives involves providing examples of situations that lead to various points of view. For instance, optical illusions like the one presented in figure I.8 can be used to show how two different viewpoints can both be correct.

Figure I.8: Optical illusion of a swan or a squirrel.
Source: Fischer, 1968.

In this image, students might see a swan with its beak tucked into its chest or a squirrel nibbling on something it holds in its paws. Ask for volunteers to share the animal that they see in the image, and then help the entire class see it both ways.

Alternatively, a teacher might describe a scenario in which two people perceive the same situation differently based on different vantage points. For example, a person who is stranded on a desert island might be thrilled to see a boat drifting in the distance, while the person floating in the boat is relieved to finally see land.

Hands-On Activities

A second, more hands-on way to teach students that different people might have different perspectives is to put students in a situation that yields different perspectives within the class. For younger students, this can be as simple as taking class polls during daily activities. After reading Dr. Seuss's *The Cat in the Hat* (1957/1985), for example, say, "Raise your hand if you would have let the Cat in the Hat into your house," and then "Raise your hand if you would not have let the Cat in." Point out that some students have one perspective, while other students have a different one, and that neither answer is right or wrong.

Older students can handle more complex activities that illuminate various perspectives among their classmates. One activity involves an imaginary scenario in which students pretend that they have been in a plane crash, leaving them stranded on a deserted island. Give students a list of characters (mechanic, hunter, plant biologist, doctor, and priest) and ask them to put the characters in order from most to least important as they try to escape the island. Students discuss their lists in pairs, then groups of four, and finally as a whole class. Guide the class to the conclusion that there is no correct or incorrect solution. Point out that students' responses are influenced by their differing beliefs and values.

Communicating Responsibly

An important skill for argumentation is the capacity to interact thoughtfully and respectfully with others during whole-class and small-group discussions. According to Marzano and Heflebower (2012), communicating responsibly depends primarily on the ability to hold oneself accountable for the outcomes of interactions. In other words, students must learn to communicate their ideas and beliefs in a way that is simultaneously honest, confident, and respectful, which means they must take responsibility for their own speech. Students who communicate responsibly exhibit the following actions:

◆ Speaking with a calm demeanor, including reasonable volume and tone of voice

◆ Listening actively (sitting up, making eye contact, nodding, and asking questions) while others are speaking

- Using disciplined and respectful word choice
- Critiquing ideas instead of individuals

Not surprisingly, the authors of the CCSS considered the ability to "participate effectively in a range of conversations and collaborations with diverse partners" to be crucial to the development of college- and career-ready students (CCRA.SL.1; NGA & CCSSO, 2010a, p. 22). They list some variation of this skill as the first Speaking and Listening standard for students of every age, from kindergarten through high school.

Many others have stressed the importance of communicating responsibly for academic success (Campbell, 2008; Hess, 2002; Matsumura, Slater, & Crosson, 2008; Miller & Pedro, 2006; Reyes, Brackett, Rivers, White, & Salovey, 2012). Sarah Michaels, Mary Catherine O'Connor, and Megan Williams Hall (2010) outlined the following elements of responsible communication from the University of Pittsburgh's Accountable Talk® program:

> When classroom talk is accountable to the learning community, students listen to one another, not just obediently keeping quiet until it is their turn to take the floor, but attending carefully so that they can use and build on one another's ideas. Students and teachers paraphrase and expand upon one another's contributions. If speakers aren't sure they understood what someone else said, they make an effort to clarify. They disagree respectfully, challenging a claim, not the person who made it. Students move the argument forward, sometimes with the teacher's help, sometimes on their own. (pp. 2–3)

The aforementioned elements of communicating responsibly can meaningfully influence the success of a classroom debate or discussion. However, as Michaels and her colleagues (2010) pointed out, productive academic discussions do not "spring spontaneously from students' mouths," but instead require "time and effort to create" (p. 1). Consequently, we recommend modeling, teaching, and practicing responsible communication skills with students before playing the games in this book, particularly those that involve discussion between students, such as Claim Capers (page 173) or Convince the Crowd (page 185).

One way teachers can help students communicate responsibly is through modeling. Michaels and her colleagues (2010) wrote:

> Teachers may press for clarification and explanation, require justifications of proposals and challenges, recognize and challenge misconceptions, demand evidence for claims and arguments, or interpret and "revoice" students' statements. Over time, students can be expected to carry out each of these conversational "moves" themselves in peer discussions. (p. 1)

A second way to guide students toward communicating responsibly is through explicit teaching. We propose the following three steps for teaching responsible communication:

1. Establish norms for communicating responsibly in the classroom.

2. Provide student-friendly examples of responsible communication.

3. Practice and deepen students' understanding of responsible communication.

Here, we provide detail about each step.

Establish Norms

Teachers should clearly establish classroom norms that support responsible communication and hold students accountable for upholding them. Humes (2012) pointed out that for students to engage successfully with controversial content, "the culture of the classroom has to be fair and open-minded" (p. 15), as well as trustworthy. He asserted that such an environment helps students feel safe and confident enough to speak up and express their own ideas. Moreover, the CCSS specifically require students to agree on and adhere to conversational norms. Second graders, for instance, are expected to "follow agreed-upon rules for discussions," which include "gaining the floor in respectful ways, listening to others with care, [and] speaking one at a time about the topics and texts under discussion" (SL.2.1; NGA & CCSSO, 2010a, p. 23). Marzano (2007) similarly suggested that every student contribute to a list of rules for effective behavior in the classroom. Students then add their signatures to this class pledge and hold themselves and each other accountable for its tenets. In keeping with these recommendations, we suggest that teachers collaborate with students to create a list of norms for responsible communication during discussion.

For younger students, Michelle Cummings (2012) suggests using a traffic light metaphor to norm behavior before a discussion. The color red represents behaviors that need to stop during discussion (such as put-downs or blaming), yellow represents behaviors that students should be careful of (such as raising one's voice), and green represents behaviors that help the discussion move forward (such as active listening or encouraging words). Teachers can even designate one student the "traffic signal," whose job it is to hold up different colored pieces of paper (red, yellow, and green) during discussion to show classmates how they are doing.

Provide Examples

Teachers can also provide students with examples of responsible, assertive discussion. Douglas Fisher, Nancy Frey, and Carol Rothenberg (2008) recommended creating question prompts and sentence frames for communicating responsibly, printing them on table cards, and placing them on desks for students to use during collaboration. They state that these easily accessible reminders "reinforce the need for holding oneself (and each other) accountable for rigorous discussion" (p. 97). Table I.19 depicts various sentence frames and stems that students can use to develop responsible communication skills.

Teachers can also display question prompts and sentence frames prominently in the classroom or distribute them via handout while a debate is in session. This strategy is particularly useful for English learners (ELs), but all students can learn from the examples, even those with lots of argumentation experience.

Table I.19: Sentence Frames and Stems for Communicating Responsibly

Clarifying	Connecting
How is this relevant to your point? Can you explain what you mean? So what you're saying is _____.	I want to say more about what _____ said about _____. I'd like to add _____. I noticed that _____. What _____ said reminded me of _____.

Agreeing	Disagreeing
I agree with _____ because _____.	I disagree with _____ because _____.
I think _____ made a great point about _____.	Couldn't it also be that _____?
Yes, and furthermore _____.	I see why _____ might say that, but _____.
Although we still disagree on the claim overall, it seems to me that we *can* agree on _____.	While I think _____ had a point that _____, I disagree with the part where he/she said _____.
	It seems to me that _____ committed an error in reasoning when he/she said _____.

Changing the Subject	Taking Responsibility
It seems to me that we're spending a lot of time discussing _____, when maybe we should be discussing _____.	I must have miscommunicated my point earlier; I apologize. What I intended to say was _____.
I'd like to change the subject to _____.	Earlier, I neglected to point out _____.
Something I think the other side has not addressed is _____.	I'm sorry, I misunderstood you. I thought you meant _____.
	You're right. Those words were hurtful and uncalled for. I shouldn't have said that.

Source: Adapted from Michaels et al., 2010.

Practice and Deepen Understanding

Finally, students practice and deepen their understanding of responsible communication. One simple and engaging method is to analyze the behavior of prominent debaters in the media. Screen clips from televised presidential debates or arguments between political pundits on programs such as CNN's *Crossfire*. Alternatively, utilize the resources that Intelligence Squared—an organization that conducts Oxford-style debates—provides on its website (http://intelligencesquaredus.org). Show your class a video of a debate, download an NPR radio podcast of one, or read, annotate, and discuss a debate transcript. Ask students to identify instances of strong and weak decorum for debate as they watch, listen, or read. Students can also complete reflection guides that contain questions, such as "What are three examples of respectful disagreement used in this clip?" or "What did it look and sound like when a debater lost control of his or her emotions? How did this affect your opinion of the debater?" Use activities like this to facilitate whole-class or small-group discussions with your students about responsible communication.

How to Use This Book

The activities and games in this book fuse two key elements of effective engagement—academic games and friendly controversy—to help students practice argumentation skills outlined in the CCSS. According to over sixty studies conducted by Marzano Research, the use of academic games in the classroom is associated with an average gain of 20 percentile points in student achievement (Haystead & Marzano, 2009). Furthermore, a study by Nancy Lowry and David Johnson (1981) demonstrated that imbuing a friendly sense of controversy into lessons leads to more curiosity, higher achievement, and more positive attitudes regarding the subject matter.

While encouraging friendly controversy, take care to avoid placing inordinate pressure on winning. Research shows that mild pressure can help people focus (Cahill, Gorski, & Le, 2003; Shors, Weiss, & Thompson, 1992; Van Honk et al., 2003) but too much pressure can have negative consequences (Ito, Larsen, Smith, & Cacioppo, 2002; Roozendaal, 2003). For example, students who feel overly compelled to win a game can be embarrassed if they lose (Epstein & Harackiewicz, 1992; Moriarty, Douglas, Punch, & Hattie, 1995; Reeve & Deci, 1996).

Fortunately, students do not need to be motivated by external pressures, prizes, or rewards to enjoy academic games. Thomas Good and Jere Brophy (2003) discussed the engaging elements of competition for its own sake:

> The opportunity to compete can add excitement to classroom activities, whether the competition is for prizes or merely for the satisfaction of winning. Competition may be either individual (students compete against everyone else) or group (students are divided into teams that compete with one another). (p. 227)

Marzano (2007) calls this type of fun, low-stakes sparring *inconsequential competition* because it has no bearing on a student's grade or status in the class.

This book contains ten argumentation activities and games for classroom use:

1. I Think, I Like, I Believe

2. Opinion Scoot

3. Fishing for Facts

4. Argument Relay

5. Rapid Fire

6. Which One Doesn't Belong?

7. Text Evidence Bingo

8. Rhetoric Memory

9. Claim Capers

10. Convince the Crowd

Activities and games are ordered by grade level, with those for younger students in earlier chapters and those for older students in later chapters. Each one involves a different combination of CCSS-based argumentation skills. The activities and games at the beginning of the book require more basic skills (such as distinguishing fact from opinion and presenting and supporting claims) than those at the end. For easy reference, the first page of each game or activity lists the appropriate age group, the argumentation skills involved, and materials needed. Teachers can also use tables I.2 (page 5) and I.3 (page 15) to see which activities and games align to specific argumentation standards. Locate the standards that correspond to your grade level in table I.2, take note of the skills associated with the standards, and choose activities and games from table I.3 that allow students to practice those skills.

Throughout the book, you will also notice teacher tips for executing each game. These tips are indicated by the light bulb icon to the left. Refer to these tips for useful hints regarding variations in gameplay and setup, solutions to potential pitfalls, and differentiation strategies to meet the needs of all students.

Remember that the activities and games are meant not to replace direct instruction in argumentation, but to provide different ways to practice and develop argumentation skills. Feel free to adapt or supplement to suit the requirements of your school, curriculum, and students. Finally—and most importantly—have fun!

1

I Think, I Like, I Believe

For lower elementary students

This circle-based game is designed to introduce young students to the concept of an opinion. It can be played three ways: (1) students practice responding to opinions, (2) students practice expressing opinions, or (3) students practice distinguishing between facts and opinions.

Setup

Arrange the place markers (see materials list) in a large circle. In addition to the facts and opinions from appendix A (page 209), teachers can come up with their own list of facts and/or opinions in advance, or make them up on the fly during the game. Teachers should be prepared to explain and provide examples of different facts and opinions.

Opinions should be simple and relatable to students so that they may decide whether or not they agree. To illustrate, a personal statement such as "I love my dog Lucky" is not a great option because students have probably never met your dog Lucky. The following list includes examples of the types of opinions teachers might generate:

- ◆ I love playing freeze tag.
- ◆ I like eating cereal for breakfast.
- ◆ I think dancing is fun.
- ◆ I love to read books.
- ◆ I believe kittens are the cutest animal.

Notice that each statement begins with a phrase that clearly signifies an opinion, such as *I like*, *I love*, *I think*, or *I believe*. Even if you do not use the game to teach

Argumentation Skills

- Distinguishing fact from opinion
- Presenting and supporting claims (stating an opinion or preference)
- Perspective taking (listening to others' opinions)

Materials

- Place marker for each student to stand on (such as rubber bases, rug sections, or chalk markings if playing outside; avoid using paper or other items on which students might slip)
- List of facts and opinions (see appendix A on page 209)

distinguishing fact and opinion, these sentence starters can help frame the basic difference between the two for students to draw on later.

Fact statements must be simple enough for young students to know they are true, based on either their background knowledge or an immediately observable source of proof. The following list includes examples of the types of facts teachers might use:

◆ Today is Monday.

◆ The four seasons are spring, summer, winter, and fall.

◆ Tomás is wearing a green shirt.

◆ The sun is shining.

Avoid fact statements that all students cannot easily observe (such as "Dillon's eyes are blue"). Furthermore, do not use factually ambiguous or incorrect statements, as students may confuse them with opinions. For instance, remarking that Erin's hair is brown—when it could also be considered dark blond or a shade of red or black—is too subjective. Right now, you simply want to help students get used to the concepts of fact and opinion, both of which are complex enough on their own. Trying to make a distinction between an opinion and a "wrong fact" at this point is likely to frustrate your students.

Play

Students form a circle by standing on their place markers. The teacher stands in the middle and reminds students that an opinion is the way someone feels about something, pointing out that opinions often begin with *I think, I like,* or *I believe.* Provide several examples of opinions to support this explanation (such as "I think chocolate is the best ice cream flavor," "I like cookies more than cake," or "I believe that kids should be paid for doing chores").

With very young students, it is best to start by giving them practice with responding to opinions. To do this, call out an opinion statement (for example, "I like going camping"). Any student who shares that opinion moves out of his or her spot. All others remain standing in their original positions. Students who have moved trade spots with other agreeing students in the circle. When students have traded, the teacher calls out a second opinion. Students who agree with the new opinion trade places. Play continues in this fashion for as long as desired. Pause the game occasionally when students are still and ask for volunteers to share reasons why they hold the opinion they do. Be sure to provide plenty of modeling yourself before asking students to share their reasons. When first introducing the game to students, teachers may also want to begin each opinion with "Move to a different spot if you . . ." so students get the hang of the rules.

 Everyone wins during this game, so there is no need for students to run from spot to spot in the circle. Explain and reiterate this rule throughout the game to avoid accidents, injuries, or hurt feelings.

When students are comfortable responding to opinions, provide practice expressing opinions. To do this, remove one of the place markers. When students move to a different spot in the circle, one student will be left without a place. This student becomes the new caller. He or she moves to the center, calls out a new opinion, and tries to find a spot. A new student becomes the caller, and so on. If you choose to play this way, be sure to stress that the person in the center has not lost the game—everyone still wins.

To give older students practice distinguishing between facts and opinions (rather than just agreeing or disagreeing with opinion statements), randomly call out opinion statements and fact statements. When an opinion is called, all students trade spots—whether they agree or disagree does not matter in this variation of the game. When a fact is called, all students remain standing in their spots. This is a great way to give students some low-stakes practice with facts and opinions. If they aren't sure of the answer, they can look around the circle and see what other students are doing. When a student mistakenly starts to leave his or her spot on a fact, offer a gentle, "Oops! Wait just a minute—are you *sure* that's an opinion? Remember—a fact is true for everyone. Can we all see that Erika is taller than Vijay?" When students are confused about a particular statement, make sure you discuss the confusion with them before moving on to the next statement.

Opinion Scoot

For middle elementary students

Opinion Scoot is based on a popular stations activity called "Scoot" (sometimes called "Scooch" or "Ske-daddle") in which students rotate from desk to desk and respond to a different question at each one. In this adaptation, we have added an element in which students vote on specific questions by dropping tokens in cups at each station. This game is designed to give elementary students practice with stating opinions and explaining their reasoning. To play, students need basic reading, writing, and counting skills. They do not need to know terms like *claim*, *grounds*, *backing*, or *qualifier*, nor do they need to be perfect spellers, fluent readers, or master grammarians.

Setup

We recommend setting up students' desks for this game before they arrive in the room. First, lay a question card face up on each desk. Teachers can use the premade question cards at the end of this chapter (see pages 63–68), or they can make their own.

Place two cups—one from each group—on each desk. Position one cup in each of the two top corners of the desk. This will save space for students to use when writing on their answer sheets. One of these cups will be for *yes* votes; the other cup will be for *no* votes. Make sure you consistently position the same cup in the same corner of every desk to prevent confusion among students. If you have distinguished the cups by color, for instance, you might place all of the blue cups

Argumentation Skills

- Presenting and supporting claims (write an opinion and reasons)
- Organizing an argument (use linking words—such as *because*, *and*, *also*, and so on—to connect opinion and reasons)

Materials

- Question card for each student in class (see reproducibles on pages 63–68)
- Two class sets of cups—each set should be visibly distinct from the other (for example, one red cup and one blue; one labeled *yes* and the other labeled *no*)
- Sandwich bag for each student with the same number of tokens (such as beads, plastic chips, tiddlywinks, foam pieces, pretzels, and so on) as rounds to be played
- Answer sheet for each student (see reproducible on page 62)
- Pen or pencil for each student
- Stopwatch or timer (optional)

Creating your own yes-or-no questions for Opinion Scoot allows you to design them around issues that are specific to your school or community (for example, "Should our neighborhood get a public swimming pool?"). Questions that address controversies in your own school are also good because they resonate with all students. For instance, if your school has recently banned throwing snowballs at recess, you could include a question that directly addresses this issue: "Should kids be allowed to throw snowballs at recess?" If there is a tradition in your school that the fifth graders get to run the after-school bake sale, then address that: "Should kids from other grades get to help out at the bake sale?" If you do decide to create your own questions, remember that they must be yes-or-no questions written in student-friendly language (all students should be able to read them independently). Keep in mind that long, complex questions are more likely to result in student frustration and rotation traffic jams during the game. Clear, straightforward questions are best.

in the top left corner of the desk and all of the red cups in the top right corner. If you have not physically written *yes* and *no* on the cups, write a key or legend on the board (for example, blue cup = yes, red cup = no) to help students remember which is which.

The cups can be visually marked in any way you like, as long as they look different. For instance, you might use a permanent marker to write yes on every cup in the first set and no on every cup in the second set, although this can be time consuming. You could also obtain a class set of red cups and a class set of blue cups. To illustrate, for a class of twenty-four students, you would need forty-eight cups in total, with twenty-four red cups and twenty-four blue cups. Figure 2.1 illustrates the way a prepared student desktop might look. When students arrive, pass out a bag of tokens and a blank answer sheet (see reproducible on page 62) to each student. Students will use the answer sheet to record their reasoning after every third rotation.

Play

Opinion Scoot follows the same basic structure as any rotating stations activity. Students spend a few minutes completing an activity in one place, then move to another place to complete a slightly different activity, then move to another, and another, until each student has been to every station or time runs out. In this particular game, each student spends time individually answering a question and voting at his or her own desk, then moves to a different student's desk to consider a new question and vote, and so on. For every third question, students record an explanation of their reasoning on an answer sheet.

Each student starts at his or her own desk. Explain that students will use their tokens to vote on a new question at every desk and that they will use their answer sheet to write down their reasoning at every third desk. Emphasize that there are no right or wrong answers in this game. Tell students that the game is about figuring out your own opinion—a personal feeling, thought, or belief—and explaining why you feel that way. Point out that different people can have different opinions, and give a few examples that are extremely relatable for your students. For instance, you might say, "Let's say you want some ice cream, but there are two choices: chocolate and vanilla. Is chocolate better than vanilla? Raise your hand if you think it is. Now raise your hand if you think it isn't. See? Demetria thinks chocolate is

"Yes" cup   Question card   "No" cup

Figure 2.1: Desktop layout for a game of Opinion Scoot.

better than vanilla, but Chase doesn't. Demetria is not wrong for liking chocolate, and Chase is not wrong for liking vanilla. Some people like both or neither. There is no right answer. Everyone has his or her own opinion about which flavor is best."

Other example questions you could ask include:

- Is spring better than autumn?
- Is Coca-Cola better than Pepsi?
- Is football better than soccer?
- Is TV better than video games?
- Are puppies better than kittens?

Once students understand that the questions on each desk are opinions, and that they are expected to vote at each desk, ask them to vote on the question at their own desk by dropping a token in either the *yes* cup or the *no* cup. Then prompt students to think about their reasoning. You might say, "Now think to yourself, 'Why do I think my opinion is right?'" In response, a student might think, "TV isn't better than video games because you can control what happens in a video game." Do not have students write anything on their answer sheets yet, but do remind them to take their sheets with them when they move to the next desk.

After students have voted at their own desks and thought of a reason for their vote, give explicit directions about how to rotate to the next desk. Include specific instructions about when, where, and how you want them to move. For the *when*, emphasize that students may only move over to the next desk when they hear you say, "Scoot!" Explain that even if they finish early, they must remain seated until you give this signal.

 If your students are still learning to read, offer to read a question aloud if they are having trouble decoding the words. Students can even raise their hands to ask you to read the question to them. After all, the primary purpose of the game is not to test students' reading skills but to get younger students to generate claims and evidence. To proactively lessen the number of students asking you for help with reading, you can quickly read through each of the question cards before beginning the game. Just walk around the room, pick up the card at each desk, read it aloud for the class, and set it back down.

The *where* will obviously depend on the layout of your classroom. Arranging desks in a circle is easiest for younger students, but is not necessary. If desks are arranged in rows, students can each move one desk to the right during rotation. Students at the end of a row move to the desk farthest to the left in the row behind them. Figure 2.2 (page 56) depicts a row rotation arrangement.

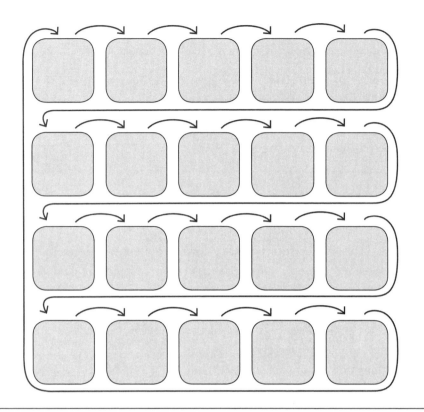

Figure 2.2: Rotation procedure for desks arranged in rows.

If desks are arranged in pods of four, rotation is trickier but still possible with some extra teacher guidance. Students rotate clockwise around the pod first, then bounce over to a new pod. Figure 2.3 shows this pod rotation arrangement.

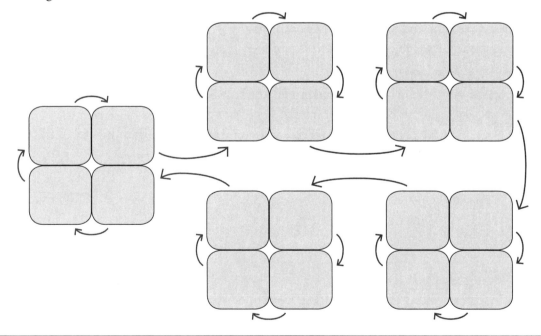

Figure 2.3: Rotation procedure for desks arranged in pods of four.

These routines may take some practice, but students will get the idea. You can proactively mitigate rotation confusion by pausing the game to ask students where they are supposed to go next—*before* they leave their seats. During the first few rotations, ask students to silently point to their new destination before cueing them to move.

Presenting expectations for *how* students ought to behave when rotating can be more complicated because there are multiple behaviors to address. The most important expectations to remember include keeping hands to oneself, keeping mouths closed, and walking from desk to desk instead of running or jumping.

When a student arrives at a new desk, he or she proceeds through four steps:

1. Read the question.

2. Answer the question in your head.

3. Vote for your answer by dropping a token in one of the cups.

4. Think up a "why" for your answer in your head.

Remind students that they have a set number of tokens in their plastic bag, and therefore can only afford to "spend" one vote at each desk. This will help prevent students from voting more than once at a desk. Depending on the age and reading ability of your students, provide somewhere between thirty seconds and two minutes for students to complete these four steps. For as long as it takes, walk the class carefully through each step to help them get used to how the game works. You may want to consider posting the steps somewhere in the classroom for students to see. When it is time for students to rotate to a new desk, say, "Scoot!" At this moment, everyone moves to the next desk in the rotation, carrying along their writing utensil, bag of tokens, and answer

Model the process of recording opinions and reasoning. Use a copy of the answer sheet and a document camera or overhead projector to show students exactly what you want them to do. Perform a metacognitive think-aloud to guide students through your thought process. Say something like the following: *This time, I am going to use my answer sheet to circle my answer and, most importantly, stop-and-jot my "why." First, I am going to read the question. It says, "Do you like scary stories?" Now I am going to ask myself, "Do I think yes, or do I think no to this question?" Okay, I think no, I don't like scary stories. So I am going to circle no—like this—on my answer sheet. Next, I'm going to vote with my token. I'll put it in this blue cup because I know the blue cup stands for no. And last, I'm going to think of my "why." So I am thinking to myself, "Why do I dislike scary stories?" Well, I know that scary stories give me nightmares sometimes, and when I have nightmares, I can't fall asleep. So I have my "why"! I'm going to write the "why" on these lines, like this . . .*

sheet. Repeat the process: give students time to read the question, consider their answer, cast their vote, and think up a "why"—a reason for their vote. Call out the steps to students to guide them through the game.

The answer sheet is used when students reach their third desk and question. Students use their tokens to vote on the question, as usual. However, after reading the question, voting for their opinion with a token, and thinking about their reasoning, students circle *yes* or *no* on the first space on the answer sheet and write a few words or—depending on age—a few sentences explaining their opinion. This allows them to practice generating grounds for their claims. Give students a few extra minutes to record their votes and their reasoning on their answer sheets.

Figure 2.4 shows a second-grade student's answer sheet after the class has rotated three times.

Figure 2.4: A second grader's answer sheet after three rotations of Opinion Scoot.

 The main goal of this activity is not to increase fluency of reading and writing. Fluency is absolutely an important learning target for elementary students, but this is not the most useful activity for accomplishing that particular task. Instead, the goal of Opinion Scoot is to provide an opportunity for children to get comfortable with making and defending claims at an early age.

Marquise's answer was in response to the question, "Is it okay to keep wild animals as pets?" As shown in figure 2.4, Marquise believes that it is not okay to keep wild animals as pets and therefore has circled *no* on his answer sheet. Notice that, when prompted with the word *because*, he was able to justify his reasoning in only a few words: "because it is scary and it can bite you." Remind students that they do not need to fill in all of the space on the lines with writing, as long as they provide a "why" that makes sense. We recommend that you limit the number of times students must physically write down a "why" to avoid overwhelming emerging readers and writers.

Have students rotate a fourth and fifth time without writing on their answer sheets. During the sixth rotation, prompt them to record their "why" a second time. Figure 2.5 shows the same second grader's answer sheet after six rounds.

Name: Marquise

YES or (NO)	because *it is scary and it can bite you.*
(YES) or NO	because *who nose you mite like it.*
YES or NO	because _____

Figure 2.5: A second grader's answer sheet after six rotations of Opinion Scoot.

Marquise's sixth question was, "Is it good to try new foods, even if you may not like them?" As shown in figure 2.5, Marquise believes that it is good to try new foods because you will never know whether you like them unless you give them a fair chance. Again, his answer does not use proper syntax, and the words are not spelled correctly; regardless, Marquise has demonstrated that he knows how to express an opinion and support it with reasoning.

Game play continues until students reach their ninth desk and question, where they again record their opinion and reasoning. Table 2.1 (page 60) illustrates the pattern of activity during rotations.

As shown, students use tokens to vote at every single desk they visit; that is, they read, consider, and mentally respond to each question they read. However, students only use their answer sheets to record their "why" at every third desk.

Table 2.1: Pattern of Activity During Rotations in Opinion Scoot

Number of Rotations	1	2	3	4	5	6	7	8	9	10	11	12
Student votes with token and thinks about reasoning	X	X	X	X	X	X	X	X	X	X	X	X
Student circles answer and records reasoning on answer sheet			X			X			X			X

Play continues until students have used all their tokens. Adjust the token count in each student's plastic bag before the game to match the number of rounds you intend to play. At the end of the game, plastic cups will contain multiple tokens, and answer sheets will be filled with opinions and reasons (claims and grounds). After eighteen rotations, a student's completed answer sheet might look like figure 2.6.

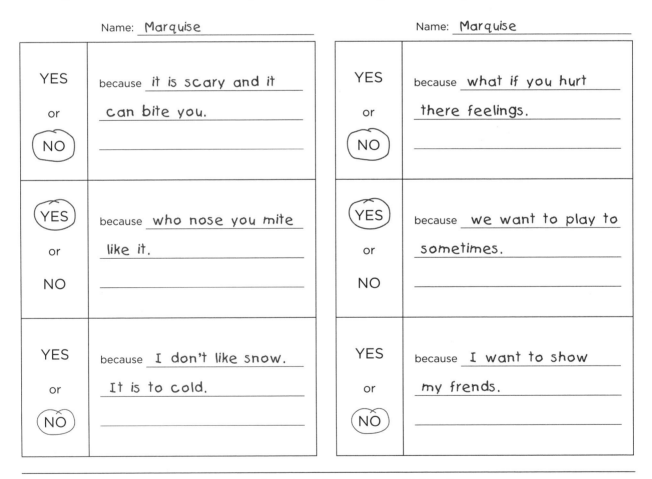

Figure 2.6: A second grader's double-sided answer sheet after eighteen rotations of Opinion Scoot.

Throughout the game, Marquise has voted on a total of eighteen questions and recorded his reasoning for a total of six questions. His third, fourth, fifth, and sixth recorded answers are in response to the following questions:

◆ Is winter the best season?

◆ Is it ever okay to lie?

◆ Should kids have longer recess?

◆ If you had magical powers, would you keep them secret?

At the end of the game, students return to their own desks and count the votes (tokens) in each of the cups. Ask them to determine whether the most votes were for *yes* or *no* and then ask every student to read aloud the question at his or her desk and to share the winner—yes or no—with the class. For each question, you can ask students from the winning side to raise their hands to share their "why," or grounds for their opinion, with the class. This gives you a great opportunity to provide feedback and coaching on making and defending claims. Collect the answer sheets to evaluate student performance during the game. Use the sheets as unobtrusive assessment data to guide further instruction.

When you first begin playing Opinion Scoot, you will probably notice some insufficient responses from students. If the question is "Should kids have to take cooking classes in school?" a student might write something like "Yes, because then they will learn how to cook." This response does not provide any grounds for the benefits of learning to cook. While the game is in play, wander around the room to monitor student responses. If the issue is limited to a few students, look over their shoulders and ask probing questions like "Why is it important for kids to learn how to cook?" "What will be good about cooking class?" "What new things will kids be able to do once they know how to cook?" If the issue is widespread, pause the game and explain what a good "why" looks like.

Student Answer Sheet for Opinion Scoot

YES or NO	because _____ _____ _____ _____
YES or NO	because _____ _____ _____ _____
YES or NO	because _____ _____ _____ _____

Question Cards for Opinion Scoot

The following reproducibles contain question cards for Opinion Scoot. The cards are organized by grade level, but teachers should feel free to make changes to this organization based on the needs of their students. Alternatively, teachers can create their own question cards using index cards, slips of scrap paper, and so on.

Grades 2–3

If you find $100, should you keep it?	Are movies better in 3-D?	Is winning more important than being nice?
Should kids have to do chores?	Does being older make you smarter?	Would you eat a bug if someone gave you $5?
Is riding a bike better than riding in a car?	Is TV good for you?	Is it okay to keep animals in zoos?
Is soccer the best sport?	If someone dares you to do something, should you do it no matter what?	Is it okay to keep wild animals as pets?
Is winter the best season?	Is it okay for an animal to go extinct?	Are video games better than board games?

page 1 of 6

If you break something by accident, should you tell?	Should there be more holidays from school?	Would you do something even if you were scared (like go down a big slide)?
Is it good to try new foods, even if you may not like them?	Should parents make kids eat vegetables?	If you could go to the future, would you?
Do you learn more in class when kids listen to the teacher?	Is inside beauty better than outside beauty?	Are cats better than dogs?
Is it ever okay to lie?	Is Halloween the best holiday?	Is playing inside better than playing outside?
If someone cheats, should you tell?	If a friend hurt you, would you forgive that friend?	Would you trade lives with a movie star?
Should all kids learn karate?	Is reading important?	If you had magical powers, would you keep them secret?

If you could read people's minds, would you do it?	Is it okay to take whales from their ocean homes to live at SeaWorld?	Do you like scary stories?
Should hats be allowed in school?	Are iPads better than books?	Can jokes still be funny if they hurt someone's feelings?
If you could go back in time, would you?	Is it okay to keep lightning bugs (fireflies) in jars?	Should kids have longer recess?
Is it okay to fool people with magic tricks?	Can a robot take a human's place?	Should we dump our trash into outer space?

Grades 4–5

Should parents get in trouble if their kids break the law?	Should kids be paid for going to school?	Are computers better than teachers?
Should students have to take cooking classes in school?	Is it okay for kids to skip subjects in school that they don't like?	Should kids have to wear uniforms to school?
Is it more important for a president to be smart than to be kind?	Should countries be ruled by kings and queens?	Should kids be allowed to get tattoos?
Should it be against the law for people to smoke cigarettes?	Should kids in elementary school have to take Spanish class?	Does homework help kids learn?
Should schools ban peanut butter because some people have allergies?	Is kickball better than dodgeball?	Do kid celebrities have easy lives?
Should fifth grade be a part of middle school?	Are fireworks and sparklers safe for kids?	Is it important to know more than everyone else does?

Should schools ban cell phones?	Is it important to learn to play an instrument (like the piano, the drums, or the flute)?	Should kids have more field trips at school?
Would year-round school help kids learn?	Should the driving age be lowered?	Is homeschooling better for kids than public schooling?
Should kids get to choose their own bedtime?	Are all-girl or all-boy classrooms better for kids than mixed classrooms?	Should school begin later in the morning and end around dinnertime?
Should it be illegal to ride a bike without a helmet?	Should schools offer fast food (like nachos or hamburgers) in lunchrooms?	Are music and art classes important for kids?
Is it okay for kids under thirteen to watch PG-13 movies?	Should all kids have to go to gym class?	Is it okay for kids and teachers to pray in school?
Should it be against the law to not recycle?	Should textbooks be replaced with iPads?	Are sports stars paid too much money?

page 5 of 6

Should students have to show their work in math class?	Is it okay for kids to date before they get to high school?	Should the United States lower the voting age?
Is it okay for parents to take their kids out of school to travel?	Should schools stop selling chocolate milk?	Is it okay for girls to play football with boys?
Is it okay for scientists to use animals to test new medicines?	Should parents control what their kids see on TV and the Internet?	Should kids be allowed to use electronics (like cell phones, iPods, and tablets) during recess?
Should elementary schools have their own sports teams (like middle and high schools)?	Should students be allowed to eat in class?	Should kids be forced to stand during the Pledge of Allegiance if they don't want to?

3 Fishing for Facts
For upper elementary students

Fishing for Facts is designed to give elementary students practice with the foundational skill of distinguishing fact from opinion. This game is loosely based on Apple Picking, a physical education game in Susan L. Kasser's (1995) book *Inclusive Games: Movement Fun for Everyone!* In that game, students hurry from one area of the gymnasium to another, grab a puffball, hurry back, and toss it into a crate. Students playing Fishing for Facts similarly rush from one area of the classroom to another, but with the added element of sorting facts and opinions into two separate buckets. To play, students must be fairly independent in their ability to distinguish facts from opinions. Teachers' ability to provide guidance depends on the number of teams the class is split into, with fewer teams allowing for more teacher coaching.

Setup

First, divide students into teams. The simplest option is to split the class into two teams, but you can have as many teams as you like. Each team needs two buckets, with one labeled "Facts" and one labeled "Opinions." Students line up behind their team's buckets on one side of the room.

On the other side of the room, create "ponds" of fact and opinion cards ("fish") using age-appropriate facts and opinions from appendix A (page 209). Each team will have its own pond. Half of the cards in each pond should be facts and half should be opinions. There should be at least as many cards in each pond as there are students on each team (so everyone gets a turn). Figure 3.1 (page 70) depicts this arrangement for two teams playing the game.

Argumentation Skill

- Distinguishing fact from opinion

Materials

- Two buckets per team (baskets, hats, shoeboxes, or similar items are also fine); label one Facts and the other Opinions
- Cards with facts or opinions (see appendix A on page 209)

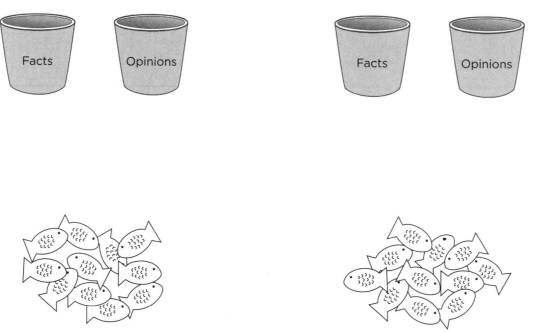

Figure 3.1: Setup of a two-team Fishing for Facts game.

Some teachers may wish to use additional materials to expand on the fishing theme and make the game more engaging for students. Depending on how much prep time you want to invest, setup can be as simple or as elaborate as you like. Design your own additions or select the variation that best suits your needs from the following list:

- **Minimal prep**—Make a photocopy of the age-appropriate set of facts and opinions in appendix A and use a paper cutter to slice the list into individual slips. Spread the slips in two areas (or more, if you have more than two teams) on the floor or on a tabletop to form the ponds. During the game, students pick them up with their fingers.

- **Some prep**—Make as many photocopies of the fish template on page 72 as you have facts and opinions. If your school has a die-cutter, you may also create your own fish cutouts out of blue or gray construction paper. Cut and paste (or handwrite) one fact or opinion on each fish. Tape the fish to two different sections of the chalkboard or place them in two separate pocket charts to form ponds. Have students pull them off the board or grab them out of the charts with their fingers.

- **High prep**—Write facts and opinions on fish as described in the previous bullet. Fasten a paper clip to each one and spread the fish in two different areas on the classroom floor. Attach a small magnet to an arms-length piece of string to create a fishing rod. Create one fishing rod for each team. Students will dangle the string over a paper clip to "catch" a fish and place it in its appropriate bucket.

Play

Before beginning to play, make sure teams understand which pond is theirs and which bucket is which—ask them to point—and remind them often. You don't want students accidentally taking fish from another team's pond, placing opinions in the fact bucket by mistake, and so on. Tell students that when people go fishing, they pay attention to the kinds of fish they are catching. Explain that reading is similar—students should be on the lookout for facts and be able to separate them from opinions—and that you're going to put their fishing skills to the test.

When you say go, the first student in each team's line rushes to his or her team's pond on the opposite side of the room, "catches" a fish, reads it (silently or aloud—it's up to you), and decides whether it is a fact or opinion. Then, students rush back to their respective teams and place their fish in the appropriate buckets. When the first student is done, the next student in line rushes to the pond and catches a new fish. The object of the game is to catch and sort all of the fish in your team's pond as quickly as possible. Whichever team does so the fastest is declared the winner of the round.

When the first team clears its pond of fish, pause the game to check the students' work (you could ask all students to be seated). If the fish have all been correctly sorted, the team wins. If there are errors, remove the incorrectly sorted fish, put them back in that team's pond, and resume play. If another team correctly sorts all its fish before the first team clears its pond, the other team wins.

After a team has been declared the winner of the round, students carry their fish back to the opposite side of the room and "release" them back into their ponds. Then, teams swap ponds and play another round with new—to them—facts and opinions.

 Students who are still learning to read may need help decoding the statements on their fish. If this is the case, stand beside the pond and offer assistance to students during the game. The game does also give students practice with reading, but in the end, the primary goal is to help them practice with facts and opinions. Do not hesitate, therefore, to read aloud to students who are struggling readers—regardless of their reading abilities, they still must learn to distinguish fact from opinion. You might also ask guiding questions to students who are able to read, but are just having a hard time with the classification aspect of the game. For example, a struggling student whose fish reads "Spider-Man is the best superhero" might catch on with the help of questions such as "Might someone else think Batman is a better superhero?" "Is this true for just some people, or is it true for everyone?" and "Can we actually prove that Spider-Man is best?"

4 Argument Relay

For upper elementary, middle school, and high school students

This game takes the form of a traditional relay race, in which each teammate completes one part of the race before being relieved by a different teammate. In this version, teams of students race to form a complete argument, with each teammate adding a different element to a teacher-provided claim. Playing Argument Relay gives students opportunities to generate grounds for claims with which they may or may not themselves agree. This prompts students to consider various perspectives on an issue. To enhance the rigor of the game, teachers can also ask students to identify errors in reasoning.

Setup

First, divide the class into teams. We recommend including four students on each team, although teams can be as large or as small as you want, so long as you adjust the number of grounds needed to win the relay (for example, if there are five students instead of four, teams will need to generate five grounds instead of four). Each team sits in a row, either at desks or on the floor (if students are sitting on the floor, each will need a hard surface, like a clipboard, to write on). Give a recording sheet to the first student in each row. Stand at the front of the room with your list of selected claims (see appendix B on page 215).

Play

Briefly establish some guidelines for game play (for example, no conferring with teammates during the game, remarks within and among teams must always

Argumentation Skills

- Presenting and supporting claims
- Perspective taking
- Organizing an argument
- Identifying errors in reasoning (optional)

Materials

- List of grade-appropriate claims (see appendix B on page 215)
- Age-appropriate recording sheet for each team (see reproducibles on pages 75–76)
- Pen or pencil for each student

If you choose to create your own claims instead of using those in appendix B, make sure that your students are able to generate grounds for them. Claims must either be general enough that all students have some degree of background knowledge about them or so domain specific that students can draw from previously taught content to support them.

be positive, students raise their hands silently if they need help, and so on). Then read a claim from your list aloud to the class. The first student in each row writes the claim in the appropriate space at the top of the recording sheet. When all students are finished writing, say "Go!" On your cue, student 1 passes the sheet of paper to the second person in the row. Student 2 reads the claim and, as quickly as possible, writes one reason that supports it (grounds) beneath it. Then student 2 passes the sheet to the third teammate. Student 3 writes another reason that supports the claim (grounds) on the same sheet of paper before passing it to the next student. The last student in line brings the paper back to the first student, who writes the final grounds. When student 1 finishes writing, the entire team stands up.

Pause the game while you check the winning team's argument. All other teams must stop working on their arguments until the teacher has either determined the argument to be sound (at which point the team is declared the winner and a new round begins with a new claim) or not sound (play resumes). If the teacher finds flaws in the argument, the team does not win. However, the team can race to revise its argument before another team stands up.

Errors in Reasoning

To incorporate the additional skill of identifying errors in reasoning into the game, explain to students before beginning that they may notice reasoning errors or false or irrelevant statements in the grounds their teammates have generated. If this happens, the student who notices the error may go to that teammate, explain his or her reasoning, and collaborate with the teammate to correctly rewrite the grounds or generate alternative grounds for the claim. This is the only situation in which teammates may confer with one another about grounds.

Extensions

To make the game more difficult for older students who are already familiar with how to play, ask them to generate more than just grounds for a claim. For example, older students might be asked to generate grounds, backing, and qualifiers for a claim. If this is the case, teams will need to send their recording sheet through the row multiple times. The first time, students record grounds; the second time, they add backing; and the final time, they add qualifiers. To accommodate this more complex version of the game, we provide a recording sheet template with additional sections

You know your students best! The following list of game play variations is designed to help you cater to the specific needs of your class:

- Scaffold for your English learners by displaying claims on the board instead of reading them aloud. Write each one manually with chalk or present a PowerPoint slide show containing a different claim on each slide.

- Prewrite each claim on the recording sheet before making copies. Place the recording sheets face down on desks and only allow students to turn them over when you say, "Go!"

- Give students more autonomy in the game to help you focus less on hosting and more on offering guidance. Write different claims on cards and give each team a different claim card at the beginning of the game. Then simply have rows trade cards between rounds. Teachers do not have to attend to displaying a new claim each round, which frees them up to move about the room and help students.

for backing and qualifiers (see page 76). Teachers can collect and review recording sheets at the end of the game to monitor students' understanding of the argumentation process and structure.

Argument Relay (Grounds)

Team Members: _____ _____ _____

_____ _____ _____

Claim: _____

Grounds: _____

_____

Grounds: _____

_____

Grounds: _____

_____

Grounds: _____

_____

Argument Relay (Grounds, Backing, and Qualifiers)

Team Members: _____ _____ _____

_____ _____ _____

Claim: _____

Grounds: _____

   Backing: _____

      Qualifier: _____

Grounds: _____

   Backing: _____

      Qualifier: _____

Grounds: _____

   Backing: _____

      Qualifier: _____

Grounds: _____

   Backing: _____

      Qualifier: _____

5

Rapid Fire

For upper elementary, middle school, and high school students

Rapid Fire is a fast-paced dueling game in which pairs of students race to answer a question. The game is based on the head-to-head version of Pepper from Doug Lemov's (2010) book *Teach Like a Champion* and has been modified for use as an argument game. Rapid Fire is meant to be a review, not an introduction to new material. It is specifically intended to develop students' fluency with argumentation—in other words, their ability to recognize elements of a strong argument almost automatically (Marzano, 2007). Teachers can also use Rapid Fire as a filler activity. Start a pickup game while students are standing in line, before the bell rings, or during any other brief period of downtime, such as a warm-up or a brain break.

Setup

To play, elementary students need to be familiar with distinguishing facts from opinions. Middle school students need to understand the difference between a claim and backing and be able to recognize the three different types of backing (expert opinion, research results, and factual information). High school students need to understand the three types of backing and be able to recognize qualifiers.

Aside from preteaching the aforementioned argumentation concepts, this game requires no setup unless teachers wish to incorporate optional tools. To set up a countdown timer, visit a website such as Online Stopwatch (www.online-stopwatch.com) and program the timer to count backward for however long you want the

Argumentation Skills

- Distinguishing fact from opinion
- Presenting and supporting claims
- Explaining the relationship between claims, grounds, and backing

Materials

- Age-appropriate clues (see pages 81–88)
- Stopwatch or timer (optional)
- Random student selection tool (for example, a jar containing students' names written on Popsicle sticks) or digital name generator (optional)

game to last. Display the countdown using a projector. Teachers with interactive whiteboards can also use the countdown tools in the accompanying software. To set up a random name generator, visit a website such as Instant Classroom (www.superteachertools.com/instantclassroom/random-name-generator.php) and type in your class roster. Teachers can also use random name generator tools in interactive whiteboard software.

Play

To play, two students stand up from their seats, the teacher gives a clue, and the first student to respond correctly remains standing to face a new opponent. It is important to clearly articulate which skill the clues will focus on before beginning play. For example, you might say, "Remember that when I read a clue, you need to say whether it is a fact or an opinion" or "You need to determine which clues are claims and which are backing." For elementary students, teachers can use the facts and opinions in appendix A. Students simply need to distinguish whether the clue is a fact or an opinion. For middle school students, the teacher can use the clues at the end of this chapter and ask students either to distinguish between claims and backing (simpler) or to distinguish between specific types of backing (more complex). For high school students, teachers can use the clues at the end of this chapter, asking students to identify each clue as expert opinion, research results, factual information, or a qualifier.

 Once students get the hang of the game, teachers can also take volunteers to compete. Beware the inevitable: some students will never raise their hands, and you'll have to mitigate this by calling on them anyway. Also, keep in mind that modifications like using randomizer tools and taking volunteers can slow the pace of the game, despite their advantages. Select the combination of tools and strategies that provides the best fit for the class, or mix and match these ideas to make each game feel unique to students.

Begin a round of Rapid Fire by selecting two students to stand up at their desks. Teachers' methods of selection will vary; they may decide to call on students themselves or use a tool that helps them select randomly. Give students just enough time to stand up—usually about two seconds—before moving right into reading a clue.

Next, read a clue to the two standing students. The goal is to be the first of the pair to arrive at the correct response and say it aloud. Whoever says the correct answer first is declared the winner. He or she remains standing, and the teacher selects a new student to be the next challenger. For example, the teacher selects student A and student B to answer a question. Students A and B stand up, and the teacher reads the clue, "Aaron Rodgers is the best quarterback in the NFL." Student A cries, "Claim!" which is the correct answer. Because student A answered correctly, she continues to stand. Student B either did not know the answer or was too late in saying it, so he is eliminated and sits down.

The teacher selects a new student to stand up and face student A, and the process repeats. If student A answers the question incorrectly, the teacher reads the entire clue again, and student B has a chance to steal. In the case that student B gets the correct answer, he or she stays standing and student A is eliminated. If both students in a pair answer a question incorrectly, they both sit down and two new students are selected to stand. Ask the same question to a different pair later in the game.

There are two keys to a successful game of Rapid Fire: maintaining a lively pace and randomness. These elements work together to energize students and ensure that they never know for sure who will be picked next, keeping them engaged and ready to respond to a clue at any moment. Do not prioritize one element over the other, as this will diminish the effectiveness of the game. Optimal speed and minimal randomness, for instance, will not work as well as if both were evenly matched.

The fastest method of selecting students is to begin at one end of a row, call on the first two students in the row to compete, and then move one by one down the row through different challengers. When it comes to sheer speed, the down-the-row method is superior. When considering randomness, however, this method seems less ideal. No matter how interested students are in the wins and losses of their classmates, engagement will almost certainly drop if the progression of competition consistently snakes one by one through each row. Students will always know who is next in line, and as one row competes, the remaining rows have little incentive to consider the questions at all.

Repeat clues occasionally to keep students on their toes. Returning to a tough question provides a review opportunity for students who answered incorrectly—whether aloud or in their heads—the first time the question was raised. This technique also rewards attentive students and can reduce distracting behavior. The possibility of losing a round on what should have been a giveaway answer can encourage students to pay close attention, even when it is not their turn.

Sacrifice the small amount of speed gained from the down-the-row method in favor of unpredictability. Select students at random using Popsicle sticks, or at least create the illusion of randomness using a popcorn-style method. Call on students from all over the room, as randomly as possible, and mentally keep a running track of those who have participated. At the same time, do not waste time picking students. Long, uncertain pauses and hesitant sounds like "um," "ah," and "eh" swing the pendulum too far in the opposite direction, slowing the pace to the detriment of the game. By the time an eliminated student sits, a new student should already be getting out of his or her seat.

Students will develop a knack for identifying signal words and phrases as the game progresses. Because Rapid Fire is essentially a race, they will learn to notice signal words right away and may call out the answer before a teacher finishes reading the clue. Do not chastise students for interrupting mid-clue to call out the answer; this is part of the game. Consider the following clue: "In the summer of 2013, the Egyptian military overthrew democratically elected President Mohamed Morsi." This is an example of factual information. Two students (Cam'ron and Pete) stand, and the teacher begins reading the clue aloud. As soon as he reaches the date *2013*, Cam'ron interrupts and calls out the correct answer. Cam'ron recognized that the use of a date can signal factual information. Because he has beaten his opponent to the correct response, he remains standing while Pete takes a seat.

A teacher's ability to cultivate a sense of fun and friendly competition can seriously enhance or detract from students' enjoyment. Call for contestants to stand and give clues using a voice like a game show host or sports announcer. Build suspense by teaching students to give a "desktop drumroll"—students rap their hands on the desktops in rapid succession until the teacher gives a cue to stop. Teachers can train students to automatically begin a desktop drumroll every time a new contestant is announced, or they can prompt students with a phrase like, "Drumroll, please!" Silence the class in one beat using a nonverbal cue. Extend both arms and sweep them to the sides like an umpire calling a player safe at base or hold up a closed fist like an orchestra conductor. Practice cues with students multiple times to squelch inappropriate or over-the-top behavior before it escalates past the point of control. Finally (and most importantly), do not underestimate students' willingness to be silly. The latent goofiness of older, "cooler" students may surprise you.

Developing fluency with argumentation concepts and signal words and phrases is the primary goal of the game. Nevertheless, teachers must also show students that, while useful, signal words and phrases are merely guiding hints, not hard-and-fast rules. Signal words and phrases often overlap among different categories. For instance, an expert opinion may contain the signal phrase *according to*, because it refers to the advice of an individual. On the other hand, a research result can also begin with *according to*, particularly when the phrase refers to the people or organization that conducted the study. Therefore, students must assess signal words and phrases within the context of the entire clue.

When a student immediately identifies a signal word and calls out the answer before listening to the whole clue, there is no guarantee that the rest of the clue will align with his or her answer.

To illustrate, let's say the teacher reads another clue for Cam'ron and his new challenger, Rosa. The entire clue reads: "In the fall of 2012, a higher percentage of Hispanic (69 percent) than white (67 percent) high school graduates enrolled in college, according to the Pew Research Center's 2013 report." This is an example of a research result. However, the clue begins with the phrase *In the fall of 2012*, which prompts Cam'ron to call out, "Factual information!" He had recognized a nearly identical signal phrase to the one from the previous clue, which provided factual information. If he had listened to the rest of the clue, Cam'ron would have realized that his first thought was incorrect. As previously mentioned, factual information sometimes does contain a date, but in the context of the entire sentence, it is clear that this particular clue is not a fact. The teacher reads the entire clue again and gives Rosa a chance to steal. When Rosa hears words like *percentage* and *research*, she knows the correct answer is *research results*. Cam'ron takes a seat, and the teacher selects a new challenger. The risk that Cam'ron took to answer quickly is a part of the game, as well.

When students give correct answers midway through a clue, teachers might also prompt them to provide an explanation of their reasoning. To maintain a lively pace, keep these prompts simple:

- What signal word(s) made you say "claim"?
- Which part told you that it was a claim?
- Peyton, how did Mikayla know it was a claim?

For elementary students, follow-up prompts can include the following:

- What words made you say "opinion"?
- What part made you say "fact"?
- Why did Melanie say that was an opinion?

Uncomplicated follow-up questions like these can help teachers get more mileage out of a single clue, especially if the student answers after hearing only a few words. If a student cannot explain his or her answer, give the other student the opportunity to steal. If that student cannot explain the answer either, ask a seated student to explain the reasoning and give him or her the chance to steal.

Clues for Rapid Fire

This section contains clues for middle and high school teachers to use during a game of Rapid Fire (elementary clues are in appendix A). Be sure to preteach the appropriate argumentation skills and concepts before using each set of clues:

- **Elementary**—Distinguish between facts and opinions (clues in appendix A).
- **Middle school (simpler)**—Distinguish between claims and backing.
- **Middle school (more complex)**—Distinguish between claims and the three types of backing— expert opinion, research results, and factual information.
- **High school**—Distinguish between the three types of backing and be able to recognize qualifiers.

Remind students of the focus for the clues being used before beginning a round of play.

Middle School

For a simpler version of the game, simply ask students to determine if the following clues are claims or backing. For a more complex version of the game, skip over the clues that present claims—only ask clues that give backing—and ask students to classify the backing as expert opinion, research results, or factual information. To allow teachers to use the same backing clues and answers for both versions of the game, we indicate in each answer that the clue is an example of backing, and then—separated by a semicolon—we give the type of backing (for example, *backing; expert opinion*).

Clue: About 77 percent of cancers are diagnosed among people fifty-five and older, according to a 2013 report by the American Cancer Society.

Answer: backing; research results

Clue: It is wrong for scientists to test medicines and vaccines on animals.

Answer: claim

Clue: At the Wimbledon tennis tournament in the United Kingdom, competitors are expected to wear the color white.

Answer: backing; factual information

Clue: The human foot has twenty-six bones in it.

Answer: backing; factual information

Clue: School principals should have the right to perform random locker searches.

Answer: claim

Clue: In AD 79 Italy, an active volcano called Mt. Vesuvius erupted and buried the town of Pompeii in ash.

Answer: backing; factual information

Clue: An ornithologist is a person who studies birds.

Answer: backing; factual information

Clue: According to 1984 research by Deborah Feltz and Maureen Weiss, girls who play sports in high school have higher ACT scores.

Answer: backing; research results

Clue: People should not care what celebrities and politicians do in their private lives.

Answer: claim

Clue: Data show that 3,442 people died from extreme heat between 1999 and 2003, according to a 2006 report by the Centers for Disease Control and Prevention.

Answer: backing; research results

Clue: Kids can learn just as much from watching television as they can from reading books.

Answer: claim

Clue: Jennifer Lawrence is the actress who played Katniss in the *Hunger Games* movies.

Answer: backing; factual information

Clue: In 2004, David Brunsma reported findings that show school uniforms do not necessarily make schools safer or kids smarter.

Answer: backing; research results

Clue: The Beatles are the most creative band in history.

Answer: claim

Clue: As of 2013, the Beatles were still the best-selling band in history.

Answer: backing; factual information

Clue: In 2011, the U.S. Department of Agriculture recommended that people fill their plates halfway with fruits and vegetables at every meal.

Answer: backing; expert opinion

Clue: Lyrics in rap music are usually offensive.

Answer: claim

Clue: Boys and girls should be allowed to play on the same sports team.

Answer: claim

Clue: The hottest temperature ever documented, 136 degrees, was recorded in Libya.

Answer: backing; factual information

Clue: Human rights activist Harvey Milk should be honored with a national holiday.

Answer: claim

Clue: Sending emails and text messages is not harmful to students' learning.

Answer: claim

Clue: Cities with too much traffic should ban cars and make people bike or take the bus everywhere.

Answer: claim

Clue: Reality shows on television are the worst form of entertainment.

Answer: claim

Clue: Doctors say that babies need between twelve and fourteen hours of sleep, including daytime naps.

Answer: backing; expert opinion

Clue: Drinks that contain caffeine, such as coffee and soda, can make it harder to fall asleep.

Answer: backing; factual information

Clue: All middle school students in the United States should wear uniforms.

Answer: claim

Clue: When combined, people in Africa speak more than one thousand different languages.

Answer: backing; factual information

Clue: The tallest tower in the world is the Tokyo Skytree, which stands at almost two thousand feet high.

Answer: backing; factual information

Clue: The Boston Red Sox should not have won the 2013 World Series against the Cardinals.

Answer: claim

Clue: Chewing gum before a test might improve scores, according to 2011 data from Serge Onyper, Timothy Carr, John Farrar, and Brittney Floyd.

Answer: backing; research results

Clue: The teddy bear was invented in 1902 after President Roosevelt refused to shoot a black bear on a hunting trip.

Answer: backing; factual information

Clue: Justin Bieber was once booed at the Billboard Music Awards.

Answer: backing; factual information

Clue: Justin Bieber is not the greatest musician.

Answer: claim

Clue: The human nose can smell thousands of different scents.

Answer: backing; factual information

Clue: In 1987, Olympic medalist Jackie Joyner-Kersee became the first female athlete to ever be on the cover of *Sports Illustrated* magazine.

Answer: backing; factual information

Clue: People should be required to serve in the military when they reach a certain age.

Answer: claim

Clue: In 2003, Hughes and his colleagues asserted that 60 percent of the world's coral reefs will be gone by 2030, due mostly to climate change and human impact.

Answer: backing; expert opinion

Clue: About 70 percent of the Earth's surface is covered in water.

Answer: backing; factual information

Clue: In 2013, Australia was the happiest country in the world, according to surveys for the OECD Better Life Index.

Answer: backing; research results

Clue: The government should raise taxes on junk food to promote healthy eating.

Answer: claim

Clue: In 2012, 47 percent of American video gamers were women, according to a 2013 report by the Entertainment Software Association.

Answer: backing; research results

Clue: Rick Riordan's novel *The Lightning Thief* is "clever" and "perfectly paced," according to a 2005 *New York Times* book review by Polly Shulman.

Answer: backing; expert opinion

Clue: The first official baseball game took place in 1946.

Answer: backing; factual information

Clue: Ninety percent of mothers who work in restaurants do not get paid when they take sick days, according to a 2013 study by Yvonne Yen Liu.

Answer: backing; research results

Clue: The United States should change its national anthem to a dance hit.

Answer: claim

Clue: The top-selling video game of 2012 was *Call of Duty: Black Ops II*.

Answer: backing; factual information

Clue: *Call of Duty* is the best video game on the market.

Answer: claim

Clue: Eight percent of Americans have asthma according to a study by the Centers for Disease Control and Prevention in 2011.

Answer: backing; research results

Clue: Having a job is very stressful.

Answer: claim

Clue: A study by the American Psychological Association in 2009 found that 70 percent of American workers say that their job stresses them out.

Answer: backing; research results

High School

Ask students to classify the following clues as research results, expert opinion, factual information, or a qualifier. Teachers can choose whether or not to read the parenthetical citations in the clues aloud.

Clue: Economist Jared Bernstein believes that abolishing the minimum wage in the United States "would needlessly hurt millions of low wage workers" (Intelligence Squared U.S., 2013).

Answer: expert opinion

Clue: Coffee can wake you up in the morning, but only if it has caffeine in it.

Answer: qualifier

Clue: The flag of the Canadian territory Nunavut features an inuksuk—a figure constructed of stacked rocks—as its coat of arms.

Answer: factual information

Clue: The capital of China is Beijing.

Answer: factual information

Clue: In the wake of disastrous oil spills, President of the Natural Resources Defense Council Frances Beinecke recommended that the United States put a pause on offshore oil drilling in favor of clean energy, such as wind and solar power (Beinecke & Gerard, 2010).

Answer: expert opinion

Clue: Cheerios are a great option for breakfast, but to be fair, they only make up one *part* of a complete breakfast.

Answer: qualifier

Clue: Using data from 2006-2010, the Centers for Disease Control and Prevention reported a 68 percent probability that a woman's first marriage will last at least ten years (Copen, Daniels, Vespa, & Mosher, 2012).

Answer: research results

Clue: Guitarist Eric Clapton was the first musician to be inducted three times into the Rock and Roll Hall of Fame.

Answer: factual information

Clue: The Intergovernmental Panel on Climate Change (IPCC) reported that the average amount of snow in the northern hemisphere decreased by 4 percent between 1920 and 2005 (Mann & Selin, 2013).

Answer: research results

Clue: Even if every citizen of Nigeria were legally obligated to receive the polio vaccine, some people would probably still go without it.

Answer: qualifier

Clue: Former Secretary of the U.S. Department of Homeland Security Michael Chertoff opposed freedom of the press to expose state secrets because "unlike the organs of government which are accountable to the public and to each other, the press is accountable to nobody" (Intelligence Squared U.S., 2011).

Answer: expert opinion

Clue: Media tycoon Rupert Murdoch created the Fox News Channel, which aired for the first time in 1996.

Answer: factual information

Clue: Although most parents agree that kids should be able to use cell phones in school, there are still some who disagree.

Answer: qualifier

Clue: Kiev is the capital of Ukraine.

Answer: factual information

Clue: Solomon Asch (1956) discovered that when the majority of people in a group agreed on the same response to a question—even if that response was obviously incorrect—75 percent of individual participants gave the same answer.

Answer: research results

Clue: Within hours of being posted, Barack Obama's "Four More Years" victory tweet (featuring a photograph of an embrace between the Obamas) had been shared more than 400,000 times.

Answer: factual information

Clue: Film critic Roger Ebert (1998) listed Orson Welles's *Citizen Kane* (1941) as one of the ten greatest films of all time, calling it a "masterpiece," "more than just a great movie," and "a gathering of all the lessons of the emerging era of sound."

Answer: expert opinion

Clue: Sports, weather, and traffic updates make up 40 percent of the content on local television news broadcasts as opposed to in-depth stories (Jurkowitz et al., 2013).

Answer: research results

Clue: As of November 2013, super typhoon Haiyan was considered the strongest typhoon ever to reach land, though in fairness, stronger storms may have occurred earlier and gone unrecorded.

Answer: qualifier

Clue: Film director Alfred Hitchcock is widely regarded as a master and innovator in the art of using cinematic techniques to create suspense.

Answer: factual information

Clue: Data show that in 40 percent of American households with children, mothers are the sole or primary financial providers (Wang, Parker, & Taylor, 2013).

Answer: research results

Clue: Racial profiling is sometimes justified in the interest of national security.

Answer: qualifier

Clue: In the first round of Milgram's (1963) obedience experiment, 65 percent of participants were willing to follow orders to harm other participants to the fullest extent that the study allowed.

Answer: research results

Clue: French microbiologist Louis Pasteur discovered that fermentation is caused by microorganisms and invented pasteurization.

Answer: factual information

Clue: While President Barack Obama is often used as an example to show that someone can come from nothing and become president, it should be noted that he experienced many advantages throughout his youth, including an Ivy League education and an upper-middle-class upbringing.

Answer: qualifier

Clue: Between 190 and 120 BC, Greek astronomer Hipparchus was the first person to use latitude and longitude.

Answer: factual information

Clue: Despite allegations that Paul Hansen's award-winning photo of a Gaza funeral had been altered with Photoshop, digital photography expert Eduard de Kam says the photo was real (Chappell, 2013).

Answer: expert opinion

Clue: Seventeen percent of cell phone owners do most of their online browsing on their phones, rather than on computers or other devices (Smith, 2012).

Answer: research results

Clue: In the fall of 2012, a higher percentage of Hispanic (69 percent) than white (67 percent) high school graduates enrolled in college (Pew Research Center, 2013).

Answer: research results

Clue: The bite of an infected tsetse fly (pronounced SET-see) transmits a potentially fatal "sleeping sickness" among humans and other mammals.

Answer: factual information

Clue: While some people experience success from switching to barefoot or minimalist running, many people have sustained injuries as a result of the practice.

Answer: qualifier

Clue: Fifteen percent of young males (between the ages of eighteen and twenty-nine) use Reddit, a social media website (Duggan & Smith, 2013).

Answer: research results

Clue: For optimal comfort on long hikes, backpackers should load their heaviest gear close to the spine in the center of the pack, in keeping with Recreational Equipment, Inc. (REI) guidelines (Wood, 2012).

Answer: expert opinion

Clue: Marilyn Monroe's real name was Norma Jeane Mortenson.

Answer: factual information

Clue: Syria was by far the most dangerous country for journalists in 2012, with more than twice as many reporter deaths as there were in Somalia, the second-ranking nation.

Answer: factual information

Clue: During 2012–2013, more people went to Broadway shows than to all of New York and New Jersey's professional sports games combined.

Answer: factual information

Clue: In 2007, only 8 percent of the artwork in the Museum of Modern Art was created by female artists.

Answer: factual information

Clue: While three to five cups of coffee per day may seem like a lot of caffeine, registered dietitian Andrea Giancoli said this amount is "safe for most people" (Sifferlin, 2012).

Answer: expert opinion

Clue: A study of over two hundred countries shows that about 23 percent of people in the world are Muslims (Pew Research Center, 2009).

Answer: research results

Clue: Green Day bassist Mike Dirnt advised aspiring musicians to "play music with friends" rather than "just play with somebody because they happen to have a lot of skills" (Guitar Center, 2001).

Answer: expert opinion

Clue: According to a report by the FBI in 2012, about 67 percent of murders and 43 percent of robberies in the United States involve guns.

Answer: research results

Clue: A tax on junk food is not a solution to high rates of obesity in the United States, even though it may help some people.

Answer: qualifier

Clue: Skilled attackers in soccer must have confidence, speed, and quick reaction time, according to professional soccer coach Paul Fairclough (2009).

Answer: expert opinion

Clue: Escape artist Harry Houdini claimed to have been born in Appleton, Wisconsin, but he was actually born in Budapest, Hungary.

Answer: factual information

Clue: Pregnant women should eat a variety of colorful fruits and vegetables, lean meats, whole grains, and low-fat dairy products, as recommended by registered dietitians (Academy of Nutrition and Dietetics, 2013).

Answer: expert opinion

6 Which One Doesn't Belong?

For upper elementary, middle school, and high school students

Which One Doesn't Belong? is based on a segment on the children's series *Sesame Street* called "One of These Things Is Not Like the Others." In the television version of the game, a group of four items is displayed, one of which differs somehow from the other three, and young viewers choose the item that does not fit. The game has since enjoyed adaptation for use in puzzles, websites, and games, including a classroom vocabulary game (Carleton & Marzano, 2010). Unlike the television show, the spin-off described in this book is not intended for preschoolers. Instead, it is designed to help upper elementary, middle, and high school students practice recognizing the various elements of effective arguments.

Setup

To play, elementary students must be able to distinguish evidence that supports an opinion from evidence that does not. Middle school students must understand the need for backing to support grounds and claims, as well as the three different types of backing (expert opinion, research results, and factual information). High school students need to understand the concept of a qualifier. They also need to know how to identify biased language, which is part of evaluating persuasive rhetoric (pages 34–35). Some high school questions ask students to identify qualifiers; others ask them to identify biased terms in statements.

Before playing, teachers must select questions that they will use during the game. At the end of this chapter, we provide ready-to-use sets of questions for elementary,

Argumentation Skills

- Identifying insufficient or irrelevant evidence
- Identifying errors in reasoning
- Explaining the relationship between claims, grounds, and backing
- Distinguishing connotation from denotation
- Evaluating persuasive rhetoric

Materials

- Stopwatch or timer
- Projector (overhead projector or document camera/computer screen projector)
- Small whiteboard for each team
- Dry erase marker and eraser for each team

Many teachers will not have a classroom set of personal whiteboards. Don't panic—there are plenty of other low-cost, low-prep options!

- **Craft your own set of whiteboards at a lower cost.** For an inexpensive alternative to store-bought personal whiteboards, visit a hardware store. Ask an employee to cut a solid white sheet of shower board (also called melamine or tileboard) into 12 × 12 inch squares. Use electrical tape (it comes in bright colors!) to cover the sharp edges of the boards. Ask students to bring in a dry erase marker as part of their supply list, along with a dryer sheet, old sock, or handkerchief to use as an eraser.

- **Create a set of answer cards for each team.** Slice sheets of construction paper into quarters with a paper cutter. Use a magic marker to write each letter option (A, B, C, and D) on one of the four pieces of construction paper. Sets of four index cards work just as well. Distribute a set of cards to each group. On your cue, groups hold up the card that represents their answer.

- **Have students respond by holding up their fingers.** If you do not have time to create a set of answer cards for each group, just assign the numbers 1–4 to the letter options and display the matches on a chalkboard or whiteboard (such as A = 1, B = 2, C = 3, and D = 4). Instead of writing the letter on a whiteboard or holding up a card, one student from each group acts as the spokesperson and holds up the number of fingers that correspond with his or her group's answer.

middle, and high school students, each of which requires increasingly more complex argumentation skills. Prepare to display each question and its answer choices so that all students can see them (ensure that answers are not displayed). This may involve creating a slide show of the selected questions or using a document camera to project the appropriate pages from this book. Teachers without a projector can photocopy the questions and distribute them to students as cards. For sets of reproducible question cards and ready-to-play slideshow presentations, visit **marzanoresearch .com/activitiesandgames**.

Teachers may also choose to prepare their own set of multiple-choice questions in advance, particularly if they wish to make them specific to a learning goal. For instance, a civics teacher may decide to create a set of questions based on Supreme Court precedents. A language arts teacher may decide to supplement the list with claims and text evidence from a class novel. Reference the questions at the end of this chapter as a guide while creating your own list of questions. Each set of answers must contain three items that share a common attribute and one item that does not fit. A list of ten questions should be plenty, at least for one round of the game. Teachers do not need to write out the specific reasoning behind each answer as long as they consider it beforehand and are prepared to explain it.

Finally, divide the class into groups of four (one group of three or five is fine for odd-numbered rosters). Make the groups as heterogeneous as possible; attempt to vary the levels of argument proficiency among students in a group. Pass out a response board or scrap paper (along with appropriate markers/erasers or pens/pencils) to each team.

Play

To begin, start the countdown timer and present one of the questions to students. If you are an elementary teacher, read the claim and all four options aloud to the class *before* setting the timer. As previously mentioned, teachers can either display these questions via slideshow presentation, distribute reproducible question cards to each team, or simply place a copy of the questions beneath a document camera, taking care to conceal the answers. If using question cards, make sure that every team is using the same one at the same time (the cards available online are numbered to facilitate this).

In their teams, students deliberate until they have reached a consensus or time runs out. As soon as a team decides on an answer, one student writes the team's response—A, B, C, or D—on the whiteboard. Then every group member raises his or her hand to show that the team is ready. When time runs out, tell students that time is up and give them a three-second countdown to hold up their whiteboards and reveal their answers (say some-

Modify the amount of time provided for considering each question depending on students' needs. We suggest allotting one minute for team deliberation before requiring an answer. This pace may seem fast to students at first, but they should grow accustomed to it within one or two questions. However, if teams still appear strained and struggle to keep up with the timer after several questions, teachers may increase the allotment to one and one-half or two minutes. Be cautious of providing too much time for deliberation. Lulls between questions will slow the pace of the game, making it less exciting and limiting the number of questions you are able to get through. If every team reaches an answer before time elapses for a round, do not wait for the clock to finish counting down before moving on. Stop the timer and give students a three-second countdown to display their answer. Teachers could also motivate students to maintain a lively pace by awarding a bonus point to the first team to arrive at the correct answer.

thing like "Okay, everyone, time is up! Show your answers in 3 . . . 2 . . . 1 . . . now!"). Award a point to every team that answered correctly. Keep track of points on the chalkboard or whiteboard so students are aware of their team's standing.

Before playing this or any game that involves collaboration, set clear expectations for group work. The following is a list of expectations you may want to present to students:

- Give each student in the group the chance to share an opinion. If you are the most vocal person in your group, it is your duty as a leader to encourage teammates to weigh in on the decision.

- Respond graciously to disagreement. Try not to take mistakes or corrections personally.

- Before finalizing an answer, ask each teammate individually whether he or she agrees with it (or at least can live with it, as interteam disagreements will undoubtedly arise throughout the game).

- Use the responsible communication sentence stems (table I.19, page 44) to respectfully disagree, ask clarifying questions, and offer alternative suggestions.

After awarding points, call on a student from a winning team to explain the reasoning behind his or her group's answer. We recommend calling on students at this point rather than asking for volunteers. Showing that anyone can be called on to explain an answer in front of the class encourages students to make sure everyone in the group understands the reasoning behind the group's answer. If one student cannot provide an explanation for an answer, call on someone else. Accept arguments for different answers and provide explanations of your own reasoning. Unlike clues in Rapid Fire, which typically have one clear answer, the multiple-choice options in Which One Doesn't Belong? might require some follow-up discussion, clarification, or even debate, particularly as the questions advance in complexity at the middle and high school levels.

Clues for Which One Doesn't Belong?

The following clues for Which One Doesn't Belong? are divided into four sections: elementary, middle school, high school A, and high school B. Before playing the game, teachers should preteach the argumentation concepts associated with the set of clues they plan to use. The clues for each section require the following:

- ◆ **Elementary**—Students select the option that does not give grounds for the claim.

- ◆ **Middle school**—Students select the option that provides backing for the claim.

◆ **High school A**—Students select the option that provides a qualifier for the claim.

◆ **High school B**—Students select the biased word in the statement.

The elementary and middle school sections each contain twenty unique clues; each high school section contains fifteen clues. Because each round requires a period of small-group deliberation, as well as a short whole-class debrief, teachers will be able to play the game several times before running out of clues. Teachers can also create their own clues based on the formats provided for their grade level.

Elementary

Students select the option that does not give a "because" (grounds) for the claim.

1. **Claim:** Disney's *Frozen* (Del Vecho, Lasseter, Buck, & Lee, 2013) is the best movie ever.

    A. Anna (the main character) is very brave and interesting.

    B. The movie has an exciting ending!

    C. Pixar's *Brave* (Sarafian et al., 2012) is a good movie, too.

    D. The reindeer and snowman in *Frozen* are really funny.

    Answer: The correct answer is option C since it does not give a "because" (grounds) for the claim. Option C does not have anything to do with *Frozen*; it is talking about a totally different movie.

2. **Claim:** Tag is an unfair game to play in gym class.

    A. Some kids are just naturally fast, so the slower kids do not have an equal chance to win.

    B. The longest-ever game of tag has lasted for twenty-three years! (Adams, 2013).

    C. Kids can cheat and say they have not been tagged even when they have.

    D. Kids who cannot run (such as kids in a wheelchair or kids who have a broken leg) do not get to play.

    Answer: The correct answer is option B since it does not give a "because" (grounds) for the claim. Option B does not have anything to do with whether the game is fair; it is just a fun fact that has nothing to do with fairness or gym class.

3. **Claim:** The best book for kids is *The Mitten* by Jan Brett (1989).

    A. Igloos are so much fun to play in.

    B. The story has a happy ending because Nicky finds his mitten at the end.

    C. The part of the book where the animals move into the mitten is very funny!

    D. All of the pictures in the book are colorful and beautifully illustrated.

    Answer: The correct answer is option A since it does not give a "because" (grounds) for the claim. Option A does not mention the book at all. Instead, it just focuses on igloos.

4. **Claim:** If you see teasing and bullying at school, you should tell a teacher.

    A. Telling a teacher on someone makes you a tattletale.

    B. You could protect another kid from feeling bad about himself or herself and maybe even from injuries.

    C. Telling a teacher about a bully is actually a very brave thing to do.

    D. If the bully gets in trouble, he or she might think twice about picking on someone in the future.

Answer: The correct answer is option A since it does not give a "because" (grounds) for the claim. Option A is talking about bullying, but it does not give a "because" for the claim. Instead, it gives a reason why kids should *not* tell a teacher about teasing and bullying, which is a completely different claim.

5. **Claim:** Even kids can help protect the environment and save the planet.

    A. Kids can turn off the faucet to save water while they brush their teeth.

    B. Picking up trash on the playground is easy and gets rid of litter.

    C. They can remember to save trees by using both sides of a sheet of paper when they draw.

    D. Lots of people pollute the air by driving cars.

Answer: The correct answer is option D since it does not give a "because" (grounds) for the claim. It does not give a way kids can help to save the environment—it just gives a fact about cars. Plus, kids do not even drive cars, so this statement does not match the claim, which only has to do with ways that *kids* can help to save the environment.

6. **Claim:** *SpongeBob SquarePants* is the best cartoon on television.

    A. The show is not just for kids—it is so funny that even some adults like it!

    B. An actor named Tom Kenny does the voice for SpongeBob.

    C. SpongeBob is always happy and kind to others, which makes him a good role model for kids.

    D. In 2013, the show won the "Favorite Cartoon" award on Nickelodeon's *Kids' Choice Awards* for the tenth time (Viacom International, 2003, 2004, 2005, 2006, 2007, 2009, 2010, 2011, 2012, 2013).

Answer: The correct answer is option B since it does not give a "because" (grounds) for the claim. Option B is talking about the person who does voice acting for the character of SpongeBob, but it does not give a "because." Instead, it just presents facts about *SpongeBob SquarePants*; it does not give any reason to believe it is the best show.

7. **Claim:** Kids should get paid to go to school.

    A. They might try harder to get good grades in school if they know they are going to make money doing it.

    B. Parents, teachers, and other adults work for money, but kids work just as hard in school.

    C. Giving money to kids to get them to go to school will never work.

    D. Paying kids to learn might stop them from dropping out of school.

Answer: The correct answer is option C since it does not give a "because" (grounds) for the claim. Option C is talking about the topic of paying students, but it does not give a "because" for the claim. Instead, it gives a reason why kids should *not* be paid to go to school, which is a completely different claim.

8. **Claim:** Schools should give kids less time for recess.

   A. Taking away recess is not fair.

   B. Kids can get bullied or hurt at recess.

   C. If you don't have a warm coat on in the wintertime, it could be uncomfortable to be outside too long.

   D. Kids already get plenty of breaks from school during summer and weekends and do not need recess.

Answer: The correct answer is option A since it does not give a "because" (grounds) for the claim. Option A is talking about the topic of taking away recess, but it gives a "because" for a different claim. Instead, it gives a reason why schools should *not* take away kids' recess, which is a different opinion on the issue.

9. **Claim:** All kids should have to do chores at home.

   A. Chores teach kids to do things around the house (like vacuuming and doing dishes) that they will need to do on their own someday.

   B. Parents work hard all day at their jobs and deserve to have some help around the house.

   C. Chores aren't so bad—sometimes they are even kind of fun.

   D. Vacuum cleaners can be very pricey—the fanciest ones cost over $1,000!

Answer: The correct answer is option D since it does not give a "because" (grounds) for the claim. Option D is off topic. The price of vacuum cleaners has nothing to do with the claim.

10. **Claim:** Everyone should wear seat belts in the car.

    A. Wearing a seat belt can save your life!

    B. It is the law to wear a seat belt.

    C. It is quick and easy to put on a seat belt.

    D. It is also very important to wear a seat belt on a roller coaster.

Answer: The correct answer is option D since it does not give a "because" (grounds) for the claim. Option D is talking about seat belts, but it is not talking about seat belts in cars. Instead, it is talking about seat belts on roller coasters, which is not what the claim is about.

11. **Claim:** Snowball fights should be banned at recess.

    A. Kids can use snowballs to pick on other kids.

    B. Snowballs can hurt if they are too hard or have ice in them.

    C. Did you know that snow is actually just frozen water?

    D. Kids might throw snowballs at cars and make it hard for drivers to see.

Answer: The correct answer is option C since it does not give a "because" (grounds) for the claim. Option C is talking about snow, but it is not talking about throwing snowballs at recess. Instead, it is talking about how snow is made, which is not what the claim is about.

12. **Claim:** Hunting should not be banned.

  A. Hunting stops animals like deer from overpopulating and hurting the ecosystem.

  B. I went hunting with my dad last summer.

  C. Many people need to hunt in order to eat.

  D. Hunting is safe because people need a license to do it.

Answer: The correct answer is option B since it does not give a "because" (grounds) for the claim. Option B is talking about hunting, but it is not talking about why it shouldn't be banned. It is just one person's personal story and is not a fact.

13. **Claim:** Kids should choose their own bedtimes.

  A. They will be tired the next day if they stay up too late.

  B. Kids will learn about taking care of themselves if they are allowed to choose their own bedtimes.

  C. If kids choose to stay up later, they can have more time for homework and reading.

  D. It will be easier for kids to fall asleep if they just go to bed when they feel tired.

Answer: The correct answer is option A since it does not give a "because" (grounds) for the claim. Option A is talking about kids staying up too late, which is not a reason that kids should choose their own bedtimes.

14. **Claim:** Homework is important for students.

  A. Kids need homework to practice what they learn in school.

  B. Without homework, students will not learn responsibility.

  C. Homework teaches kids not to be lazy.

  D. Some teachers assign way too much homework.

Answer: The correct answer is option D since it does not give a "because" (grounds) for the claim. Option D is talking about teachers who give too much homework, which is not a reason that homework is important for students.

15. **Claim:** Reading is a very important skill to learn.

  A. When you read, you get better at concentrating.

  B. Reading helps you learn about the world around you.

  C. Kids who read a lot do better at their work in school.

  D. Books with lots of pictures are the best ones.

Answer: The correct answer is option D since it does not give a "because" (grounds) for the claim. Option D is talking about reading, but it gives an opinion about which kinds of books are best, not a reason for why reading is important.

16. **Claim:** Dogs make better pets than cats.

    A. A dog can protect your house and keep you safe.

    B. Cats are very independent, but dogs love to play with humans.

    C. The best kind of dog is a Dalmatian.

    D. Dogs will go for long walks on a leash, but cats usually won't.

Answer: The correct answer is option C since it does not give a "because" (grounds) for the claim. Option C is talking about different kinds of dogs. It does not talk about how dogs are better than cats.

17. **Claim:** We should not have school on Saturdays.

    A. Sunday is not a good time to have school, either.

    B. We need weekends to see our families.

    C. Some kids need weekends to play sports.

    D. Students need time off to relax.

Answer: The correct answer is option A since it does not give a "because" (grounds) for the claim. Option A is talking about school on Sundays, which does not have anything to do with having school on Saturday.

18. **Claim:** Kids should be allowed to vote for president.

    A. Kids might want to learn more about the world if they could vote.

    B. Kids deserve a vote—we live in this country, too!

    C. Why can't kids vote for president?

    D. It's unfair that adults can vote and kids cannot.

Answer: The correct answer is option C since it does not give a "because" (grounds) for the claim. Option C is simply asking why kids cannot vote. It does not give a reason why kids should be allowed to vote.

19. **Claim:** All kids should play sports.

    A. Playing sports helps you learn teamwork.

    B. It is healthy to be active in sports.

    C. Sports are so much fun!

    D. Soccer is probably the best sport, but football is fun, too.

Answer: The correct answer is option D since it does not give a "because" (grounds) for the claim. Option D is talking about sports, but it gives an opinion about which kinds of sports are best, not a reason for why sports are important.

20. **Claim:** Movies are better than books.

   A. You can watch movies together with friends, but only one person at a time can read a book.

   B. Some movies are too scary to watch.

   C. Everyone can watch a movie because you do not need to know how to read.

   D. Movies are more fun than books because they have sound and pictures.

Answer: The correct answer is option B since it does not give a "because" (grounds) for the claim. Option B gives a fact about movies, but it does not explain why they are better than books.

Middle School

Students select the option that provides backing for the claim. Teachers might award a bonus point to teams that can also identify the type of backing (expert opinion, research results, or factual information).

1. **Claim:** Schools should be single gendered.

   A. Students will be more focused if they attend single-gendered schools.

   B. Girls will have more opportunities in school for clubs, sports, and school leadership roles.

   C. In single-gendered schools, girls may be under less pressure to look a certain way.

   D. Studies show that in co-ed classrooms, teachers are less likely to call on girls than boys (Good & Findley, 1985; Jones & Wheatley, 1990; Sadker & Sadker, 1995).

Answer: The correct answer is option D because it provides backing in the form of research results.

2. **Claim:** Skateboarding should be allowed on public streets.

   A. Not every community has a skate park. People will have no place to skateboard if the sport is not allowed in public and there is no access to a private skating facility.

   B. According to a study published in the *New England Journal of Medicine* (Thompson, Rivara, & Thompson, 1989), bicycle helmets can reduce the risk of head injury by 85 percent.

   C. The U.S. Consumer Product Safety Commission (2008) reports that the highest number of sports-related injuries among children under fifteen occur on bicycles. There were about four times more bicycle injuries in 2006 than skateboard injuries.

   D. More children are injured on bicycles than on skateboards, but bicycles are not banned.

Answer: The correct answer is option C because it provides backing in the form of research results.

3. **Claim:** The United States should ban the death penalty.

   A. As of March 12, 2014, more than 144 prisoners have been freed from death row because they were found to be innocent (Death Penalty Information Center, 2014).

   B. There is a race gap between criminals who get the death penalty and criminals who do not.

   C. If a defendant cannot afford an experienced, successful lawyer, he or she may be more likely to get the death penalty.

   D. A life prison sentence is a more reasonable and humane option than the death penalty.

   Answer: The correct answer is option A because it provides backing in the form of factual information.

4. **Claim:** Singer-songwriter Taylor Swift is a great musician.

   A. She is extremely talented for her age.

   B. Many legendary rock and country artists love her music and say she is talented, including Neil Young, Stevie Nicks, Jon Bon Jovi, and Dolly Parton (Bon Jovi, 2010; *CMT Insider Interview*, 2009; Nicks, 2010; Stromblad, 2011).

   C. Taylor gives lots of money to charity.

   D. Although Taylor writes some songs all on her own, expert pop producers co-wrote many of her hits, including "I Knew You Were Trouble" (Swift, Martin, & Shellback, 2012a, track 4) and "We Are Never Ever Getting Back Together" (Swift, Martin, & Shellback, 2012b, track 8).

   Answer: The correct answer is option B because it provides backing in the form of expert opinion.

5. **Claim:** Students should be allowed to wear headphones during standardized tests.

   A. Students who are bad test takers may be relaxed by listening to their own music.

   B. Studies have shown that students may perform better on tests after listening to classical music (Rauscher, Shaw, & Ky, 1993).

   C. Students who finish early will have something to do besides reading a book.

   D. Students might use iPods to play back prerecorded notes to use for cheating during tests.

   Answer: The correct answer is option B because it provides backing in the form of research results.

6. **Claim:** The driving age should not be raised from sixteen to eighteen.

   A. Research indicates that men are 78 percent more likely than women to be involved in car-related deaths, but no one is trying to stop men from driving cars (Fischbeck, Gengler, Gerard, & Weinberg, 2007).

   B. Increasing the driving age will not lower the number of accidents. Instead, it will make eighteen-year-olds the inexperienced drivers (instead of sixteen-year-olds). Either way, there will be inexperienced drivers on the road.

   C. Underage drinking is known to occur on college campuses. Sixteen-year-olds do not have as many opportunities to drink and drive as college-bound eighteen-year-olds.

   D. Raising the driving age because of a few reckless teenagers unfairly punishes those who are safe.

   Answer: The correct answer is option A because it provides backing in the form of research results.

7. **Claim:** Social media websites like Facebook should stop people from posting hate speech anonymously.

   A. This is not a violation of free speech because the people at Facebook do not just delete hateful pages. Instead, they give the person who made the page a choice: either change the words on the page or reveal your identity. Facebook employee Jud Hoffman says that this system works in "the vast majority of cases" because "it requires [users] to take responsibility for [offensive] content" (cited in Henn, 2013).

   B. Even though the Supreme Court of the United States ruled in *Reno v. American Civil Liberties Union* (1997) that Internet communication is protected under the First Amendment, Facebook does not count because the company is in the private sector.

   C. If Facebook does not get rid of hate speech, teens and other users will cyberbully people by creating pages that target certain people or groups.

   D. Facebook users still have the right to protest and tell the company how they feel about the speech on the site. This means that users have a say in what is okay to post on Facebook and what is not.

Answer: The correct answer is option A because it provides backing in the form of expert opinion. Alternatively, a student might say that option A provides backing in the form of factual information because Hoffman is drawing on data from Facebook to make his case. This is an acceptable answer if the student can explain his or her reasoning.

8. **Claim:** Every state should pass the DREAM Act, which allows certain undocumented immigrants to live in the United States (kids who are brought to the United States by their parents, teens who graduate from U.S. high schools, or people who serve in the military).

   A. This is not the first time that people who are not U.S. citizens have served in the military, and new DREAM Act recruits would only make the military stronger.

   B. The DREAM Act will increase the ratio of college graduates in the United States, which will make the nation smarter and help it compete with other countries.

   C. According to the Congressional Budget Office (2010), the DREAM Act would reduce the United States' debt by $1.4 billion. Over ten years, it would earn $2.3 billion for the government.

   D. In order to be admitted through the DREAM Act, immigrants cannot have any criminal record. This will help border security officials focus on deporting criminals and other people who are actually bad for the country.

Answer: The correct answer is option C because it provides backing in the form of expert opinion.

9. **Claim:** Hollywood movie studios should stop using the Motion Picture Association of America's (MPAA) age rating system for movies (which uses ratings such as G, PG, PG-13, R, and NC-17).

    A. The ratings do not work—kids can easily watch PG-13 or R-rated movies online or at friends' houses.

    B. Age is not always the same as maturity level. One fourteen-year-old may be able to handle the violence in a war movie, but a different person of the same age may not.

    C. The MPAA claims to be fair, but it has rated movies unfairly in the past. For example, *Bully* (Lowen, Waitt, & Hirsch, 2011), a nonfiction movie about bullying in schools, received an R rating for swearing (director Lee Hirsch had to take out some of the words from the movie to get a lower rating), even though many other movies have used the same language and received a PG-13 rating (Roeper, 2012).

    D. When a movie gets an NC-17 rating, producers can have a very hard time advertising and drawing crowds to see it. This means the MPAA's ratings have the power to lower the profit the movie makes and even stop people from finding out about it at all. This is a type of censorship.

    Answer: The correct answer is option C because it provides backing in the form of factual information.

10. **Claim:** Kids should only be allowed to watch television a few times per week.

    A. Studies show that people who watch lots of television are at an increased risk for type 2 diabetes, cardiovascular disease, and death because they exercise less and eat more junk food (Grøntved & Hu, 2011).

    B. Television is rarely educational for kids.

    C. There is lots of violence on television, which may have a bad influence on kids.

    D. Watching television does not teach kids to be social, but playing outside with friends or neighbors does.

    Answer: The correct answer is option A because it provides backing in the form of research results.

11. **Claim:** To protect the environment, people should not drive cars anymore.

    A. There are more than ten times as many cars and trucks on the road polluting the air as there were in 1950 (DaimlerChrysler, 2007).

    B. People can use the bus instead.

    C. Air pollution is only getting worse.

    D. Riding a bike or walking is healthier than sitting in a car.

    Answer: The correct answer is option A because it provides backing in the form of factual information.

12. **Claim:** Teachers and principals should be allowed to censor what students write in a school newspaper.

    A. Teachers have a responsibility to protect students, so they need to make sure that hateful speech is not published.

    B. In the case *Hazelwood School District et al. v. Kuhlmeier et al.* (1988), the U.S. Supreme Court ruled that school newspapers can be censored because they are not the same as regular newspapers, which are protected by free speech.

    C. Students still have control of their speech—they can express their opinions online on Facebook or Twitter.

    D. Without censorship, students might publish untrue rumors or gossip in the paper.

   Answer: The correct answer is option B because it provides backing in the form of expert opinion or factual information (both are acceptable answers).

13. **Claim:** Sea animal amusement parks like SeaWorld are cruel and should be shut down.

    A. Giant whales are locked in tiny tanks at SeaWorld when they should be swimming freely and getting plenty of exercise in the ocean.

    B. In the book *Death at SeaWorld*, journalist David Kirby (2013) reports that yearly death rates of captive orcas are two and one-half times higher than the death rate of wild orcas.

    C. When orcas are aggressive toward one another in the ocean, they have thousands of miles to swim away and get some space, but an orca can't escape from a fight in a small SeaWorld tank.

    D. Sometimes SeaWorld splits up orca calves from their mothers, even though wild orcas stay together for life.

   Answer: The correct answer is option B because it provides backing in the form of research results.

14. **Claim:** Hollywood movies have a trend of being sexist.

    A. Blockbusters often make women seem stupid, conceited, or obsessed with finding love.

    B. Film editors can change the appearance of people in their movies to make them seem more attractive, which is misleading.

    C. Female actresses who are age forty or older often cannot find work because movies only want young actresses. However, older men are in movies all the time.

    D. In 2011, only 11 percent of the main characters in the top hundred best-selling movies were women, even though women make up about half of the population (Lauzen, 2012).

   Answer: The correct answer is option D because it provides backing in the form of factual information.

15. **Claim:** Field trips should always be educational in some way.

   A. Kids who visit museums learn critical thinking skills, according to a study of ten thousand students who toured an Arkansas art museum (Greene, Kisida, & Bowen, 2014).

   B. Field trips allow students to participate in projects that they would not be able to do in a classroom (such as hands-on science projects at a nature preserve).

   C. Some families cannot afford to see a play in the theater or pay to visit a museum—field trips make it possible for everyone to have these opportunities.

   D. Educational field trips can combine fun and learning!

   Answer: The correct answer is option A because it provides backing in the form of research results.

16. **Claim:** Students should be allowed to chew gum in school.

   A. On its website, the American Dental Association (2013) states, "Chewing sugarless gum has been shown to increase the flow of saliva, thereby reducing plaque acid, strengthening the teeth and reducing tooth decay."

   B. Kids who do not stick used gum underneath desks should not be punished because of kids who do!

   C. Many teachers do not find gum distracting during class.

   D. Gum can increase concentration and help kids do better on tests!

   Answer: The correct answer is option A because it provides backing in the form of research results.

17. **Claim:** Standardized tests are not good for students.

   A. Teachers are under a lot of pressure to teach the things that they know will be on the test and might not have time to teach students other things they should know.

   B. Computers are sometimes used to grade standardized test essays. Les Perelman, director of writing at the Massachusetts Institute of Technology, has tested these computerized grading systems and believes they will make students worse writers (TIME for Kids Staff, 2013).

   C. Some schools are getting rid of music and art programs so that they can spend even more time teaching reading and math to prepare for standardized tests.

   D. Standardized tests are not very good at measuring students' creativity.

   Answer: The correct answer is option B because it provides backing in the form of expert opinion.

18. **Claim:** Companies should be allowed to put advertisements on school lockers and buses.

   A. Ads on school buses can help earn money for districts that are facing budget cuts.

   B. Ads for things like beer, cigarettes, or politicians might be inappropriate for kids.

   C. District 11 in Colorado Springs, Colorado, earned $15,000 in 2012 from companies that used their buses for advertising (McGraw, 2013).

   D. Companies are going to be paying for advertising anyway, so the money might as well be going to a good cause (like schools).

   Answer: The correct answer is option C because it provides backing in the form of factual information.

19. **Claim:** The government should not put a high tax on soda.

   A. People should be free to make their own decisions about what they eat and drink.

   B. It is true that there are high taxes on other unhealthy substances (like cigarettes), but unlike people who smoke cigarettes, people who drink soda do not harm others around them—they are only harming themselves.

   C. Harvard economist N. Gregory Mankiw (2010) worried that a tax on soda allows the government to decide what is best for citizens and could lead to taxes on things such as "fried foods" or "mindless television shows."

   D. A tax is not going to stop people from drinking soda.

   Answer: The correct answer is option C because it provides backing in the form of expert opinion.

20. **Claim:** Physical contact games (like tackle football and dodgeball) should be banned in physical education classes.

   A. Neil Williams, professor of physical education, says that the game of dodgeball "allows the stronger kids to pick on and target the weaker kids" (as quoted in TIME for Kids Staff, 2011).

   B. Many school districts in the United States have already banned dodgeball and tackle football in gym classes.

   C. Kids who get eliminated right away from games like dodgeball do not get very much exercise, which is the whole point of gym class.

   D. Kids can learn all the athletic skills they need from other games.

   Answer: The correct answer is option A because it provides backing in the form of expert opinion.

High School A

Students select the option that provides a qualifier for the claim.

1. **Claim:** Professional and college sports teams should eliminate American Indian references from their mascots.

   A. Team names like *Braves* or *Redskins* can be very offensive to American Indians, a historically marginalized social group.

   B. In the past fifty years, many sports teams have successfully changed their mascots to eliminate American Indian stereotypes and become more socially appropriate.

   C. The National Congress of American Indians (NCAI, 2013) "strongly opposes the use of derogatory Native sports mascots" because they "present a misleading image of Indian people and feed the historic myths that have been used to whitewash a history of oppression."

   D. Despite its general opposition to American Indian sports mascots, the NCAI points out that in special cases, such team names can be acceptable. For instance, the NCAI (2013) "respects the right of individual tribal nations to work with universities and athletic programs to decide how to protect and celebrate their respective tribal heritage."

   Answer: Option D is a qualifier because it presents information that does not support the claim. Option C provides backing, and options A and B provide grounds for the claim.

2. **Claim:** Students should attend school year-round.

   A. Year-round education has been shown to lower schools' expenses, particularly schedules that use the school building all year and divide students into multiple tracks with rotating attendance (one group goes to school while the other is on vacation; Daneshvary & Clauretie, 2001). Despite this benefit, other year-round models maintain or even raise costs for schools, such as schedules that keep all students in one group and provide everyone with the same breaks (Dossett & Munoz, 2000).

   B. Data show that low-income students at year-round schools sometimes score higher than low-income students at traditional schools (Cooper, Valentine, Charlton, & Melson, 2003).

   C. Teachers can devote more time to introducing new academic content instead of reviewing material that students have already learned.

   D. Year-round schooling provides more frequent breaks instead of one long summer vacation, giving more review time to students who have fallen behind.

Answer: Option A is a qualifier because it presents information that does not support the claim. Options A and B both provide backing for the claim because they each include dates, academic sources, and phrases like "data show" and "has been shown." However, option A can be more accurately classified as backing with a qualifier because it presents an exception to evidence. C and D are grounds in that they answer the question, "Why should students attend school year-round?"

3. **Claim:** Whale hunting (whaling) should be banned internationally.

   A. Certain species of whale contain harmful contaminants (such as mercury) and are not safe to eat, particularly in excess and by high-risk people (Simmonds et al., 2002).

   B. In a 2008 study in *Marine Policy*, fewer than one in five whales were killed immediately by the harpoons used by whalers. The study showed that the harpoons took an average of ten minutes to actually kill a whale. Sometimes this process can even take a period of hours (Gales, Leaper, & Papastavrou, 2008).

   C. Some whale species have been found to possess spindle neurons, a type of brain cell that is only found in highly intelligent creatures like humans, certain apes, and bottlenose dolphins (Hof & Van der Gucht, 2007). Despite this finding, the existence of intelligent animals without the spindle neuron (such as pigs) does make it difficult to determine which animals are morally acceptable to kill.

   D. Whaling could be bad for tourist industries—such as whale watching—because the types of whales that typically approach boats may also be the easiest to hunt.

Answer: Option C is a qualifier because it presents information that does not support the claim. Options A and B provide backing in the form of research results, and option D provides grounds for the claim.

4. **Claim:** France should allow Muslim women to wear a niqab (a full-face veil) in public places.

   A. The majority of French Muslim women reported that they choose to wear the niqab. They were not forced or pressured by parents, husbands, or orthodox Muslim groups (Open Society Foundations, 2011).

   B. If Muslim women cannot wear the niqab in public, many of them might decide to leave work and school in order to stay at home, where they are still allowed to wear the niqab. This could alienate Muslim women from the rest of French society.

   C. Some feminists believe that the niqab degrades women, but not all. Many other feminists believe that a federal ban of the garment is worse because it is antidemocratic. They point out that banning the niqab is a way for men to legislate the way women dress and exercise control over women's bodies.

   D. The French government argues that the ban is a matter of national security in public spaces (such as airports, banks, and state buildings). However, French Muslim women report that they would be willing to show their faces for identification purposes when asked by a state official in such a location (Open Society Foundations, 2011).

Answer: Option C is a qualifier because it presents information that does not support the claim. Option B provides grounds. A and D provide backing in the form of research results.

5. **Claim:** Fast food and soft drink companies should not be allowed to sponsor the Olympics.

   A. Tobacco companies are not allowed to sponsor Olympic events because cigarettes are unhealthy. The same logic can be applied to fast food and soft drink companies.

   B. Jacques Rogge, president of the International Olympic Committee (IOC), raised concerns that dropping sponsors may cause financial trouble for the Games ("IOC Chief Jacques Rogge Admits 'Question Mark,'" 2012).

   C. Dr. Tony Jewell, chief medical officer for Wales, opposes sponsors like McDonald's and Coca-Cola. He said, "There is much to do to tackle obesity, and stating clearly that fast food has no place in sport sends a clear message" (cited in McWatt, 2012).

   D. The addictive potential of fast food—especially among vulnerable populations— may make it tougher for people to select healthier options (Garber & Lustig, 2011). Granting this point, individuals should still be encouraged to take personal responsibility for their health.

Answer: Option D is a qualifier because it presents information that does not support the claim. Option A provides grounds, while options B and C both provide backing in the form of expert opinion.

6. **Claim:** English should not be made the official language of the United States.

   A. Americans who speak little or no English would be disadvantaged if English were to become the official language because they might have to pay to take classes to learn the language.

   B. A government with an official language may not issue notifications in multiple languages during emergencies (such as natural disasters or medical pandemics), making life more dangerous for Americans who do not speak English.

   C. To be fair, all immigrants to the United States probably should make an effort to learn English for their own benefit, even if it does not become the official language.

   D. The United States prides itself on being a nation of immigrants. Making English the official language may jeopardize the melting pot identity of the nation.

Answer: Option C is a qualifier because it presents information that does not support the claim. Options A, B, and D all provide grounds for the claim.

7. **Claim:** The NBA should drop its minimum-age requirement for players and allow high school athletes to be included in the draft.

   A. Former high school draft picks like Kobe Bryant, Kevin Garnett, and Jermaine O'Neal have become extremely successful basketball superstars.

   B. Baseball and hockey do not have minimum-age requirements for drafted players. Basketball should not be any different.

   C. A study by legal sports analyst Michael McCann (2005) shows that of eighty-four NBA players with arrest records, only 4 percent had never been to college.

   D. Even though they are few and far between, there have been careers of high school draftees that do not end successfully.

Answer: Option D is a qualifier because it presents information that does not support the claim. Options A and B both provide grounds for the claim, and option C provides backing in the form of research results.

8. **Claim:** Assault weapons like AK-47s should be banned in the United States.

   A. Even if most gun-related crimes in the United States are carried out with handguns rather than assault weapons, this is not a reason for the government to ignore the deaths and dangers caused by assault weapons (Leshner, Altevogt, Lee, McCoy, & Kelley, 2013).

   B. The United States no longer depends on state and federal militias for defense. Therefore, the right to own an assault weapon is not protected by the Second Amendment, which states, "A well regulated Militia, being necessary to the security of a free State, the right of the people to keep and bear Arms, shall not be infringed" (U.S. Const. amend. II).

   C. The majority of the sixty-two mass murders that occurred between 1982 and 2013 in the United States involved legally obtained guns (Follman, Aronsen, & Pan, 2012).

   D. Evidence from the Harvard Injury Control Research Center suggests that nations with higher gun availability also have higher rates of homicide (Hepburn & Hemenway, 2004).

Answer: Option A is a qualifier because it presents information that does not support the claim. Option B provides grounds for the claim, and C and D provide backing in the form of factual information and research results.

9. **Claim:** Colleges and universities should abolish early-admission programs for prospective students.

   A. Still, it is a valid point that early acceptance can assuage some stress for a high school senior.

   B. William Fitzsimmons, dean of admissions at Harvard College, says, "Students who apply early are more likely to be affluent, savvy about the process, and attend high schools with resources to help them assemble their college applications" (Fitzsimmons, 2007).

   C. Low-income students depend on the opportunity to compare the different offers they receive for financial aid, which early-admission programs may prevent. If these students cannot participate in early-admission programs, they cannot compete with applicants who do.

   D. Early-admission programs may encourage students to make hasty decisions about college, which ought to be a carefully considered process.

   Answer: Option A is a qualifier because it presents information that does not support the claim. Option B provides backing in the form of an expert opinion. Options C and D offer grounds for the claim.

10. **Claim:** The United States should close the detention facility at Guantánamo Bay.

    A. Some prisoners at Guantánamo have not been tried in federal court.

    B. The American Civil Liberties Union (ACLU, n.d.) has openly called for the closing of Guantánamo, calling it a "shameful episode in American history" and "a catastrophic failure on every front."

    C. Many prisoners at Guantánamo have decided to go on hunger strikes and are being forcibly fed by prison officials as a result, which is a form of torture.

    D. It is true that many Americans who advocate for closing Guantánamo do not know the specific details about the terrorist detainees and may not truly understand the danger that they pose to national security.

    Answer: Option D is a qualifier because it presents information that does not support the claim. Options A and C offer grounds for the claim, and option B offers backing in the form of expert opinion.

11. **Claim:** The United States government should reverse its amendment to Title IX and ban single-sex education (all boys or all girls).

    A. Some single-sex schools, such as Girls Athletic Leadership School (GALS) in Denver, have been very successful in helping their students grow and improve academically.

    B. The idea that girls learn best by sitting still in quiet classrooms and boys learn best by moving around in noisier classrooms has been debunked by scientists (Halpern et al., 2011).

    C. Men and women often collaborate in the workforce, so schools should be preparing students to work together with students of other genders.

    D. The American Civil Liberties Union (ACLU, 2013) has stated that single-sex education programs teach kids dangerous stereotypes about gender.

    Answer: Option A is a qualifier because it presents information that does not support the claim. Options B and D present research results and expert opinions, respectively, and option C presents grounds.

12. **Claim:** Video games are not to blame for acts of youth violence.

   A. Game theorists argue that kids can tell the difference between play and reality, so a child who plays violent video games may not necessarily be violent in real life (Salen & Zimmerman, 2004).

   B. The Office of the U.S. Surgeon General (2001) reported that risk factors for school shootings related most strongly to mental health and home life, not exposure to violent media.

   C. To be fair, the Office of the U.S. Surgeon General (2001) also reported that kids who were exposed to violent media did demonstrate a short-term increase in physical aggression.

   D. The majority of Americans play video games (Entertainment Software Association, 2013b), so the fact that someone who commits violent acts is also a gamer does not prove much.

   Answer: Option C is a qualifier because it presents information that does not support the claim. Option A presents an expert opinion, and options B and D present research results.

13. **Claim:** U.S. high schools should not block the video-sharing website YouTube on school computers.

   A. It is true that YouTube has come under fire in the past for being used as a tool for cyberbullying.

   B. Students can create videos or tutorials about academic content and use YouTube to share them with their classmates.

   C. Teachers also benefit from being able to access YouTube at school—they can show videos that enhance their lessons.

   D. Instead of blocking YouTube outright, schools can sign up for YouTube for Schools, a program that filters out inappropriate videos and allows students to access educational ones.

   Answer: Option A is a qualifier because it presents information that does not support the claim. Options B and C provide grounds, and option D provides factual information.

14. **Claim:** All high school students should be required to take courses in the arts (such as music, theater, film, and so on).

   A. Research shows that high schools that offer students education in the arts have higher graduation rates than those that do not (Israel, 2009).

   B. Of course, supplies and materials for arts classes are often expensive—they can consume a lot of money from the school.

   C. Students in Japan, Hungary, and the Netherlands receive mandatory music education and consistently have among the highest test scores in math and science (Ponter, 1999).

   D. If students are not required to take courses in the arts, they may miss out on opportunities they may not have chosen to take themselves.

   Answer: Option B is a qualifier because it presents information that does not support the claim. Options A and C present research results, and option D presents grounds.

15. **Claim:** Homework should be banned in public schools.

    A. Out-of-class assignments can teach students valuable lessons in time management and independence.

    B. Some students' parents are able to help them with their homework, but not everyone has this opportunity—some students' parents do not speak English or have to work during the evenings and are unable to offer help.

    C. Schoolwork should be completed in school so that time after school and in the evenings can be reserved for participation in athletics, arts, and clubs.

    D. Teens who stay up late in order to study are more likely to have problems in school the next day (Gillen-O'Neel, Huynh, & Fuligni, 2013).

Answer: Option A is a qualifier because it presents information that does not support the claim. Options B and C provide grounds, and option D provides research results.

High School B

Students select the biased word (the word that subtly reveals the speaker's opinion).

1. Arthur Miller (1953/2003) depicted the shameful Salem Witch Trials of 1692 in a play called *The Crucible*, which he originally called *The Chronicles of Sarah Good*.

    A. depicted

    B. shameful

    C. originally

    D. witch

Answer: The correct answer is option B because it reveals the speaker's opinion that the Salem Witch Trials were shameful.

2. Franklin Delano Roosevelt became the thirty-second president of the United States and instituted the New Deal after bravely overcoming polio.

    A. instituted

    B. polio

    C. overcoming

    D. bravely

Answer: The correct answer is option D because it reveals the speaker's opinion that President Roosevelt was brave.

3. The unethical research of embryonic stem cells could lead to treatments for certain diseases, such as arthritis, Alzheimer's, and stroke.

     A. could

     B. embryonic

     C. certain

     D. unethical

Answer: The correct answer is option D because it reveals the speaker's opinion that stem cell research is unethical.

4. As of 2013, only four women had ever been nominated to win an Oscar for Best Director in the history of the Academy Awards.

     A. only

     B. nominated

     C. history

     D. awards

Answer: The correct answer is option A because it reveals the speaker's opinion that more women should be nominated for Academy Awards.

5. "The Necklace" is a short story by Guy de Maupassant (1885/1992) about an unsatisfied woman who learns a valuable lesson about wealth, fortune, and vanity.

     A. short

     B. unsatisfied

     C. valuable

     D. vanity

Answer: The correct answer is option C because it reveals the speaker's opinion that "The Necklace" teaches a valuable lesson.

6. During his presidency, Barack Obama imposed a number of changes on the American people, including an end to the military's Don't Ask, Don't Tell policy, an increase in funding for Pell Grant scholarships, and controversial healthcare legislation.

     A. imposed

     B. changes

     C. increase

     D. controversial

Answer: The correct answer is option A because it reveals the speaker's opinion that Barack Obama's changes were imposed on a generally unwilling public.

7. The discovery of the Pythagorean theorem ($a^2 + b^2 = c^2$) is often accredited to the brilliant Greek philosopher Pythagoras; however, some scholars believe that Babylonian mathematicians are actually responsible for the theorem.

    A. discovery

    B. accredited

    C. brilliant

    D. actually

Answer: The correct answer is option C because it reveals the speaker's opinion that Pythagoras was brilliant.

8. Award-winning Indian American author Jhumpa Lahiri received a Pulitzer Prize for *Interpreter of Maladies*, a poignant collection of short stories, and saw her autobiographical first novel—*The Namesake*—adapted for the screen.

    A. award-winning

    B. poignant

    C. autobiographical

    D. first

Answer: The correct answer is option B because it reveals the speaker's opinion that the stories in Lahiri's *Interpreter of Maladies* were poignant.

9. Christopher Columbus's voyages facilitated the transfer of smallpox to the Americas, slaughtering millions of Native Americans whose populations never recovered.

    A. facilitated

    B. slaughtering

    C. millions

    D. recovered

Answer: The correct answer is option B because it reveals the speaker's opinion that the death of the Native Americans by smallpox was a result of malicious intent.

10. During the Arab Spring, a wave of revolutionary protests and wars in North Africa and the Middle East, citizens from numerous countries recklessly challenged—and sometimes toppled—antidemocracy rulers and regimes.

    A. revolutionary

    B. recklessly

    C. toppled

    D. antidemocracy

Answer: The correct answer is option B because it reveals the speaker's opinion that the Arab Spring protests were reckless.

11. Wealthy American entrepreneur Elon Musk was one of the visionaries behind PayPal, a company that allows people to make payments online, and a founder of Tesla Motors, a company that manufactures high-end electric cars.

   A. wealthy

   B. visionaries

   C. allows

   D. high-end

   Answer: The correct answer is option B because it reveals the speaker's opinion that Elon Musk is a visionary.

12. Even though his songs are sometimes controversial, lyrical genius Jay-Z has been called one of the most influential rappers of all time.

   A. controversial

   B. lyrical

   C. genius

   D. influential

   Answer: The correct answer is option C because it reveals the speaker's opinion that Jay-Z is a genius.

13. Scientists believe that mosquitoes use moisture, body heat, and movement to seek host animals and pursue their annoying bloodsucking habits.

   A. believe

   B. seek

   C. annoying

   D. bloodsucking

   Answer: The correct answer is option C because it reveals the speaker's opinion that mosquitoes are annoying.

14. In 2001, the American energy company Enron was found to have committed accounting fraud through the use of creative and corrupt accounting practices.

   A. energy

   B. fraud

   C. creative

   D. corrupt

   Answer: The correct answer is option C because it reveals the speaker's opinion that Enron's accounting practices were creative.

15. Some people in the media have attacked pop singer Miley Cyrus for behaving inappropriately and dressing provocatively.

    A. attacked

    B. pop

    C. inappropriately

    D. provocatively

Answer: The correct answer is option A because it reveals the speaker's opinion that the media was too harsh in its criticism of Miley Cyrus.

7 Text Evidence Bingo

For upper elementary, middle school, and high school students

This game, based on the classic game of chance, gives students practice with generating claims and identifying grounds to support them, particularly those that involve citing textual evidence. The game is flexible enough to allow for ample variation in subject matter and game play. It can be modified to suit multiple content areas (language arts, science, and social studies) and works best with students who are very familiar with using textual evidence.

Setup

Prepare a set of claims about a particular text for students to fill in on their blank bingo boards. You can either (1) use one of the sets of claims provided at the end of this chapter (pages 120–158), (2) create a set of claims yourself, or (3) lead a content-related brainstorming session to create a list of claims with your class.

Make sure to come up with more claims to choose from than there are spaces on the board (that is, at least twenty-six items). The types of claims you use will vary by content area. For example, if you teach high school language arts, you could play the game to practice using textual evidence to support claims about a class novel. During a previous lesson, the class brainstorms a long list of themes present in a novel and claims that can be made about those themes. For example, if you are practicing using evidence to make claims for themes in F. Scott Fitzgerald's *The Great Gatsby*, one list item may read, "Dwelling in the past can prevent you from moving forward into the future."

Argumentation Skills

- Citing textual evidence
- Making inductive inferences
- Presenting and supporting claims
- Explaining the relationship between claims, grounds, and backing

Materials

- Twenty-five tokens for each student (plastic chips, tiddlywinks, foam pieces, pretzels, and so on)
- Blank bingo board for each student (see reproducible on page 159)
- List of claims about a particular text (displayed on chalkboard, whiteboard, chart paper, or with a projector; see resources at end of chapter)
- List of textual evidence from a particular text (see resources at end of chapter)
- Note-taking materials for each student

As previously mentioned, this list of claims should contain at least twenty-six items by the end of the brainstorming session, because you want students' boards to be as varied as possible to avoid ties.

To accelerate the brainstorming process, you might decide to have students work in small groups to brainstorm themes before meeting as a whole class to consolidate a list. If you create a set with your class, we recommend having this brainstorming session during an earlier class period before you play bingo to give you time to prepare corresponding clues for the items.

If the class is struggling to come up with twenty-six claims, there are a few different ways to proceed. First, divide students up into groups and assign each group a salient topic in the novel (for example, gender roles, violence, economics, and so on) to guide the students in producing a longer list. This can spark new thoughts about themes in the novel. Second, assign each group a character in the novel (for example, Nick Carraway, Daisy Buchanan, Jay Gatsby, Myrtle Wilson, and so on) and encourage them to discuss and record their opinions about these characters, their values, their personalities, their relationships, and so on. For instance, a student might say, "I hate Daisy. She's so shallow and lazy, and she dumps Gatsby in the end just because he's not 'old money,'" prompting a second student to disagree: "I agree that she's shallow, but I don't think you can blame her, because she was raised to value money and marry rich." A third student might point out that because of this rigid social structure, not to mention the limitations imposed on her by her gender, one could actually claim that Daisy is trapped. A fourth might add that Gatsby's obsession with Daisy actually reflects his own materialism and pursuit of the American Dream, for which Daisy is a symbol, and so to argue that Gatsby is a victim of Daisy's materialism would be a hypocritical claim. All of these are claims worthy of recording and adding to the whole-class list. If students are still stuck, you might prompt them with thematically inspired questions about the novel: "Is Gatsby a heroic figure?" "Why does Daisy ultimately stay with Tom?" "Is Nick a reliable narrator?" "Who is to blame for Gatsby's murder at the end of the novel?" "What do you think Jordan means when she says that she prefers large parties because they are more intimate than small parties, where there isn't any privacy?"

Display the list of claims so that the whole class can read it by writing it out on a chalkboard, projecting it on a screen or interactive whiteboard, or writing it on a large piece of chart paper. You will also need to prepare a list containing pieces of textual evidence to use as clues during the game. This might include direct quotes, symbols, motifs, facts, or details—anything that can be found right in the text. Keep the textual evidence clues ready and available for your own use as the "caller," but do not display them for the class to see. Finally, pass out twenty-five tokens and a blank bingo board to each student.

Play

Give students five minutes to select claims from this list and write them in their empty bingo templates in any order they choose. Allowing students to fill in their own grids provides them with a degree of agency in a game normally contingent on luck. It also ensures that each student will have a unique arrangement of claims on his or her board. To begin the game, students use one of their tokens to mark off the "free space" on their bingo boards.

Next, the teacher "calls clues" by reading items aloud from the list of textual evidence. Players listen to the pieces of evidence and use their tokens to mark off claims for which the evidence provides support. For instance, you might say, "In the final line of F. Scott Fitzgerald's *The Great Gatsby*, narrator Nick Carraway says, 'So we beat on, boats against the current, borne back ceaselessly into the past.'" If a student has chosen to write the claim "Dwelling in the past can prevent you from moving forward into the future" in one of her spaces, she recognizes that the quote you just read provides textual evidence for that claim and places a token on that space on her bingo board. Students will need to take notes about which textual evidence they are using to support each claim so that they can defend their answers at the end of the game.

Next, you might read a clue that says, "The colors *yellow* and *gold*—Gatsby's yellow car; Daisy 'the golden girl'; Jordan's 'slender golden arms'; Daisy's 'little gold pencil'; T. J. Eckleburg's yellow glasses." Again, students examine their boards to see if they have a claim that can be supported by that textual evidence, cover it with a token if they do, and make notes to help them remember which textual evidence they used to support that claim.

Keep moving down your list of clues, giving students about thirty seconds of think time between each one, until someone is able to mark five spaces (claims) in a row (horizontally, vertically, or diagonally). The free space in the center of the board can count as one of these five spaces. Make sure to remind students that they may only mark one space (that is, one claim) per piece of evidence, even if that piece of evidence could lend support to multiple different claims.

When a student gets five in a row, she shouts, "Bingo!" At this point, the student must justify *every one* of her answers in order to win; that is, she must explain how each claim she marked was supported by a piece of evidence read by the teacher. This is when students' notes will become necessary. For example:

Student: Bingo!

Teacher: Okay. Let's hear what you marked and why.

Student: First, I marked "Dwelling in the past can prevent you from moving forward into the future," which is supported by the metaphor you read, in which Nick compares himself and the other characters to boats against the current. Furthermore, this quote's position at the very end of the book highlights its importance and lends support to the argument for this theme as one of the most prominent in the novel.

Teacher: Good. Next?

Student: Next, I marked "Old American aristocrats distinguish themselves from the newly wealthy," which is supported by the yellow and gold colors you mentioned. Fitzgerald uses gold colors in writing about Daisy and Jordan, who have been rich since birth, and yellow colors when writing about Gatsby, who was born poor and became rich. T. J. Eckleburg's yellow glasses also support this claim, because the Eckleburg billboard looms over the Valley of Ashes, a place that could represent the upper class's disregard of the working class.

Teacher: Excellent. And third?

If a student can't justify one of his space markings, he does not earn a bingo. He is not eliminated from the game, but he must remove his marker from that particular space, and the game continues.

In order to keep the game interesting throughout guided practice or a review session, mix it up using the variations on traditional bingo presented in table 7.1 (page 118).

Table 7.1: Variations in Bingo Game Play

Variation	Description	Example
Traditional	Five spaces are marked on the board in a horizontal, vertical, or diagonal line. The free space in the center of the board may count toward a bingo.	
Six Pack	The board is marked with a pattern of six connected spaces (three spaces from two rows arranged horizontally or vertically). The free space in the center of the board may count toward a bingo.	
Bullseye	The free space in the center of the board is surrounded by marked spaces.	
Postage Stamps	Four spaces are marked to create a square in a corner of the board. To make the game last longer, mark a total of eight spaces to create two squares in separate corners of the board.	
Flying Kite	Four spaces are marked to create a square in a corner of the board. From here, three spaces are marked diagonally from the corner space to an opposite corner of the board, resembling a kite. The free space counts toward a bingo.	
Sandwich	The entire top and bottom rows of the board are marked.	
Railroad	The entire left and right columns of the board are marked.	

Inverted Bingo	In this twist, any player who gets a bingo is knocked out of the game. The player who marks the most spaces on his or her board without getting a bingo is the winner. A fun way to play this game is to begin with all students standing at their seats, then sit when they are eliminated. The free space counts toward a bingo.	
Blackout	All spaces on the board are marked. This variation can take a lot of time and works best at the end of a bingo session.	

Sample Bingo Board Items for Text Evidence Bingo

Here we provide sets of claims and textual evidence for the upper elementary, middle school, and high school levels. Each set contains the following elements:

◆ Bingo space items (claims) that students can use to fill in their blank bingo boards

◆ Teacher clues (evidence) that teachers read aloud to students during the game

Each sample set of bingo items is based on a grade-level-appropriate text recommended by the Common Core State Standards (NGA & CCSSO, 2010c). Therefore, teachers can use either (1) the sets provided here (if their class is studying one of the featured books) or (2) sets they create themselves for specific texts their classes are studying. If teachers design their own sets, they can use the sets provided here as a guide. The sample sets correspond to the following texts.

Grades 4–5:

◆ *Bud, Not Buddy* by Christopher Paul Curtis

◆ *Tuck Everlasting* by Natalie Babbit

Grades 6–8:

◆ *A Wrinkle in Time* by Madeleine L'Engle

◆ *Roll of Thunder, Hear My Cry* by Mildred D. Taylor

Grades 9–10:

◆ *To Kill a Mockingbird* by Harper Lee

◆ *The Tragedy of Macbeth* by William Shakespeare

Grades 11–12:

◆ *Pride and Prejudice* by Jane Austen

◆ *The Great Gatsby* by F. Scott Fitzgerald

You may notice that different grade levels contain different types of bingo space items (claims). High school claims, for the most part, are symbolic or thematic; they can be applied to life outside the text (for example,

"Materialism and consumption do not always lead to happiness"). Because younger students are still learning to use text evidence, the claims at the elementary level are not as complex. They generally pertain to events that occur within the context of the novel and may or may not apply universally outside it (for example, "Bud is very brave for a ten-year-old kid"). Middle school claims contain a mix of these two types.

Finally, please note that in the following tables we have not used the traditional (author, page number) format for citing direct quotations. All of the texts we selected from the CCSS have been published multiple times, and different editions of the texts may have different paginations. To ensure that all teachers can use these sets (no matter which edition of a book they have), we do not refer to page numbers when citing direct quotations. Instead, citations of quotes from novels follow the format (chapter.paragraph). To illustrate, a line from the second paragraph in chapter 3 would be cited as (3.2). Citations of quotes from plays follow the format (act.scene.line). Line breaks are indicated with the symbol /. In Shakespeare's *Macbeth*, for instance, the Act 4, Scene 1 line "Double, double toil and trouble / Fire burn, and cauldron bubble" would be cited as follows: (4.1.10–11).

Grades 4–5

Bud, Not Buddy by Christopher Paul Curtis

Bingo Space Items (Claims)	Teacher Clues (Textual Evidence)
Bud can't be sad anymore because he has already been sad so often in his life.	But the tears coming out doesn't happen to me anymore, I don't know when it first happened, but it seems like my eyes don't cry no more (1.17). Here we go again (1.1, 1.17, 1.45).
The negative changes that Bud thinks happen to people when they turn six actually happened because Momma died.	I couldn't help but feel sorry for Jerry. . . . being six is a real rough age to be at. Most folks think you start to be a real adult when you're fifteen or sixteen years old, but that's not true, it really starts when you're around six (1.24). It's at six that grown folks don't think you're a cute little kid anymore. . . . it's around six that grown folks stop giving you little swats and taps and jump clean up to giving you slugs that'll knock you right down (1.25). Six is real tough. That's how old I was when I came to live here in the Home. That's how old I was when Momma died (1.31).
Bud is a good friend.	Jerry sat on his bed and I could tell that he was losing the fight not to cry. . . . I sat down next to him and said, "I know being in a house with three girls sounds terrible, Jerry, but it's a lot better than being with a boy who's a couple of years older than you." . . . Jerry couldn't help but smile. I said, "You're going to be great" (1.18–22). Bugs said, "Hurry, I'll wait." "I'll catch you, go ahead" (8.216–217).
Bud has had bad experiences in previous foster homes.	And you'd best understand too, if you aren't looking for some real trouble, 'cause it's around six that grown folks stop giving you little swats and taps and jump clean up to giving you slugs that'll knock you right down and have you seeing stars in the middle of the day. The first foster home I was in taught me that real quick (1.25). Here we go again (1.45).

The "Herman E. Calloway" flyer is one of Bud's most prized possessions.	I did what I do every night before I go to sleep, I checked to make sure everything was there. . . . I had to make sure no one had run off with any of my things. First I pulled my blanket out and saw that everything was where it was supposed to be. At the bottom of my suitcase were the flyers. I took the blue flyer out and looked at it again (1.33–34).
	The paper was starting to wear out from me looking at it so much (1.35).
	I got a whole lot calmer when I picked [my suitcase] up and it was the right weight, I didn't think they'd taken anything out of it (4.2).
We can predict that Momma knew someone on the blue flyer.	I remember Momma bringing this flyer with her when she came from working one day, I remember because she got very upset when she put it on the supper table and kept looking at it and picking it up and putting it back and moving it around (1.41).
	This one really got her jumpy. The only difference I could see between the blue one and the [other flyers] was that the others didn't say anything about Flint on them (1.41).
Bud does not trust adults very much.	You tell some adult about what's happening but all they do is say it's normal (1.29).
	You Have to Give Adults Something That They Think They Can Use to Hurt You by Taking It Away (2.57).
	If a Adult Tells You Not to Worry, and You Weren't Worried Before, You Better Hurry Up and Start 'Cause You're Already Running Late (5.46).
Todd and Bud both lie, but it is worse when Todd does it.	Todd coughed out, "Oh, Mother . . ." He took in two jumbo breaths. "I was only trying to help. . . . and look what it's gotten me" (2.9).
	She didn't have to worry, I'd apologize. One beating from these Amoses was enough for me (2.44).
	I put my head down and started shooting apologies out like John Dillinger shoots out bullets. I aimed at Todd first. . . . And if I didn't lie good enough [Mrs. Amos] was going to use that strap on me (2.50–53).
The Amoses are bad people, but they think they are good people.	This was wrong. They'd promised they'd keep [my suitcase] safe and not look in it. They'd laughed at me when I made them promise, but they did promise (2.36).
	"Boy," Mrs. Amos said, "I am not the least bit surprised at your show of ingratitude. Lord knows I have been stung by my own people before. But take a good look at me because I am one person who is totally fed up with you and your ilk. I do not have time to put up with the foolishness of those members of our race who do not want to be uplifted" (2.37).
	Shucks, you'd think that with the Amoses being so doggone mean they'd worry about leaving a big old gun like that out in the open (4.3).
Bud is a very quick thinker.	I put my head down and started shooting apologies out like John Dillinger shoots out bullets (2.50).
	"Please don't call the Home, please don't send me back." Shucks, going back to the Home was just what I wanted to do, but I was being just like Brer Rabbit in one of the books Momma used to read to me at night when he yelled out, "Please, Brer Fox, don't throw me into the pricker patch, please, please!" (2.55).

Continued on next page →

Sometimes Bud pretends to be brave even when he is afraid.	I squeezed my tongue between my teeth to hold it still 'cause I know a lot of times your brain might want to be brave but your mouth might let some real chicken-sounding stuff fall out of it (2.69).
	I looked down at the floor. If I was a normal kid I would've busted out crying, but I just stood there breathing hard. . . . They were really going to make me sleep in a shed with a patch of blood from that kid who had disappeared out of here a couple of weeks ago! (2.75).
Bud loves to read because of his Momma.	I was being just like Brer Rabbit in one of the books Momma used to read to me at night (2.55).
	I took two more breaths and pretended I was hearing Momma reading to me about the Billy Goats Gruff or the Fox and the Grapes or the Dog That Saw His Reflection in the Water or some other story she'd checked out of the library (8.205).
Bud has learned to blame himself for things that aren't his fault.	[Mrs. Amos] looked at her husband. "Mr. Amos will show you to the shed tonight and you can come back in tomorrow for breakfast before you go. I do hope your conscience plagues you because you may have ruined things for many others. I do not know if I shall ever be able to help another child in need" (2.38).
	I was mad at the Amoses, but most of all I was mad at me for believing there really was a vampire in the shed and for getting trapped like this where there wasn't anybody who cared what happened to me (3.53).
Bud tries to see things from other points of view.	I can't all the way blame Todd for giving me trouble. . . . If I had a regular home with a mother and father I wouldn't be too happy about other kids living in my house either (4.6).
	I couldn't really blame him, I don't think I'd be real happy about sharing my brown sugar and my folks with any strange kids either (6.48).
	Even though it might seem kind of mean, you can't really blame the librarians for tossing drooly folks out 'cause there's nothing worse than opening a book and having the pages all stuck together from some-body's dried-up slobber (7.5).
Bud is generally a gentle person.	I took the gun outside and put it on the back porch in a corner where they wouldn't be able to see it until daytime. I felt a lot better when it was out of my hands (4.16).
Bud has been to the library many times before.	The air in the library isn't like the air anywhere else . . . no other place smells anything like it (7.1–2).
	I opened my eyes to start looking for Miss Hill (7.6).
Bud trusts the adults in the library because they care about him.	The only hope I had was the north side library. If I got there maybe Miss Hill would be able to help me, maybe she'd understand and would be able to tell me what to do (5.3).
	[Miss Hill] wasn't at the lending desk so I left my suitcase with the white lady there. I knew it would be safe (7.6).
	The librarians call Bud "young man" (7.10) and help him look up informa-tion in books (7.26–35).

Being too proud to ask for help can end up hurting you.	The baby sounded like all those new sick babies at the Home, it was coughing like it was a half-dead little animal (8.36).
	"They been invited, but my daddy said you got to feel sorry for them. . . . When someone took them some food and blankets, the man said, 'Thank you very much, but we're white people. We ain't in need of a handout'" (8.186).
Bugs and the people in the Hooverville feel like family to Bud.	I spit a big glob in my hand and said, "We're brothers forever, Bugs!" (8.27).
	"This here is the right place for y'all to be 'cause we're all in the same boat. And you boys are nearer to home than you'll ever get. . . . If you two boys are from Flint, this is the right Hooverville for you" (8.77–79).
	Man, I'd found some family and he was gone before we could really get to know each other (8.243).
People who take good care of Bud's suitcase earn his respect.	This was wrong. They'd promised they'd keep [my suitcase] safe and not look in it. They'd laughed at me when I made them promise, but they did promise (2.36).
	I went to the woman with my suitcase. It was in the same spot I'd left it and the knots in the twine were the kind I tie. I said, "Thank you very much, ma'am." She said, "I told you not to worry" (8.188–190).
	"Please promise that you won't look inside of it, sir." [Lefty Lewis] raised his hand. "You've got my word" (12.115–116).
Bud's suitcase is a symbol for his own heart.	"I guess you sort of carry your family around inside of you, huh?" "I guess I do. Inside my suitcase, too" (8.141–142).
	Man, this is one tough suitcase, you couldn't even tell what it had been through, it still looked exactly the same (8.241).
Bud thinks kids are more honest than adults.	It's one thing to lie to a grown-up, most times adults want to hear something that lets them take their attention off you and put it on something else. That makes it easy and not too bad to lie to them. . . . It's different when you lie to another kid. Most times kids really do want to know what they're asking you (11.123–124).
Bud tends to trust people who have a sense of humor.	I knew I was going to be safe, because I'd never heard of a vampire that could drive a car and I'd never seen one that had such a good sense of humor (11.66).
	"Right, me and Bud-not-Buddy are too dang hungry to hear any more of your lip." Of all the Dusky Devastators of the Depression or the Nubian Knights, Steady Eddie is my favorite (13.84–85).
Bud cries at the table with the band because he finally feels at home.	All of a sudden I knew that of all the places in the world that I'd ever been in this was the one. That of all the people I'd ever met these were the ones. This was where I was supposed to be (14.92).
	I wasn't sure if it was her lips or her hand, but something whispered to me in a language that I didn't have any trouble understanding, it said, "Go ahead and cry, Bud, you're home" (14.99).

Continued on next page →

Bud loves Miss Thomas because she reminds him of his mother.	She pulled me out of my chair into her lap and wrapped her arms around me and bounced me up and down on her knee. . . . She said, so quiet that I was the only one who could hear it, "OK, baby, OK. I know, sweetheart, I know" (14.97–98).
	My clothes were all folded up in a neat pile the same way Momma used to fold them (16.3).
	I noticed too that even without the rings Miss Thomas still had to be the most beautiful woman in the world (16.22).
	She stood up, grabbed both my arms and looked right hard in my face, just like Momma used to (16.64).
African Americans in the 1930s did not have the same opportunities as white people.	[The sign] showed a gigantic picture of a family of four rich white people sitting in a car driving somewhere. . . . My pretend daddy read it and said, "Uh-uh-uh, well, you got to give them credit, you wouldn't expect that they'd have the nerve to come down here and tell the truth" (6.30–33).
	But all the cops I'd ever seen were white so I knew this guy must be a soldier (10.12).
	"Bud, Mr. C. has always got a white fella in the band, for practical reasons." . . . "Why does he always keep one white guy in the band?" Deed said, "It's the way of the world, Sleepy. It's against the law for a Negro to own any property out where the Log Cabin is so Mr. C. put it in my name" (18.5–9).

Tuck Everlasting by Natalie Babbit

Bingo Space Items (Claims)	Teacher Clues (Textual Evidence)
Without death, we cannot live life to the fullest.	"You can't have living without dying. So you can't call it living, what we got. We just *are*, we just *be*, like rocks beside the road" (12.10).
	"But dying's part of the wheel, right there next to being born. You can't pick out the pieces you like and leave the rest. Being part of the whole thing, that's the blessing" (12.10).
	"I want to grow again," [Tuck] said fiercely, "and change. And if that means I got to move on at the end of it, then I want that, too" (12.11).
Living forever has been a curse, not a blessing, for the Tucks.	"I was more'n forty by then," said Miles sadly. "I was married. I had two children. But, from the look of me, I was still twenty-two. My wife, she finally made up her mind I'd sold my soul to the Devil. She left me. She went away and she took the children with her" (7.15).
	"[Our friends] come to pull back from us. There was talk about witchcraft. Black magic. Well, you can't hardly blame them, but finally we had to leave the farm. We didn't know where to go. We started back the way we come, just wandering" (7.17).
	"I want to grow again," [Tuck] said fiercely, "and change. And if that means I got to move on at the end of it, then I want that, too" (12.11).

What you do with your life is more important than how long it lasts.	"Someday," said Miles, "I'll find a way to do something important" (17.27).
	"The way I see it," Miles went on, "it's no good hiding yourself away, like Pa and lots of other people. And it's no good just thinking of your own pleasure, either. People got to do something useful if they're going to take up space in the world" (17.29).
Winnie's ideas about being immortal change throughout the novel.	[Winnie] raged against it, helpless and insulted, and blurted at last, "I don't want to die" (12.9).
	"It'd be nice," [Winnie] said, "if nothing ever had to die" (17.18).
	Winnie pulled out the cork from the mouth of the bottle, and kneeling, she poured the precious water, very slowly and carefully, over the toad. . . . The little bottle was empty now. It lay on the grass at Winnie's feet (25.15–17).
	[Tuck] had wanted [the gravestone] to be there, but now that he saw it, he was overcome with sadness. He knelt and read the inscription: *In Loving Memory* *Winifred Foster Jackson* *Dear Wife* *Dear Mother* *1870–1948* (epilogue.21–22).
By keeping the immortality spring a secret, the Tucks are not being selfish; they are actually trying to protect people.	"And we figured it'd be very bad if everyone knowed about that spring," said Mae. "We begun to see what it would mean" (7.24).
	"If people knowed about the spring down there in Treegap, they'd all come running like pigs to slops. They'd trample each other, trying to get some of that water. . . . The wheel would keep on going round, the water rolling by to the ocean, but the people would've turned into nothing but rocks by the side of the road. 'Cause they wouldn't know till after, and then it'd be too late" (12.11).
	"It'd be nice," [Winnie] said, "if nothing ever had to die." "Well, now, I don't know," said Miles. "If you think on it, you come to see there'd be so many creatures, including people, we'd all be squeezed in right up next to each other before long" (17.18–19).
Jesse asks Winnie to drink the immortality spring water because he believes he is doing her a favor.	"Winnie—isn't it peculiar? And kind of wonderful? Just think of all the things we've seen in the world! All the things we're going to see!" (8.4).
Jesse asks Winnie to drink the immortality spring water because he wants an immortal companion his own age.	"But the thing is, you knowing about the water already, and living right next to it so's you could go there any time, well, listen, how'd it be if you was to wait till you're seventeen, same age as me—heck, that's only six years off—and then you could go and drink some, and then you could go away with me! We could get married, even. That's be pretty good, wouldn't it! We could have a grand old time, go all around the world, see everything" (14.26).
	"Winnie, listen—I won't see you again, not for ages. Look now—here's a bottle of water from the spring. You keep it. And then, no matter where you are, when you're seventeen, Winnie, you can drink it, and then come find us. We'll leave directions somehow. Winnie, please say you will!" (22.20).
	"Poor Jesse" (epilogue.26).

Continued on next page →

Winnie did the right thing by not drinking the immortality spring water.	And then [Tuck's] throat closed. For it was there. He had wanted [Winnie's gravestone] to be there, but now that he saw it, he was overcome with sadness (epilogue.21).
	"Good girl," [Tuck] said aloud. And then he turned and left the cemetery, walking quickly (epilogue.23).
Winnie decides not to drink the spring water because of Tuck.	"But dying's part of the wheel, right there next to being born. You can't pick out the pieces you like and leave the rest. Being part of the whole thing, that's the blessing" (12.10).
	Instead, [Tuck] was gazing at the body on the ground, leaning forward slightly, his brows drawn down, his mouth a little open. It was as if he were entranced and—yes, envious—like a starving man looking through a window at a banquet. Winnie could not bear to see him like that (20.12).
The novel is set in the late 1800s.	So the road went humbly by and made its way, past cottages more and more frequent but less and less forbidding, into the village. But the village doesn't matter, except for the jailhouses and the gallows (1.2).
	In Loving Memory *Winifred Foster Jackson* *Dear Wife* *Dear Mother* *1870–1948* (epilogue.22).
The toad in the novel is a symbol for freedom.	"Why should you [a toad] have to be cooped up in a cage, too? It'd be better if I could be like you, out in the open and making up my own mind. . . . I'll never be able to do anything important if I stay in here like this" (3.8).
	[Winnie] stooped and put her hand through the fence and set the toad free. "There!" she said. "You're safe. Forever" (25.17).
The water in the pond is a symbol for life.	"Life. Moving, growing, changing, never the same two minutes together. This water, you look out at it every morning, and it *looks* the same, but it ain't. All night long it's been moving, coming in through the stream back there to the west, slipping out through the stream down east here, always quiet, always new, moving on" (12.4).
Tuck's rowboat is a symbol for the Tuck family's situation.	"But this rowboat now, it's stuck. If we didn't move it out ourself, it would stay here forever, trying to get loose, but stuck. That's what us Tucks are, Winnie. Stuck so's we can't move on" (12.8).
In the novel, wheels are symbols for time.	The first week of August hangs at the very top of summer, the top of the live-long year, like the highest seat of a Ferris wheel when it pauses in its turning (prologue.1).
	But things can come together in strange ways. The wood was at the center, the hub of the wheel. All wheels must have a hub. A Ferris wheel has one, as the sun is the hub of the wheeling calendar. Fixed points they are, and best left undisturbed, for without them, nothing holds together. But sometimes people find this out too late (prologue.6).

In the novel, wheels are symbols for the circle of life.	"It's a wheel, Winnie. Everything's a wheel, turning and turning, never stopping. . . . Always coming in new, always growing and changing, and always moving on. That's the way it's supposed to be. That's the way it *is*" (12.6).
	"But dying's part of the wheel, right there next to being born. You can't pick out the pieces you like and leave the rest. Being part of the whole thing, that's the blessing. . . . If I knowed how to climb back on the wheel, I'd do it in a minute" (12.10).
	[Mae's] strong arms swung the shotgun round her head, like a wheel. The man in the yellow suit jerked away, but it was too late. With a dull cracking sound, the stock of the shotgun smashed into the back of his skull (19.37).
We can predict that people will make mistakes in the novel.	These are strange and breathless days, the dog days, when people are led to do things they are sure to be sorry for after (prologue.1).
	But the village doesn't matter, except for the jailhouses and the gallows. The first house only is important; the first house, the road, and the wood (1.2).
The way Winnie feels about the woods is just like the way the Tucks feel about immortality.	Winnie, the only child of the house, never went [to the woods], though she sometimes stood inside the fence, carelessly banging a stick against the iron bars, and looked at it. But she had never been curious about it. Nothing ever seems interesting when it belongs to you—only when it doesn't (1.6).
Tuck wants to help Winnie make the decision to stay mortal because it's too late for him to change his own life anymore.	"I want to grow again," [Tuck] said fiercely, "and change. And if that means I got to move on at the end of it, then I want that, too. Listen, Winnie, it's something you don't find out how you feel until afterwards." . . . He peered at her, and Winnie saw that his face was pinched with the effort of explaining. "Do you see, now, child? Do you understand? Oh, Lord, I just got to make you understand!" (12.11).
	And then [Tuck's] throat closed. For it was there. He had wanted [Winnie's gravestone] to be there, but now that he saw it, he was overcome with sadness (epilogue.21).
Angus Tuck wishes he could be mortal again.	"Things just are, and fussing don't bring changes. Tuck, now, he's got a few other ideas, but I expect he'll tell you" (10.12).
	"I want to grow again," [Tuck] said fiercely, "and change. And if that means I got to move on at the end of it, then I want that, too" (12.11).
Mae Tuck does not seem to care whether she is mortal or immortal.	"Life's got to be lived, no matter how long or short," [Mae] said calmly. "You got to take what comes. . . . Funny—we don't feel no different. Leastways, I don't. Sometimes I forget about what's happened to us, forget it altogether" (10.12).
Miles Tuck wants to use his immortality to do something good for the world.	"Someday," said Miles, "I'll find a way to do something important" (17.27).
	"The way I see it," Miles went on, "it's no good hiding yourself away, like Pa and lots of other people. And it's no good just thinking of your own pleasure, either. People got to do something useful if they're going to take up space in the world" (17.29).
Jesse Tuck seems excited about being immortal.	"Winnie—isn't it peculiar? And kind of wonderful? Just think of all the things we've seen in the world! All the things we're going to see!" (8.4).

Continued on next page →

The two brothers (Miles and Jesse) feel differently about their immortality because Miles has lost something and Jesse has not.	"I was more'n forty by then," said Miles sadly. "I was married. I had two children. But, from the look of me, I was still twenty-two. My wife, she finally made up her mind I'd sold my soul to the Devil. She left me. She went away and she took the children with her" (7.15). "I'm glad *I* never got married," Jesse put in (7.16).
It is worth it to make sacrifices for people you love.	"Why didn't you take them to the spring and give them some of the special water?" . . . "I wanted to, heaven knows. But, Winnie, how'd it have been if I had? My wife was nearly forty by then. And the children—well, what was the use? They'd have been near growed theirselves. They'd have had a pa close to the same age *they* was. No, it'd all have been so mixed up and peculiar, it just wouldn't have worked" (17.13–14). Over and over [Winnie's parents] asked her, shocked at first and then wistful: why had she *done* such a thing? *Why?* . . . They did not understand. And finally she had sobbed the only truth there was into her mother's shoulder, the only explanation: the Tucks were her friends. She had done it because—in spite of everything, she loved them (25.7).
Sometimes lying is okay, but sometimes it is not.	Jesse Tuck's face was instantly serious. "Oh, that. No—no, it's not," he said quickly. "You mustn't drink from it. Comes right up out of the ground. Probably pretty dirty" (5.40). The man in the yellow suit sighed. "But of course I had to find out where they were taking her," he explained patiently. "I came right back after that. And the Fosters are friends of mine. They've—uh—sold me their wood" (16.4).

Grades 6–8

A Wrinkle in Time by Madeleine L'Engle

Bingo Space Items (Claims)	Teacher Clues (Textual Evidence)
Things are not always what they seem.	Even though [Meg] was used to Mrs. Whatsit's odd getup (and the very oddness of it was what made her seem so comforting), she realized with a fresh shock that it was not Mrs. Whatsit herself that she was seeing at all . . . it was only the tiniest facet of all the things Mrs. Whatsit *could* be (6.17). There's something phoney in the whole setup, Meg thought. There is definitely something rotten in the state of Camazotz (7.132). "If this [food] isn't real, it's the best imitation you'll ever get." Charles Wallace took a bite, made a face, and spit out his mouthful. . . . "Still tastes like sand," he said (7.143–147).

Eyeglasses are a symbol for seeing things clearly.	"Listen, you go right on wearing your glasses. I don't think I want anybody else to see what gorgeous eyes you have" (3.174).
	Then the voice was directed to Meg. "To you I leave my glasses, little blind-as-a-bat. But do not use them except as a last resort" (6.90).
	Suddenly [Meg] shoved Mrs. Who's glasses down her nose and peered over them, and immediately she was in complete and utter darkness. She snatched them off her face and thrust them at her father. . . . "Can you see now, Father?" "Yes," he said. "Yes. . . . How extraordinary!" (9.51–54).
Not everything can be seen with the eyes.	An enormous shudder shook Charles Wallace. For a brief flash his eyes seemed to see (8.45).
	"We do not know what things *look* like, as you say," the beast said. "We know what things *are* like. It must be a very limiting thing, this seeing" (11.50).
	[Meg] knew that to try to explain anything that could be seen with the eyes would be impossible, because the beasts in some way saw, knew, understood, far more completely than she, or her parents, or Calvin, or even Charles Wallace (11.57).
	"We look not at the things which are what you would call seen, but at the things which are not seen. For the things which are seen are temporal. But the things which are not seen are eternal" (11.85).
Love is the most powerful force in the universe.	Charles Wallace slipped his hand confidingly into Meg's, and the sweet, little-boy gesture warmed her so that she felt the tense knot inside her begin to loosen. *Charles* loves me at any rate, she thought (2.70).
	Happiness at their concern was so strong in [Meg] that her panic fled, and she followed Charles Wallace into the dark recesses of the house without fear (2.133).
	She knew! Love. That was what she had that IT did not have. . . . But how could she use it? What was she meant to do? . . . She could love Charles Wallace (12.137–147).
Meg learns to embrace her flaws and overcome her insecurities.	"I wish I were a different person," Meg said shakily. "I hate myself" (3.168).
	"I think I'm a biological mistake" (3.171).
	"But I'm always trying to get rid of my faults!" "Yes," Mrs. Whatsit said. "However, I think you'll find they'll come in very handy on Camazotz" (6.85–86).
	What were her greatest faults? Anger, impatience, stubbornness. Yes, it was to her faults that [Meg] turned to save herself now (9.132).
	She knew! Love. That was what she had that IT did not have (12.137–139).
Meg learns to find bravery and confidence inside herself, instead of always depending on others.	Happiness at their concern was so strong in [Meg] that her panic fled, and she followed Charles Wallace into the dark recesses of the house without fear (2.133).
	[Meg] wanted to reach out and grab Calvin's hand, but it seemed that ever since they had begun their journeyings she had been looking for a hand to hold, so she stuffed her fists into her pockets and walked along behind the two boys.—I've got to be brave, she said to herself.—I *will* be (8.37).
	"I wanted you to do it all for me. I wanted everything to be all easy and simple. . . . So I tried to pretend that it was all your fault . . . because I was scared, and I didn't want to have to do anything myself—" (12.84).

Continued on next page →

We can predict that there may be a battle in the sky later in the novel.	Behind the trees clouds scudded frantically across the sky. Every few moments the moon ripped through them, creating wraithlike shadows that raced along the ground (1.2).
	"It was a star," Mrs. Whatsit said sadly. "A star giving up its life in battle with the Thing. It won, oh, yes, my children, it won. But it lost its life in the winning" (6.8).
We can predict that Meg may go on a journey through time.	"Maybe if Father were here he could help you, but I don't think I can do anything till you've managed to plow through some more time. . . . Just give yourself time, Meg" (1.67–70).
Meg does not do well in school because she dislikes the focus on rules and memorization over knowledge and creativity.	"Who *cares* about the imports and exports of Nicaragua, anyhow?" [Meg] muttered (2.19).
	"Do they care *how* you do it?" [Meg] asked. "I mean, can you work it out your own way?" "Well, sure, as long as I understand and get the answer right." "Well, *we* have to do it *their* way. Now look, Calvin, don't you see how much easier it would be if you did it *this* way?" Her pencil flew over the paper (3.38–40).
	"I suppose I should stop being surprised by now, but you're supposed to be dumb in school" . . . "The trouble with Meg and math," Mrs. Murry said briskly, "is that Meg and her father used to play with numbers and Meg learned far too many shortcuts. So when they want her to do problems the long way around at school she gets sullen and stubborn and sets up a fine mental block for herself" (3.43–45).
The greatest knowledge is accepting that you cannot understand everything.	"No, Meg. Don't hope it was a dream. I don't understand it any more than you do, but one thing I've learned is that you don't have to understand things for them to *be*" (2.7).
	"Goethe. *I do not know everything; still many things I understand.* That is for you, Charles. Remember that you do not know everything" (6.90).
Meg learns to value more than logic and science.	"Oh, Calvin, I'm not any good at English" (3.64).
	"And Shakespeare," Charles Wallace called out, "and Bach! And Pasteur and Madame Curie and Einstein!" Now Calvin's voice rang with confidence. "And Schweitzer and Gandhi and Buddha and Beethoven and Rembrandt and St. Francis!" "Now you, Meg," Mrs. Whatsit ordered. "Oh, Euclid, I suppose. . . . and Copernicus" (5.119–122).
	[The music] seemed to travel with [Meg], to sweep her aloft in the power of song, so that she was moving in glory among the stars, and for a moment she, too, felt that the words Darkness and Light had no meaning, and only this melody was real (11.73).
Meg is very impatient.	Meg was in such an agony of impatience that her voice grated irritably. . . . Meg went over to Mrs. Which and stamped as though she were as young as Charles Wallace (5.122–124).
	"My, but the little miss is impatient! Patience, patience, young lady" (7.90).

Individuality is better than everyone being the same.	The men all wore nondescript business suits, and though their features were as different one from the other as the features of men on earth, there was also a sameness to them (7.14).
	"On Camazotz we are all happy because we are all alike. Differences create problems" (8.65).
	"Why do you think people get confused and unhappy? Because they all live their own, separate, individual lives. I've been trying to explain to you in the simplest possible way that on Camazotz individuals have been done away with. . . . And that's why everybody's so happy and efficient" (8.80).
Charles Wallace's pride is his downfall when he faces IT.	"Remember that you do not know everything" (6.90).
	"Charles Wallace, the danger here is greatest for you" (6.94).
	"Beware of pride and arrogance, Charles, for they may betray you" (6.96).
	"But it is only the little boy whose neurological system is complex enough. If you tried to conduct the necessary neurons your brains would explode" (7.123).
We cannot rely on intelligence alone—we also need emotion.	IT was a brain. A disembodied brain. An oversized brain, just enough larger than normal to be completely revolting and terrifying. A living brain (9.124–125).
Just like the Man with the Red Eyes, some people on Earth do not understand love.	"They can't understand plain, ordinary love when they see it" (3.152).
	"Why do you want your father?" "Didn't you ever have a father yourself?" Meg demanded. "You don't want him for a *reason*. You want him because he's your *father*" (7.87).
Meg's "happy medium" is a balance between rigid conformity and uniqueness.	"You don't know the meaning of moderation, do you, my darling?" Mrs. Murry asked. "A happy medium is something I wonder if you'll ever learn" (1.63).
	"You know that's the reason you're not happy at school. Because you're different." . . . "Maybe I don't like being different," Meg said, "but I don't want to be like everybody else, either" (8.67–71).
The author compares the total conformity of Camazotz to Meg's school.	"Do you enjoy being the most belligerent, uncooperative girl in school?" (2.46).
	Meg reacted [to the Man with the Red Eyes] as she sometimes reacted to Mr. Jenkins at school (7.113).
	"Why are you being so belligerent and uncooperative?" (7.169).
Meg learns to embrace oddity and imperfection.	"I'm not sure *what* they are, but they're not robots. I can feel minds there. I can't get at them at all, but I can feel them sort of pulsing" (6.164).
	"I know our world isn't perfect, Charles, but it's better than this" (8.85).
Physical force is usually not a solution.	Charles Wallace began to pull away with a power that was not his own. . . . Calvin the athlete, Calvin the boy who split firewood and brought it in for his mother, whose muscles were strong and controlled, let go Charles Wallace's wrist and tackled him as though he were a football (8.13–14).
	"We've been trying to fight Charles physically, and that isn't any good" (8.39).

Continued on next page →

We need pain and unhappiness in order to feel comfort and happiness.	"Nobody suffers here," Charles intoned. "Nobody is ever unhappy." "But nobody's ever happy, either," Meg said earnestly. "Maybe if you aren't unhappy sometimes you don't know how to be happy" (8.86–87). "You're hurting me!" "Then you're feeling again," her father said quietly. "I'm afraid it *is* going to hurt, Meg" (10.72–73).
Evil can be external (outside us) or internal (within us).	Disappointment was as dark and corrosive in [Meg] as the Black Thing. The ugly words tumbled from her cold lips even as she herself could not believe that it was to her father, her beloved, longed-for father, that she was talking to in this way. . . . She did not realize that she was as much in the power of the Black Thing as Charles Wallace (10.66–67).
Meg learns that parents are human, too, and do not know everything.	She was frozen, and Charles Wallace was being devoured by IT, and her omnipotent father was doing nothing (10.67). "My daughter, I am not a Mrs. Whatsit, a Mrs. Who, or a Mrs. Which. . . . I am a human being, and a very fallible one" (10.68).
Mr. Murry learns to let Meg grow up.	"But I wanted to do it for you," Mr. Murry said. "That's what every parent wants." He looked into her dark, frightened eyes. "I won't let you go, Meg. I am going." "No. . . . You are going to allow Meg the privilege of accepting this danger. You are a wise man, Mr. Murry. You are going to let her go" (12.85–86).
Sometimes words are not enough to communicate.	For a brief flash [Charles Wallace's] eyes seemed to see. Then his whole body twirled wildly, and went rigid. He started his marionette's walk again. "I should have known better," he said. "If you want to see Murry you'd better come with me and not try any more hanky-panky" (8.46). Aunt Beast was puzzled. "Oh, child, your language is so utterly simple and limited that it has the effect of extreme complication" (11.87). Something completely and indescribably and incredibly delicious was put to Meg's lips (11.64). If it was impossible to describe sight to Aunt Beast, it would be even more impossible to describe the singing of Aunt Beast to a human being (11.73).
Our choices—not fate—determine our future.	"You mean you're comparing our lives to a sonnet? A strict form, but freedom within it?" "Yes," Mrs. Whatsit said. "You're given the form, but you have to write the sonnet yourself. What you say is completely up to you" (12.72–73).

Roll of Thunder, Hear My Cry by Mildred D. Taylor

Bingo Space Items (Claims)	Teacher Clues (Textual Evidence)
Little Man and Cassie are very proud.	"Miz Crocker," I said, "I don't want my book neither." The switch landed hard upon Little Man's upturned bottom. Miss Crocker looked questioningly at me as I reached up to her desk and placed the book upon it. Then she swung the switch five more times and, discovering that Little Man had no intention of crying, ordered him up. "All right Cassie," she sighed, turning to me, "come on and get yours" (1.153–155). Big Ma looked at me again, her voice cracking as she spoke. "Go on child . . . apologize." "But, Big Ma—" Her voice hardened. "Do like I say." . . . "I'm sorry," I mumbled. "I'm sorry, *Miz* Lillian Jean," demanded Mr. Simms. "Big Ma!" I balked. "Say it, child." A painful tear slid down my cheek and my lips trembled. "I'm sorry . . . M-Miz . . . Lillian Jean" (5.102–111).
Even though slavery was illegal, the government of Mississippi still had racist tendencies in the early 1900s.	In the very center of the expansive front lawn, waving red, white, and blue with the emblem of the Confederacy emblazoned in its upper left-hand corner, was the Mississippi flag. Directly below it was the American flag (1.89). [Jeremy and Lillian Jean] were headed for the Jefferson Davis County School, a long white wooden building looming in the distance (1.89).
Characters change their speech to fit in with certain groups of people.	"Yes, ain't that something?" Miss Crocker said, forgetting her teacher-training-school diction in her indignation. "The very idea! That's on all the books, and why they got so upset about it I'll never know" (1.162). "You sure giving folks something to talk 'bout with that car of yours, Hammer," Mr. Granger said in his folksy dialect as he sat down with a grunt across from Papa. In spite of his college education he always spoke this way (7.165).
We can predict that something bad involving a mob might happen in the novel.	But I remained silent. I never did approve of group responses (1.109).
The Logan children are a loyal team.	"Miz Crocker, don't, please!" I cried. Miss Crocker's dark eyes warned me not to say another word. "I know why he done it!" "You want part of this switch, Cassie? . . . Sit down!" she ordered as I hurried to her with the open book in my hand (1.141–144). "Cassie, you start digging over there on that side of the road right across from me. . . . Christopher-John, you and Little Man start scooping out mud from the middle of the road." . . . Now understanding Stacey's plan, we worked wordlessly until the water lay at the same level as the road (3.64–67).
People of different races cannot be true friends.	"Far as I'm concerned, friendship between black and white don't mean that much 'cause it usually ain't on a equal basis. . . . Maybe one day whites and blacks can be real friends, but right now the country ain't built that way" (7.108–110).

Continued on next page →

People of different races can be true friends.	But we did not relent and as I glanced back at [Jeremy] standing alone in the middle of the crossing, he looked as if the world itself was slung around his neck. It was only then that I realized that Jeremy never rode the bus, no matter how bad the weather (3.48).
Stacey wishes he could be friends with Jeremy.	"Actually, he's much easier to get along with than T. J.," Stacey went on. "And I s'pose if I let him, he could be a better friend than T. J." (7.107). As I stood in the doorway, [Stacey] lingered over the [flute], then, carefully rewrapping it, placed it in his box of treasured things. I never saw that flute again (7.112).
The Logan family values education.	"Now how could [Little Man] know what it says? He can't read." "Yes'm, he can. He been reading since he was four" (1.146–147). "You jus' keep on studyin' and get yo'self a good education and you'll be all right" (3.12). Nothing compared to the books. . . . [Little Man] lay upon the deerskin rug looking at the bright, shining pictures of faraway places, turning each page as if it were gold (7.74). I volunteered to sacrifice school and help them. My offer was refused and I trudged wearily to school for another week (9.2). "But he'd promised your grandmama 'fore she died to see that your mama got an education, and when your mama 'come high school age, he sent her up to Jackson to school, then on to teacher training school" (8.134).
The Logans's land ownership gives them more power than other families to protest the mistreatment of the black community.	"For the past year now, our family's been shopping down at Vicksburg. There are a number of stores down there and we've found several that treat us well." "Vicksburg?" Mr. Turner echoed, shaking his head. "Lord, Miz Logan, you ain't expectin' me to go all the way to Vicksburg? That's an overnight journey in a wagon down there and back" (4.208–209). "Y'all got it better'n most the folks 'round here 'cause y'all gots your own place and y'all ain't gotta cowtail to a lot of this stuff. But you gotta understand it ain't easy for sharecroppin' folks to do what you askin'" (4.213). "Them men, they doing what they've gotta do. You got any idea what a risk they took just to go shopping in Vicksburg in the first place? They go on that chain gang and their families got nothin'. . . . You were born blessed, boy, with land of your own" (9.88–89).
The author portrays the school bus as a monstrous creature to show how important it is to the Logan children.	Little Man turned around and watched saucer-eyed as a bus bore down on him spewing clouds of red dust like a huge yellow dragon breathing fire (1.68). Then [the bus] sputtered a last murmuring protest and died, its left front wheel in our ditch, its right wheel in the gully, like a lopsided billy goat on its knees (3.88).
Nonviolent words and actions can fight oppression.	"In this family, we don't shop at the Wallace store" (2.60). *Roll of thunder / hear my cry / Over the water / bye and by / Ole man comin' / down the line / Whip in hand to / beat me down / But I ain't gonna let him / Turn me 'round* . . . On the front porch Mr. Morrison sat singing soft and low into the long night, chanting to the approaching thunder (11.1).

Mama is secretly proud of Cassie's behavior in Miss Crocker's class.	Mama glanced at the book I had rejected and opened the front cover so that the offensive pages of both books faced her. "You say Cassie said it was because of this front page that she and Little Man didn't want the books?" Mama asked quietly (1.161).
	"Of course you [had a right to punish them], Daisy," Mama said, turning back to the books again. "They disobeyed you." But her tone was so quiet and noncommittal that I knew Miss Crocker was not satisfied with her reaction (1.165).
Stacey has a strong sense of honor.	"Well, whether she knew it or not, she sho' 'nough whipped [Stacey]. . . . Course, now, she give him a chance to get out of it when he said he wasn't cheatin' and she asked him how he got them cheat notes. But Stacey wouldn't tell on ole T. J." (4.106).
	Despite our every effort to persuade Stacey otherwise, when Mama came home he confessed that he had been fighting T. J. at the Wallace store and that Mr. Morrison had stopped it. He stood awkwardly before her, disclosing only those things which he could honorably mention. He said nothing of T. J.'s cheating or that Christopher-John, Little Man, and I had been with him (4.192).
The schools in Spokane County, Mississippi, are separate and unequal in the novel.	But even so, after today a number of the older students would not be seen again for a month or two, not until the last puff of cotton had been gleaned from the fields, and eventually most would drop out of school altogether (1.90).
	Holding the book up to her, I said, "See, Miz Crocker, see what it says. They give us these ole books when they didn't want 'em no more" (1.145).
People should respect differential treatment based on age, but not race.	"Ain't never no reason good enough to go disobey your mama" (4.141).
	I spied Mr. Barnett wrapping an order of pork chops for a white girl. Adults were one thing; I could almost understand that. They ruled things and there was nothing that could be done about them. But some kid who was no bigger than me was something else again (5.55).
Throughout the novel, Cassie realizes that she is being treated differently solely because of her race.	Certainly, Mr. Barnett had simply forgotten about T. J.'s order. I decided to remind him . . . "You get her out of here," [Mr. Barnett] said [to Stacey] with hateful force. "And make sure she don't come back till yo' mammy teach her what she is" (5.55–71).
	"I didn't say that Lillian Jean *is* better than you. I said Mr. Simms only *thinks* she is." . . . "Just 'cause she's his daughter?" I asked, beginning to think Mr. Simms was a bit touched in the head. "No, baby, because she's white" (6.81–83).

Continued on next page →

Few white people were not hateful to blacks.	Jeremy nodded slightly as if he did not know how to accept [Mama's] thanks, and stiffly handed a slender, paper-wrapped object to Stacey. "Made this for ya," he said. . . . "M-made it myself." Stacey slid his fingers down the smooth, sanded back of a wooden flute (7.84–85).
	"I'm a Southerner, born and bred, but that doesn't mean I approve of all that goes on here, and there are a lot of other white people who feel the same" (7.140).
	"If you and so many others feel that way," said Uncle Hammer with a wry sneer, "then how come them Wallaces ain't in jail?" "Hammer—" Big Ma started. "Because," answered Mr. Jamison candidly, "there aren't enough of those same white people who would admit how they feel, or even if they did, would hang a white man for killing a black one. It's as simple as that" (7.141–143).
The author believes that people who are different can be united by a common goal.	Moving across the field, slowly, mechanically, as if sleepwalking, was a flood of men and women dumping shovels of dirt on fire patches which refused to die. They wore wide handkerchiefs over their faces and many wore hats, making it difficult to identify who was who, but it was obvious that the ranks of the fire fighters had swelled from the two dozen townsmen to include nearby farmers. I recognized Mr. Lanier by his floppy blue hat working side by side with Mr. Simms, each oblivious of the other, and Papa near the slope waving orders to two of the townsmen (12.91).
The law favors white people over black people.	"The way I hears it," said Mr. Lanier, "they been after John Henry ever since he come back from the war and settled on his daddy's place up by Smellings Creek." . . . Big Ma shook her head. "[He was] just in the wrong place at the wrong time" (2.52).
	"When Henrietta went to the sheriff and told him what she'd seed, he called her a liar and sent her on home. Now I hear tells that some of them men that done it been 'round braggin' 'bout it" (2.58).
	"It may not be real justice, but it'll hurt them and we'll have done something" (7.58).
	"There aren't enough of those same white people who would admit how they feel, or even if they did, would hang a white man for killing a black one. It's as simple as that" (7.143).
	It seemed to me that since the Wallaces had attacked Papa and Mr. Morrison, the simplest thing to do would be to tell the sheriff and have them put in jail, but Mama said things didn't work that way. . . . If we did not [remain silent], Mr. Morrison could be charged with attacking white men, which could possibly end in his being sentenced to the chain, or worse (10.88).
Sharecropping is basically a legal form of slavery.	"When cotton-pickin' time comes, he sells my cotton, takes half of it, pays my debt up at that store and my interest for they credit, then charges me ten to fifteen percent more as 'risk' money for signin' for me in the first place. This year I earned me near two hundred dollars after Mr. Montier took his half of the crop money, but I ain't seen a penny of it. In fact, if I manages to come out even without owin' that man nothin', I figures I've had a good year" (4.211).
	"Mr. Granger making it hard on us, David. Said we gonna have to give him sixty percent of the cotton, 'stead of fifty . . . The way cotton sells these days, seems the more we plant, the less money we get anyways" (9.70).

The church is a key social center for the black community.	In fact, [Mama] said, the county provided very little and much of the money which supported the black schools came from the black churches (3.5). "They live way over on the other side of Smellings Creek. They come up to church sometimes" (1.32). It was to this church that many of the school's students and their parents belonged (1.91).
Papa teaches the Logan children to fight for their rights because he has hope for the future of the civil rights movement.	"The sad thing is, you know in the end you can't beat him or the Wallaces." Papa looked down at the boys and me awaiting his reply, then nodded slightly, as if he agreed. "Still," he said, "I want these children to know we tried, and what we can't do now, maybe one day they will" (7.157–158). "We keep doing what we gotta, and we don't give up. We can't" (9.93).
The fig tree is a symbol for the civil rights movement.	"That oak and walnut, they're a lot bigger and they take up more room and give so much shade they almost overshadow that little ole fig. But that fig tree's got roots that run deep, and it belongs in that yard as much as that oak and walnut. It keeps on blooming, bearing good fruit year after year, knowing all the time it'll never get as big as them other trees. Just keeps on growing and doing what it gotta do. It don't give up. It give up, it'll die. There's a lesson to be learned from that little tree, Cassie girl, 'cause we're like it" (9.93).
Cars stand for privilege and power in the novel.	"One day you'll have a plenty of clothes and maybe even a car of yo' own to ride 'round in" (3.12). Big Ma stammered, "Hammer, you—you went and got a car like Harlan Granger's?" Uncle Hammer smiled a strange, wry smile. "Well, not exactly like it, Mama. Mine's a few months newer. Last year when I come down here, I was right impressed with that big ole Packard of Mr. Harlan Filmore Granger's and I thought I'd like to own one myself. It seems that me and Harlan Granger just got the same taste." He winked slyly at Stacey. "Don't it, Stacey?" (6.14–15). The driver of the truck stopped, and for no more than a second hesitated on the bridge, then without a single honk of protest backed off so that we could pass. "Hammer!" Big Ma cried. "They think you're Mr. Granger." . . . As we came off the bridge, we could see the Wallaces, all three of them—Dewberry, Thurston, and Kaleb—touch their hats respectfully, then immediately freeze as they saw who we were. Uncle Hammer, straight-faced and totally calm, touched the brim of his own hat in polite response and without a backward glance sped away, leaving the Wallaces gaping silently after us (6.165–168). Beyond the Avery house bright lights appeared far away on the road near the Granger mansion. For a breathless second they lingered there, then plunged suddenly downward toward the Averys'. The first set of lights was followed by a second, then a third, until there were half a dozen sets of headlights beaming over the trail. . . . Two pickups and four cars rattled into the yard, their lights focused like spotlights on the Avery front porch. Noisy, angry men leaped from the cars and surrounded the house (11.59–61).

Grades 9–10

To Kill a Mockingbird by Harper Lee

Bingo Space Items (Claims)	Teacher Clues (Textual Evidence)
People learn to be compassionate (or not); they are not born with it.	"He ain't company, Cal, he's just a Cunningham—" "Hush your mouth! Don't matter who they are, anybody sets foot in this house's yo' comp'ny, and don't you let me catch you remarkin' on their ways like you was so high and mighty! Yo' folks might be better'n the Cunninghams but it don't count for nothin' the way you're disgracin' 'em" (3.27–28).
	"You never really understand a person until you consider things from his point of view . . . until you climb into his skin and walk around in it" (3.85–87).
	"Do you want to tell us what happened?" But [Mayella] did not hear the compassion in his invitation (18.167).
People are born with compassion.	This was as much as I heard of Mr. Gilmer's cross-examination, because Jem made me take Dill out. For some reason, Dill had started crying and couldn't stop; quietly at first, then his sobs were heard by several people in the balcony (19.151).
	"The way [Mr. Gillmer] called [Tom Robinson] 'boy' all the time an' sneered at him, an' looked around at the jury every time he answered—" "Well, Dill, after all he's just a Negro." "I don't care one speck. It ain't right, somehow it ain't right to do 'em that way" (19.163–165).
	[Mr. Raymond] jerked his head at Dill: "Things haven't caught up with that one's instinct yet. Let him get a little older and he won't get sick and cry. Maybe things'll strike him as being—not quite right, say, but he won't cry, not when he gets a few years on him. . . . Cry about the hell white people give colored folks, without even stopping to think that they're people, too" (20.20–22).
Justice is not always a right—sometimes it is a privilege.	"There's something in our world that makes men lose their heads—they couldn't be fair if they tried. In our courts, when it's a white man's word against a black man's, the white man always wins. They're ugly, but those are the facts of life" (23.38).
	"Don't see how any jury could convict on what we heard—" "No don't you be so confident, Mr. Jem, I ain't ever seen any jury decide in favor of a colored man over a white man" (20.29–30).
People must fight for their morals and never give up.	"Atticus, are we going to win it?" "No, honey." "Then why—" "Simply because we were licked a hundred years before we started is no reason for us not to try to win" (9.22–25).
	"I wanted you to see what real courage is, instead of getting the idea that courage is a man with a gun in his hand. It's when you know you're licked before you begin but you begin anyway and you see it through no matter what. You rarely win, but sometimes you do" (11.153).
	"Link, that boy might go to the chair, but he's not going till the truth's told" (15.23).

The American justice system is flawed.	"The one place where a man ought to get a square deal is in a courtroom, be he any color of the rainbow, but people have a way of carrying their resentments right into a jury box" (23.40).
	"I am not [going to court]. 't's morbid, watching a poor devil on trial for his life. Look at all those folks, it's like a Roman carnival" (16.43).
	"Well, what if—say, Mr. Link Deas had to decide the amount of damages to award, say, Miss Maudie, when Miss Rachel ran over her with a car. Link wouldn't like the thought of losing either lady's business at his store, would he? So he tells Judge Taylor that he can't serve on the jury because he doesn't have anybody to keep store for him while he's gone. So Judge Taylor excuses him" (23.49).
	"Scared of arrest, scared you'd have to face up to what you did?" "No suh, scared I'd hafta face up to what I didn't do" (19.147–148).
The American justice system reflects the morals of the community.	"I'm no idealist to believe firmly in the integrity of our courts and in the jury system—that is no ideal to me, it is a living, working reality. Gentlemen, a court is no better than each man of you sitting before me on this jury" (20.52).
	Atticus had used every tool available to free men to save Tom Robinson, but in the secret courts of men's hearts Atticus had no case. Tom was a dead man the minute Mayella Ewell opened her mouth and screamed (25.28).
Vigilante justice is more effective than justice in a courtroom.	"How could they do it [convict Tom Robinson], how could they?" "I don't know, but they did it. They've done it before and they did it tonight and they'll do it again and when they do it—seems that only children weep" (22.16–17).
	"There's a black boy dead for no reason, and the man responsible for it's dead. Let the dead bury the dead this time, Mr. Finch. Let the dead bury the dead" (30.60).
Kids turn out just like their parents.	The adults in Maycomb never discussed the case with Jem and me; it seemed that they discussed it with their children, and their attitude must have been that neither of us could help having Atticus for a parent, so their children must be nice to us in spite of him (26.10).
	Never take a check from a Delafield without a discreet call to the bank; Miss Maudie Atkinson's shoulder stoops because she was a Buford; if Mrs. Grace Merriweather sips gin out of Lydia E. Pinkham bottles it's nothing unusual—her mother did the same (13.34).
Adults often underestimate children.	"Don't talk like that, Dill," said Aunt Alexandra. "It's not becoming to a child. It's—cynical." "I ain't cynical, Miss Alexandra. Tellin' the truth's not cynical, is it?" (22.32–33).
Identity is not solidified in childhood; it changes over time.	Then [Jem] rose and broke the remaining code of our childhood. . . . "Dill, I had to tell [Atticus]," he said. "You can't run three hundred miles off without your mother knowin'" (12.79–90).
	One time [Atticus] said you never really know a man until you stand in his shoes and walk around in them. Just standing on the Radley porch was enough (31.31).

Continued on next page →

Children are naturally just, fair, and accepting.	"It ain't right, somehow it ain't right to do 'em that way. Hasn't anybody got any business talkin' like that—it just makes me sick" (19.165).
	He jerked his head at Dill: "Things haven't caught up with that one's instinct yet. Let him get a little older and he won't get sick and cry. Maybe things'll strike him as being—not quite right, say, but he won't cry, not when he gets a few years on him. . . . Cry about the hell white people give colored folks, without even stopping to think that they're people, too" (20.20–22).
	"How could they do it, how could they?" "I don't know, but they did it. They've done it before and they did it tonight and they'll do it again and when they do it—seems that only children weep" (22.16–17).
A moral person is not necessarily a good person (with *bad* morals instead of *no* morals).	"There are just some kind of men who—who're so busy worrying about the next world they've never learned to live in this one" (5.44).
	"I tell you there are some good but misguided people in this town. Good, but misguided. Folks in this town who think they're doing right, I mean" (24.48).
Honesty is the highest virtue.	"Link, that boy might go to the chair, but he's not going till the truth's told" (15.23).
	"If this thing's hushed up it'll be a simple denial to Jem of the way I've tried to raise him. . . . If I connived at something like this, frankly I couldn't meet his eye, and the day I can't do that I'll know I've lost him" (30.37).
Sometimes it is okay not to be honest.	I said I would like it very much, which was a lie, but one must lie under certain circumstances and at all times when one can't do anything about them (13.20).
	"No," he said. "You've had enough scaring for a while. This is too—" "Atticus, I wasn't scared" (31.45–46).
People will destroy innocent lives rather than disturb the social order.	"Serving on a jury forces a man to make up his mind and declare himself about something. Men don't like to do that. Sometimes it's unpleasant" (23.52).
	He likened Tom's death to the senseless slaughter of songbirds by hunters and children (25.27).
Justice that serves no practical purpose is unnecessary cruelty.	"Mockingbirds don't do one thing but make music for us to enjoy. They don't eat up people's gardens, don't nest in corncribs, they don't do one thing but sing their hearts out for us. That's why it's a sin to kill a mockingbird" (10.9).
	He likened Tom's death to the senseless slaughter of songbirds by hunters and children (25.27).
	"Yes sir, I understand," I reassured [Atticus]. "Mr. Tate was right." Atticus disengaged himself and looked at me. "What do you mean?" "Well, it'd be sort of like shootin' a mockingbird, wouldn't it?" (30.66–68).
Gender roles are not innate, but socially constructed and governed by social rules.	I felt the starched walls of a pink cotton penitentiary closing in on me, and for the second time in my life I thought of running away (14.24).
	I walked home with Dill and returned in time to overhear Atticus saying to Aunty, ". . . in favor of Southern womanhood as much as anybody, but not for preserving polite fiction at the expense of human life" (15.39).
	"[Mayella] did something that in our society is unspeakable: she kissed a black man. . . . No code mattered to her before she broke it, but it came crashing down on her afterwards" (20.45).

Being masculine means being unafraid.	"Cry about what, Mr. Raymond?" Dill's maleness was beginning to assert itself (20.21).
	Jem wanted Dill to know once and for all that he wasn't scared of anything. . . . Besides, Jem had his little sister to think of. When he said that, I knew he was afraid (1.76–77).
	"There has been a request," Judge Taylor said, "that this courtroom be cleared of spectators, or at least of women and children" (17.97).
	"[Tom Robinson] took advantage of me an' if you fine fancy gentlemen don't wanta do nothin' about it then you're all yellow stinkin' cowards, stinkin' cowards, the lot of you" (18.168).
Jem views masculinity as honorable, but femininity as shameful.	Jem told me I was being a girl, that girls always imagined things, that's why other people hated them so (4.119).
	"I declare to the Lord you're gettin' more like a girl every day!" With that, I had no option but to join them (6.24).
	"Don't pay any attention to her, just hold your head high and be a gentleman" (11.21).
Scout learns that being a woman also involves unique skills.	[Calpurnia] seemed glad to see me when I appeared in the kitchen, and by watching her I began to think there was some skill involved in being a girl (12.8).
	[Aunt Alexandra] looked at a tray of cookies on the table and nodded at them. I carefully picked up the tray and watched myself walk to Mrs. Merriweather. With my best company manners, I asked her if she would have some. After all, if Aunty could be a lady at a time like this, so could I (24.94–95).
Children are more perceptive than adults.	"When a child asks you something, answer him, for goodness' sake. . . . Children are children, but they can spot an evasion quicker than adults, and evasion simply muddles 'em" (9.175).
The majority is not always right.	"Scout, I couldn't go to church and worship God if I didn't try and help [Tom Robinson]." "Atticus, you must be wrong. . . ." "How's that?" "Well, most folks seem to think they're right and you're wrong" (11.53–56).
	"The one thing that doesn't abide by majority rule is a person's conscience" (11.57).
	"[Mayella] did something that in our society is unspeakable: she kissed a black man. . . . No code mattered to her before she broke it, but it came crashing down on her afterwards" (20.45).
	"As you grow older, you'll see white men cheat black men every day of your life, but let me tell you something and don't you forget it—whenever a white man does that to a black man, no matter who he is, how rich he is, or how fine a family he comes from, that white man is trash" (23.40).

Continued on next page →

Family determines status and identity.	Somewhere, I had received the impression that Fine Folks were people who did the best they could with the sense they had, but Aunt Alexandra was of the opinion, obliquely expressed, that the longer a family had been squatting on one patch of land the finer it was (13.29).
	There was indeed a caste system in Maycomb, but to my mind it worked this way: the older citizens, the present generation of people who had lived side by side for years and years, were utterly predictable to one another: they took for granted attitudes, character shadings, even gestures, as having been repeated in each generation and refined by time (13.34).
	"Background doesn't mean Old Family," said Jem. "I think it's how long your family's been readin' and writin'" (23.112).
All people deserve compassion.	"You never really understand a person until you consider things from his point of view . . . until you climb into his skin and walk around in it" (3.85–87).
	"Son, I have no doubt that you've been annoyed by your contemporaries about me . . . but to do something like this to a sick old lady is inexcusable. I strongly advise you to go down and have a talk with Mrs. Dubose" (11.43).
	"Jem, see if you can stand in Bob Ewell's shoes a minute. I destroyed his last shred of credibility at that trial, if he had any to begin with" (23.15).
Justice and kindness can exist together; they are not mutually exclusive.	"[Mayella] has committed no crime, she has merely broken a rigid and time-honored code of our society, a code so severe that whoever breaks it is hounded from our midst as unfit to live with. She is the victim of cruel poverty and ignorance, but I cannot pity her: she is white. She knew full well the enormity of her offense, but because her desires were stronger than the code she was breaking, she persisted in breaking it" (20.43).
Being compassionate can lead to trouble.	"You felt sorry for her, you felt sorry for her?" Mr. Gilmer seemed ready to rise to the ceiling. [Tom Robinson] realized his mistake and shifted uncomfortably in the chair. But the damage was done (19.126–127).
	"Jem, see if you can stand in Bob Ewell's shoes a minute. I destroyed his last shred of credibility at that trial, if he had any to begin with" (23.15).
	Somehow, I could think of nothing but Mr. Bob Ewell saying he'd get Atticus if it took him the rest of his life. Mr. Ewell almost got him, and it was the last thing he did (29.2).
	"Mr. Finch, there's just some kind of men you have to shoot before you can say hidy to 'em. Even then, they ain't worth the bullet it takes to shoot 'em" (29.33).

The Tragedy of Macbeth by William Shakespeare

Bingo Space Items (Claims)	Teacher Clues (Textual Evidence)
Humans are inherently murderous and ambitious.	Stay, you imperfect speakers, tell me more. / By Sinel's death I know I am Thane of Glamis. / But how of Cawdor? The Thane of Cawdor lives, / A prosperous gentleman, and to be king / Stands not within the prospect of belief, / No more than to be Cawdor (1.3.67–73).
	The prince of Cumberland—that is a step / On which I must fall down or else o'erleap, / For in my way it lies (1.4.48–50).
	Glamis thou art, and Cawdor, and shalt be / What thou art promised. Yet do I fear thy nature. / It is too full o' th' milk of human kindness / To catch the nearest way (1.5.13–16).
	I have no spur / To prick the sides of my intent, but only / Vaulting ambition which o'erleaps itself / And falls on th' other (1.7.25–28).
Being masculine is about being cruel, violent, and unfeeling.	When you durst do it, then you were a man (1.7.49).
	Art thou afeard / To be the same in thine own act and valour / As thou art in desire? (1.7.39–41).
	Bring forth men-children only, / For thy undaunted mettle should compose / Nothing but males (1.7.72–74).
Good men are also able to feel emotion.	I shall do so [dispute it], / But I must also feel it as a man. / I cannot but remember such things were / That were most precious to me (4.3.222–225).
	My plenteous joys, / Wanton in fullness, seek to hide themselves / In drops of sorrow (1.4.33–35).
Once one becomes a murderer, one cannot stop.	For mine own good / All causes shall give way. I am in blood / Stepped in so far that, should I wade no more, / Returning were as tedious as go o'er (3.4.134–137).
	Blood will have blood (3.4.121).
Life is meaningless.	Life's but a walking shadow, a poor player / That struts and frets his hour upon the stage, / And then is heard no more. It is a tale / Told by an idiot, full of sound and fury, / Signifying nothing (5.5.23–27).
Powerful women are "un-sexed"; that is, they are not feminine.	Come, you spirits / That tend on mortal thoughts, unsex me here, / And fill me from the crown to the toe top-full / Of direst cruelty (1.5.38–41).
	Bring forth men-children only, / For thy undaunted mettle should compose / Nothing but males (1.7.72–74).
Kindness is a feminine trait.	Glamis thou art, and Cawdor, and shalt be / What thou art promised. Yet do I fear thy nature. / It is too full o' th' milk of human kindness / To catch the nearest way (1.5.13–16).
Guilt can fester and destroy us.	You see her eyes are open. / Ay, but their sense is shut (5.1.21–22).
	Out, damned spot! (5.1.30).
	The Thane of Fife had a wife. Where is she now? / What, will these hands ne'er be clean? (5.1.36–37).

Continued on next page →

Emotion makes a person weak and vulnerable.	My plenteous joys, / Wanton in fullness, seek to hide themselves / In drops of sorrow (1.4.33–35).
	Besides, this Duncan / Hath borne his faculties so meek (1.7.16–17).
An ideal king should be somewhere between naïve and tyrannical.	This castle hath a pleasant seat. The air / Nimbly and sweetly recommends itself / Unto our gentle senses (1.6.1–3).
	Besides, this Duncan / Hath borne his faculties so meek (1.7.16–17).
	The son of Duncan / From whom this tyrant holds the due of birth (3.6.24–25).
	We'll have thee as our rarer monsters are, / Painted upon a pole, and underwrit / "Here may you see the tyrant" (5.10.25–27).
We cannot control our own fates.	All hail, Macbeth! Hail to thee, Thane of Glamis! / All hail, Macbeth! Hail to thee, Thane of Cawdor! / All hail, Macbeth, that shalt be king hereafter! (1.3.46–48).
	Macbeth, Macbeth, Macbeth, beware Macduff, / Beware the Thane of Fife. Dismiss me. Enough (4.1.87–88).
	Be bloody, bold, and resolute. Laugh to scorn / The power of man, for none of woman born / Shall harm Macbeth (4.1.95–97).
	Macbeth shall never vanquished be until / Great Birnam Wood to high Dunsinane Hill / Shall come against him (4.1.108–110).
Murder disturbs the order and law of nature.	Thou seest the heavens, as troubled with man's act, / Threatens his bloody stage. By th' clock 'tis day, / And yet dark night strangles the travelling lamp. / Is 't night's predominance or the day's shame / That darkness does the face of Earth entomb / When living light should kiss it? (2.4.5–10).
	'Tis unnatural, / Even like the deed that's done. On Tuesday last / A falcon, tow'ring in her pride of place, / Was by a mousing owl hawked at and killed (2.4.10–13).
	And Duncan's horses—a thing most strange and certain— / Beauteous and swift, the minions of their race, / Turned wild in nature, broke their stalls, flung out, / Contending 'gainst obedience, as they would / Make war with mankind (2.4.14–18).
Life is cyclical (history repeats itself).	All hail, Macbeth! Hail to thee, Thane of Glamis! / All hail, Macbeth! Hail to thee, Thane of Cawdor! / All hail, Macbeth, that shalt be king hereafter! (1.3.46–48).
	Hail, King of Scotland! (5.11.25).
Power corrupts people.	No more that Thane of Cawdor shall deceive / Our bosom interest. Go pronounce his present death, / And with his former title greet Macbeth. / I'll see it done. / What he hath lost, noble Macbeth hath won (1.2.63–67).
	We'll have thee as our rarer monsters are, / Painted upon a pole, and underwrit / "Here may you see the tyrant" (5.10.25–27).
Murder is justified in cases of revenge, but not ambition.	So clear in his great office, that his virtues / Will plead like angels, trumpet-tongued against / The deep damnation of his taking-off (1.7.18–20).
	Hail, King, for so thou art. Behold where stands / Th' usurper's cursèd head. The time is free. / I see thee compassed with thy kingdom's pearl, / That speak my salutation in their minds, / Whose voices I desire aloud with mine: / Hail, King of Scotland! (5.11.20–25).

Women are dangerous and can destroy men.	Come, you spirits / That tend on mortal thoughts, unsex me here, / And fill me from the crown to the toe top-full / Of direst cruelty (1.5.38–41).
	Bring forth men-children only, / For thy undaunted mettle should compose / Nothing but males (1.7.72–74).
	Hie thee hither, / That I may pour my spirits in thine ear / And chastise with the valor of my tongue / All that impedes thee from the golden round (1.5.23–26).
Violence begets violence; once it begins, it never ends.	For mine own good / All causes shall give way. I am in blood / Stepped in so far that, should I wade no more, / Returning were as tedious as go o'er (3.4.134–137).
	Blood will have blood (3.4.121).
	Hail, King, for so thou art. Behold where stands / Th' usurper's cursèd head. The time is free (5.8.20–21).
Organized violence (war) is acceptable, but acts of individual violence are not.	And with his former title greet Macbeth. / I'll see it done. / What he hath lost, noble Macbeth hath won (1.2.65–67).
	Thou hast it now: King, Cawdor, Glamis, all / As the weird women promised; and I fear / Thou played'st most foully for 't (3.1.1–3).
	'Tis unnatural, / Even like the deed that's done (2.4.10–11).
	Hail, King, for so thou art. Behold where stands / Th' usurper's cursèd head. The time is free (5.8.20–21).
Humans misinterpret language to suit their own desires (we hear what we want to hear).	Fair is foul, and foul is fair (1.1.10).
	None of woman born / Shall harm Macbeth (4.1.96–97).
	Macbeth shall never vanquished be until / Great Birnam Wood to high Dunsinane Hill / Shall come against him (4.1.108–110).
	And be these juggling fiends no more believed, / That palter with us in a double sense, / That keep the word of promise to our ear / And break it to our hope (5.10.19–22).
Ambition is only rewarded when it is selfless.	Let me find him [Macbeth], fortune, / And more I beg not (5.8.9–10).
	For mine own good / All causes shall give way (3.4.134–135).
The illusion of fate blinds us to the fact that we make our own choices.	Is this a dagger which I see before me, / The handle toward my hand? . . . Thou marshall'st me the way that I was going, / And such an instrument I was to use (2.1.33–43).
	And be these juggling fiends no more believed, / That palter with us in a double sense, / That keep the word of promise to our ear / And break it to our hope (5.10.19–22).
Even those who are most good can be seduced by ambition.	Yet it was said / It should not stand in thy posterity, / But that myself should be the root and father / Of many kings. If there come truth from them— / As upon thee, Macbeth, their speeches shine— / Why by the verities on thee made good / May they not be my oracles as well, / And set me up in hope? (3.1.3–10).

Continued on next page →

Loyalty to king and country is one of the best qualities a person can have.	O Scotland, Scotland! (4.3.101). Fit to govern? / No, not to live. O nation miserable, / With an untitled tyrant bloody-sceptered, / When shalt thou see thy wholesome days again, / Since that truest issue of thy throne / By his own interdiction stands accursed / And does blaspheme his breed? / . . .These evils thou repeat'st upon thyself / Hath banished me from Scotland (4.3.103–114).
Try as they might, humans cannot control time.	Thy letters have transported me beyond / This ignorant present, and I feel now / The future in the instant (1.5.54–56). To beguile the time, / Look like the time (1.5.61–62). Boundless intemperance in nature is a tyranny. It hath been / Th'untimely emptying of the happy throne / And fall of many kings (4.3.67–70). Behold where stands / Th' usurper's cursèd head. The time is free (5.11.20–21).

Grades 11–12

Pride and Prejudice by Jane Austen

Bingo Space Items (Claims)	Teacher Clues (Textual Evidence)
Romantic love is not a right; it is a privilege.	"When [Jane] is secure of [Bingley], there will be leisure for falling in love as much as she chooses" (6.6). [Marriage] was the only honourable provision for well-educated young women of small fortune, and however uncertain of giving happiness, must be their pleasantest preservative from want. This preservative [Charlotte] had now obtained; and at the age of twenty-seven, without having ever been handsome, she felt all the good luck of it (22.3). [Elizabeth] had always felt that Charlotte's opinion of matrimony was not exactly like her own, but she could not have supposed it possible that when called into action, she would have sacrificed every better feeling to worldly advantage (22.18).
Economic security should be the first priority in a marriage.	Miss Lucas, who accepted [Mr. Collins] solely from the pure and disinterested desire of an establishment, cared not how soon that establishment were gained (22.2). [Marriage] was the only honourable provision for well-educated young women of small fortune, and however uncertain of giving happiness, must be their pleasantest preservative from want (22.3).
Lust is transient.	Had Elizabeth's opinion been all drawn from her own family, she could not have formed a very pleasing picture of conjugal felicity or domestic comfort. Her father captivated by youth and beauty, and that appearance of good humour, which youth and beauty generally give, had married a woman whose weak understanding and illiberal mind had very early in their marriage put an end to all real affection for her. Respect, esteem, and confidence had vanished for ever; and all his views of domestic happiness were overthrown (42.1).

Love is necessary to happiness.	[Elizabeth] had always felt that Charlotte's opinion of matrimony was not exactly like her own, but she could not have supposed it possible that when called into action, she would have sacrificed every better feeling to worldly advantage. Charlotte the wife of Mr. Collins, was a most humiliating picture!—And to the pang of a friend disgracing herself and sunk in her esteem, was added the distressing conviction that it was impossible for that friend to be tolerably happy in the lot she had chosen (22.18).
Love is not necessary to contentment.	"I am not romantic you know. I never was. I ask only a comfortable home; and considering Mr. Collins's character, connections, and situation in life, I am convinced that my chance of happiness with him is as fair, as most people can boast on entering the marriage state" (22.17).
True, romantic love is not necessarily logical.	"My reasons for marrying are, first, that I think it a right thing for every clergyman in easy circumstances (like myself) to set the example of matrimony in his parish. Secondly, that I am convinced that it will add very greatly to my happiness; and thirdly—which perhaps I ought to have mentioned earlier, that it is the particular advice and recommendation of the very noble lady whom I have the honour of calling patroness. . . . And now nothing remains for me but to assure you in the most animated language of the violence of my affection" (19.10). "There certainly was some great mismanagement in the education of those two young men. One has got all the goodness, and the other all the appearance of it" (40.15).
Love at first sight does not exist.	Mr. Darcy had at first scarcely allowed [Elizabeth] to be pretty; he had looked at her without admiration at the ball; and when they next met, he looked at her only to criticise. But no sooner had he made it clear to himself and his friends that she hardly had a good feature in her face, than he began to find it was rendered uncommonly intelligent by the beautiful expression of her dark eyes. . . . He began to wish to know more of her (6.12–13). "There certainly was some great mismanagement in the education of those two young men. One has got all the goodness, and the other all the appearance of it" (40.15). "When I said that [Mr. Darcy] improved on acquaintance, I did not mean that either his mind or his manners were in a state of improvement, but that from knowing him better, his disposition was better understood" (41.36). If gratitude and esteem are good foundations of affection, Elizabeth's change of sentiment will be neither improbable nor faulty. But if otherwise, if the regard springing from such sources is unreasonable or unnatural, in comparison of what is so often described as arising on a first interview with its object, and even before two words have been exchanged, nothing can be said in her defence, except that she had given somewhat of a trial to the latter method, in her partiality for Wickham, and that its ill success might perhaps authorise her to seek the other less interesting mode of attachment (46.24). "Will you tell me how long you have loved him?" "It has been coming on so gradually, that I hardly know when it began" (59.15–16).

Continued on next page →

People who view relationships as solely practical and transactional cannot love.	"But the fact is, that being, as I am, to inherit this estate after the death of your honoured father, (who, however, may live many years longer), I could not satisfy myself without resolving to choose a wife from among his daughters" (19.10).
	[Elizabeth] could not have supposed it possible that when called into action, [Charlotte] would have sacrificed every better feeling to worldly advantage (22.18).
People who are of a high-class status are not necessarily classy in their behaviors.	Mr. Darcy soon drew the attention of the room by his fine, tall person, handsome features, noble mien; and the report which was in general circulation within five minutes after his entrance, of his having ten thousand a year. . . . He was looked at with great admiration for about half the evening, till his manners gave a disgust which turned the tide of his popularity; for he was discovered to be proud, to be above his company, and above being pleased; and not all his large estate in Derbyshire could then save him from having a most forbidding, disagreeable countenance, and being unworthy to be compared with his friend (3.5).
	[The Bingley ladies] were rather handsome, had been educated in one of the first private seminaries in town, had a fortune of twenty thousand pounds, were in the habit of spending more than they ought, and of associating with people of rank; and were therefore in every respect entitled to think well of themselves, and meanly of others (4.11).
Mr. Darcy represents pride; Elizabeth represents prejudice.	"Yes, vanity is a weakness indeed. But pride—where there is a real superiority of mind, pride will be always under good regulation" (11.24).
	"And *your* defect is a propensity to hate every body." "And yours," [Darcy] replied with a smile, "is wilfully to misunderstand them" (11.31–32).
	"How despicably have I acted!" [Elizabeth] cried.—"I, who have prided myself on my discernment!—I, who have valued myself on my abilities!" (36.8).
More wealth means more opportunity.	"If she is really headstrong and foolish, I know not whether she would altogether be a very desirable wife to a man in my situation, who naturally looks for happiness in the marriage state. If therefore she actually persists in rejecting my suit, perhaps it were better not to force her into accepting me, because if liable to such defects of temper, she could not contribute much to my felicity" (20.4).
	[Marriage] was the only honourable provision for well-educated young women of small fortune, and however uncertain of giving happiness, must be their pleasantest preservative from want (22.3).
Men are also hindered by the economic stipulations of marriage.	"Our habits of expense make us too dependant, and there are not many in my rank of life who can afford to marry without some attention to money" (33.14).
	It is a truth universally acknowledged, that a single man in possession of a good fortune, must be in want of a wife (1.1).

Women can be more than petty, foolish, and competitive; they are multidimensional.	"But my feelings are not only cordial towards [Wickham]; they are even impartial towards Miss King. I cannot find out that I hate her at all, or that I am in the least unwilling to think her a very good sort of girl" (26.29). And to the pang of a friend disgracing herself and sunk in her esteem, was added the distressing conviction that it was impossible for that friend to be tolerably happy in the lot she had chosen (22.18). [Elizabeth and Georgiana] were able to love each other even as well as they intended (61.11). By Elizabeth's instructions [Georgiana] began to comprehend that a woman may take liberties with her husband, which a brother will not always allow in a sister more than ten years younger than himself (61.11).
A good parent gives children a balance of freedom and restriction.	"From this day you must be a stranger to one of your parents.—Your mother will never see you again if you do *not* marry Mr. Collins, and I will never see you again if you *do*" (20.19). "If you, my dear father, will not take the trouble of checking her exuberant spirits, and of teaching her that her present pursuits are not to be the business of her life, she will soon be beyond the reach of amendment. Her character will be fixed, and she will, at sixteen be the most determined flirt that ever made herself and her family ridiculous" (41.18).
Parents' actions have significant effects on their children.	But [Elizabeth] had never felt so strongly as now, the disadvantages which must attend the children of so unsuitable a marriage, nor ever been so fully aware of the evils arising from so ill-judged a direction of talents; talents which rightly used, might at least have preserved the respectability of his daughters, even if incapable of enlarging the mind of his wife (42.2). "And we mean to treat you all," added Lydia; "but you must lend us the money, for we have just spent ours at the shop out there." Then shewing her purchases: "Look here, I have bought this bonnet. I do not think it is very pretty; but I thought I might as well buy it as not" (39.3).
Good manners do not a good person make.	As to [Wickham's] real character, had information been in [Elizabeth's] power, she had never felt a wish of enquiring. His countenance, voice, and manner had established him at once in the possession of every virtue (36.4). "There certainly was some great mismanagement in the education of those two young men. One has got all the goodness, and the other all the appearance of it" (40.15).
People often deceive themselves.	"As I must therefore conclude that you are not serious in your rejection of me, I shall choose to attribute it to your wish of increasing my love by suspense, according to the usual practice of elegant females" (19.19). As to [Wickham's] real character, had information been in [Elizabeth's] power, she had never felt a wish of enquiring. His countenance, voice, and manner had established him at once in the possession of every virtue (36.4).

Continued on next page →

Social norms get in the way of constructive behavior and conversation.	"I know it to be the established custom of your sex to reject a man on the first application, and perhaps you have even now said as much to encourage my suit as would be consistent with the true delicacy of the female character." "Really, Mr. Collins," cried Elizabeth . . . "If what I have hitherto said can appear to you in the form of encouragement, I know not how to express my refusal in such a way as may convince you of its being one" (19.17–18).
	"Pray, my dear aunt, what is the difference in matrimonial affairs, between the mercenary and the prudent motive? Where does discretion end, and avarice begin? Last Christmas you were afraid of [Wickham's] marrying me, because it would be imprudent; and now, because he is trying to get a girl with only ten thousand pounds, you want to find out that he is mercenary" (27.9).
Pride is a virtue when it is deserved and used for good.	"[Mr. Darcy's] pride," said Miss Lucas, "does not offend *me* so much as pride often does, because there is an excuse for it. One cannot wonder that so very fine a young man, with family, fortune, every thing in his favour, should think highly of himself. If I may so express it, he has a *right* to be proud" (5.18).
	"A person may be proud without being vain. Pride relates more to our opinion of ourselves, vanity to what we would have others think of us" (5.20).
	"Yes, vanity is a weakness indeed. But pride—where there is a real superiority of mind, pride will be always under good regulation" (11.24).
	"It *is* wonderful,"—replied Wickham,—"for almost all his actions may be traced to pride;—and pride has often been his best friend. It has connected him nearer with virtue than any other feeling" (16.39).
	"Can such abominable pride as [Mr. Darcy's], have ever done him good?" "Yes. It has often led him to be liberal and generous,—to give his money freely, to display hospitality, to assist his tenants, and relieve the poor. Family pride, and *filial* pride, for he is very proud of what his father was, have done this. . . . He has also *brotherly* pride, which with *some* brotherly affection, makes him a very kind and careful guardian of his sister" (16.40–41).
Actions speak louder than words.	"If you were aware," said Elizabeth, "of the very great disadvantage to us all, which must arise from the public notice of Lydia's unguarded and imprudent manner; nay, which has already arisen from it, I am sure you would judge differently in the affair" (41.16).
	"When I said that [Mr. Darcy] improved on acquaintance, I did not mean that either his mind or his manners were in a state of improvement, but that from knowing him better, his disposition was better understood" (41.36).
	It was but just done, to give pleasure to Miss Darcy, who had taken a liking to the room, when last at Pemberley. "He is certainly a good brother," said Elizabeth (43.43–44).

High status is a fragile identity that must be shored up and reinforced.	"Do not make yourself uneasy, my dear cousin, about your apparel. Lady Catherine is far from requiring that elegance of dress in us, which becomes herself and her daughter. . . . She likes to have the distinction of rank preserved" (29.6).
	But Lady Catherine seemed gratified by their excessive admiration, and gave most gracious smiles, especially when any dish on the table proved a novelty to them (29.14).
First impressions can be misleading.	Every body was pleased to think how much they had always disliked Mr. Darcy before they had known anything of the matter (24.30).
	"Your sister I also watched.—Her look and manners were open, cheerful and engaging as ever, but without any symptom of peculiar regard, and I remained convinced from the evening's scrutiny, that though she received his attentions with pleasure, she did not invite them by any participation of sentiment.—If *you* have not been mistaken here, *I* must have been in an error" (35.5).
	"How despicably I have acted!" [Elizabeth] cried.—"I, who have prided myself on my discernment!—I, who have valued myself on my abilities!" (36.8).
Pride is the worst quality a person can have.	[Darcy's] sense of [Elizabeth's] inferiority—of its being a degradation—of the family obstacles which judgment had always opposed to inclination, were dwelt on with a warmth which . . . was very unlikely to recommend his suit (34.5).
	"Had I been in love, I could not have been more wretchedly blind. But vanity, not love, has been my folly" (36.8).
Prejudice is the worst quality a person can have.	[Elizabeth] grew absolutely ashamed of herself.—Of neither Darcy nor Wickham could she think, without feeling that she had been blind, partial, prejudiced, absurd (36.7).
	As to [Wickham's] real character, had information been in [Elizabeth's] power, she had never felt a wish of enquiring. His countenance, voice, and manner had established him at once in the possession of every virtue (36.4).
	"And *your* defect is a propensity to hate every body." "And yours," [Darcy] replied with a smile, "is wilfully to misunderstand them" (11.31–32).
The novel portrays class prejudice as arbitrary and ridiculous.	"And is *such* a girl to be my nephew's sister? Is *her* husband, is the son of his late father's steward, to be his brother? Heaven and earth! —of what are you thinking? Are the shades of Pemberley to be thus polluted?" (56.62).
	"In marrying your nephew, I should not consider myself as quitting that sphere. He is a gentleman; I am a gentleman's daughter; so far we are equal" (56.51).
	"I thought it my duty to give the speediest intelligence of this to my cousin, that she and her noble admirer may be aware of what they are about, and not run hastily into a marriage which has not been properly sanctioned" (57.22).

Continued on next page →

True love requires humility and respect.	"Be not alarmed, Madam, on receiving this letter, by the apprehension of its containing any repetition of those sentiments, or renewal of those offers, which were last night so disgusting to you. I write without any intention of paining you, or humbling myself, by dwelling on wishes" (35.4).
	"Pleased with the preference of one, and offended by the neglect of the other, on the very beginning of our acquaintance, I have courted prepossession and ignorance, and driven reason away, where either were concerned. Till this moment, I never knew myself" (36.8).
	"We will not quarrel for the greater share of blame annexed to that evening," said Elizabeth. "The conduct of neither, if strictly examined, will be irreproachable; but since then, we have both, I hope, improved in civility" (58.13).
	"I know your disposition, Lizzy. I know that you could be neither happy nor respectable, unless you truly esteemed your husband . . . Your lively talents would place you in the greatest danger in an unequal marriage. . . . My child, let me not have the grief of seeing *you* unable to respect your partner in life" (59.35).

The Great Gatsby by F. Scott Fitzgerald

Bingo Space Items (Claims)	Teacher Clues (Textual Evidence)
American aristocrats (people from "old money") distinguish between themselves and the upwardly mobile (people from "new money").	[Daisy] was appalled by West Egg, this unprecedented "place" that Broadway had begotten upon a Long Island fishing village—appalled by its raw vigor that chafed under the old euphemisms and by the too obtrusive fate that herded its inhabitants along a short cut from nothing to nothing (6.96).
	"A lot of these newly rich people are just big bootleggers, you know" (6.100).
	"Come on, Daisy," said Tom, pressing her with his hand toward Gatsby's car. "I'll take you in this circus wagon" (7.115).
	"An Oxford man!" [Tom] was incredulous. "Like hell he is! He wears a pink suit" (7.130).
Women have a limited number of choices in life.	"[The nurse] told me it was a girl, and so I turned my head away and wept. 'All right,' I said. 'I'm glad it's a girl. And I hope she'll be a fool—that's the best thing a girl can be in this world, a beautiful little fool'" (1.118).

Wealth does not equal morality (that is, having lots of money does not always make you a good person).	Some time toward midnight Tom Buchanan and Mrs. Wilson stood face to face discussing in impassioned voices whether Mrs. Wilson had any right to mention Daisy's name. "Daisy! Daisy! Daisy!" shouted Mrs. Wilson. "I'll say it whenever I want to! Daisy! Dai———" Making a short deft movement, Tom Buchanan broke her nose with his open hand (2.125–127).
	"Meyer Wolfsheim? No, he's a gambler." Gatsby hesitated, then added coolly: "He's the man who fixed the World's Series back in 1919" (4.112).
	"[Tom] won't touch [Daisy]," I said. "He's not thinking about her." "I don't trust him, old sport." "How long are you going to wait?" "All night, if necessary. Anyhow, till they all go to bed" (7.401–404).
	I called up Daisy half an hour after we found [Gatsby], called her instinctively and without hesitation. But she and Tom had gone away early that afternoon, and taken baggage with them (9.4).
	They were careless people, Tom and Daisy—they smashed up things and creatures and then retreated back into their money or their vast carelessness, or whatever it was that kept them together, and let other people clean up the mess they had made (9.145).
The reckless pursuit of pleasure and spending of money is not sustainable enough to last forever; instead, it leads to decay.	This is a valley of ashes—a fantastic farm where ashes grow like wheat into ridges and hills and grotesque gardens; where ashes take the forms of houses and chimneys and rising smoke and, finally, with a transcendent effort, of men who move dimly and already crumbling through the powdery air. Occasionally a line of gray cars crawls along an invisible track, gives out a ghastly creak, and comes to rest, and immediately the ash-gray men swarm up with leaden spades and stir up an impenetrable cloud, which screens their obscure operations from your sight (2.1).
	The night had made a sharp difference in the weather and there was an autumn flavor in the air. . . . "I'm going to drain the pool today, Mr. Gatsby. Leaves'll start falling pretty soon and then there's always trouble with the pipes." "Don't do it to-day," Gatsby answered. He turned to me apologetically. "You know, old sport, I've never used that pool all summer?" (8.31–33).
	A small gust of wind that scarcely corrugated the surface was enough to disturb its accidental course with its accidental burden. The touch of a cluster of leaves revolved it slowly, tracing, like the leg of transit, a thin red circle in the water (8.112).
	So when the blue smoke of brittle leaves was in the air and the wind blew the wet laundry stiff on the line I decided to come back home (9.126).
Materialism and consumption do not always lead to happiness.	"They're a rotten crowd," I shouted across the lawn. "You're worth the whole damn bunch put together" (8.45).
	After Gatsby's death the East was haunted for me like that, distorted beyond my eyes' power of correction. . . . I decided to come back home (9.126).

Continued on next page →

Dwelling in the past can prevent you from moving forward into the future.	"I wouldn't ask too much of [Daisy]," I ventured. "You can't repeat the past." "Can't repeat the past?" [Gatsby] cried incredulously. "Why of course you can!" He looked around him wildly, as if the past were lurking here in the shadow of his house, just out of reach of his hand. "I'm going to fix everything just the way it was before," he said, nodding determinedly. "She'll see" (6.129–132).
	"I'm going to drain the pool today, Mr. Gatsby. Leaves'll start falling pretty soon and then there's always trouble with the pipes." "Don't do it to-day," Gatsby answered. He turned to me apologetically. "You know, old sport, I've never used that pool all summer?" (8.32–33).
	So we beat on, boats against the current, borne back ceaselessly into the past (9.152).
People cannot escape from their actions—a conscience or higher power is always watching.	"I spoke to her," [Wilson] muttered, after a long silence. "I told her she might fool me but she couldn't fool God. I took her to the window"—with an effort he got up and walked to the rear window and leaned with his face pressed against it—"and I said 'God knows what you've been doing, everything you've been doing. You may fool me, but you can't fool God!'" Standing behind him, Michaelis saw with a shock that he was looking at the eyes of Doctor T. J. Eckleburg, which had just emerged, pale and enormous, from the dissolving night (8.102–103).
Morality and good intentions are not always enough to prevail.	"Was Daisy driving?" "Yes," [Gatsby] said after a moment, "but of course I'll say I was" (7.396–397).
	"Then he killed her," said Wilson. His mouth dropped open suddenly. . . . "It was the man in that car. She ran out to speak to him and he wouldn't stop" (8.87–94).
	It was after we started with Gatsby toward the house that the gardener saw Wilson's body a little way off in the grass, and the holocaust was complete (8.113).
Humans invest things with symbols and meaning that, in reality, are empty.	"If it wasn't for the mist we could see your home across the bay," said Gatsby. "You always have a green light that burns all night at the end of your dock." Daisy put her arm through his abruptly, but he seemed absorbed in what he had just said. Possibly it had occurred to him that the colossal significance of that light had now vanished forever. Compared to the great distance that had separated him from Daisy it had seemed very near to her, almost touching her. It had seemed as close as a star to the moon. Now it was again a green light on a dock. His count of enchanted objects had diminished by one (5.121–122).
	"'You may fool me, but you can't fool God!'" Standing behind him, Michaelis saw with a shock that [Wilson] was looking at the eyes of Doctor T. J. Eckleburg, which had just emerged, pale and enormous, from the dissolving night. . . . "That's an advertisement," Michaelis assured him. Something made him turn away from the window and look back into the room. But Wilson stood there a long time, his face close to the window pane, nodding into the twilight (8.102–105).

Only fools fall in love.	It passed, and [Gatsby] began to talk excitedly to Daisy, denying everything, defending his name against accusations that had not been made. But with every word she was drawing further and further into herself, so he gave that up and only the dead dream fought on as the afternoon slipped away, trying to touch what was no longer tangible, struggling unhappily, undespairingly, toward that lost voice across the room (7.291). "Go on. He won't annoy you. I think he realizes that his presumptuous little flirtation is over." They were gone, without a word, snapped out, made accidental, isolated, like ghosts, even from our pity (7.297–298).
Marriage is a flawed institution.	"You see," cried Catherine triumphantly. She lowered her voice again. "It's really [Tom's] wife that's keeping [Tom and Myrtle] apart" (2.97). [Wilson] had discovered that Myrtle had some sort of life apart from him in another world, and the shock had made him physically sick. I stared at him and then at Tom, who had made a parallel discovery less than an hour before—and it occurred to me that there was no difference between men (7.159).
The individualist philosophy of the American Dream breeds isolation and alienation.	The bar is in full swing, and floating rounds of cocktails permeate the garden outside, until the air is alive with chatter and laughter, and casual innuendo and introductions forgotten on the spot, and enthusiastic meetings between women who never knew each other's names (3.4). "Anyhow, he gives large parties," said Jordan, changing the subject with an urbane distaste for the concrete. "And I like large parties. They're so intimate. At small parties there isn't any privacy" (3.89). But with every word she was drawing further and further into herself, so he gave that up, and only the dead dream fought on as the afternoon slipped away, trying to touch what was no longer tangible, struggling unhappily, undespairingly, toward that lost voice across the room (7.291). They smashed up things and creatures and then retreated back into their money or their vast carelessness, or whatever it was that kept them together (9.145).
Education is a more important mark of status than wealth.	"[Gatsby] went to Oggsford College in England. You know Oggsford College?" "I've heard of it" (4.94–95). "An Oxford man!" [Tom] was incredulous. "Like hell he is! He wears a pink suit" (7.130). "That's a great expression of yours, isn't it?" said Tom sharply [to Gatsby]. "What is?" "All this 'old sport' business. Where'd you pick that up?" (7.184–186).

Continued on next page →

Capitalism and the desire for wealth have replaced religion.	"You see," cried Catherine triumphantly. She lowered her voice again. "It's really his wife that's keeping them apart. She's a Catholic, and they don't believe in divorce." Daisy was not a Catholic, and I was a little shocked at the elaborateness of the lie (2.97–98).
	"'You may fool me, but you can't fool God!'" Standing behind him, Michaelis saw with a shock that [Wilson] was looking at the eyes of Doctor T. J. Eckleburg, which had just emerged, pale and enormous, from the dissolving night. . . . "That's an advertisement," Michaelis assured him. Something made him turn away from the window and look back into the room. But Wilson stood there a long time, his face close to the window pane, nodding into the twilight (8.102–105).
Money cannot solve all of life's problems.	He looked around him wildly, as if the past were lurking here in the shadow of his house, just out of reach of his hand. "I'm going to fix everything just the way it was before," he said, nodding determinedly. "She'll see" (6.130–131).
	[Wilson] had discovered that Myrtle had some sort of life apart from him in another world, and the shock had made him physically sick. I stared at him and then at Tom, who had made a parallel discovery less than an hour before—and it occurred to me that there was no difference between men (7.159).
Nick is a reliable narrator.	I am still a little afraid of missing something if I forget that, as my father snobbishly suggested, and I snobbishly repeat, a sense of the fundamental decencies is parceled out unequally at birth (1.3).
Nick is an unreliable narrator.	"Whenever you feel like criticizing any one," [my father] told me, "just remember that all the people in this world haven't had the advantages that you've had." He didn't say any more, but we've always been unusually communicative in a reserved way, and I understood that he meant a great deal more than that. In consequence, I'm inclined to reserve all judgments (1.2–3).
	Everyone suspects himself of at least one of the cardinal virtues, and this is mine: I am one of the few honest people that I have ever known (3.171).
Dreamers finish last.	But with every word she was drawing further and further into herself, so he gave that up, and only the dead dream fought on as the afternoon slipped away, trying to touch what was no longer tangible, struggling unhappily, undespairingly, toward that lost voice across the room (7.291).
	[Gatsby] must have felt that he had lost the old warm world, paid a high price for living too long with a single dream. He must have looked up at an unfamiliar sky through frightening leaves and shivered as he found what a grotesque thing a rose is and how raw the sunlight was upon the scarcely created grass. A new world, material without being real, where poor ghosts, breathing dreams like air, drifted fortuitously about . . . like that ashen, fantastic figure gliding toward him through the amorphous trees (8.110).
	And as I sat there, brooding on the old, unknown world, I thought of Gatsby's wonder when he first picked out the green light at the end of Daisy's dock. He had come a long way to this blue lawn, and his dream must have seemed so close that he could hardly fail to grasp it. He did not know that it was already behind him, somewhere back in that vast obscurity beyond the city, where the dark fields of the republic rolled on under the night (9.150).

The wealthy are violent, careless people who leave destruction in their wake and think nothing of it.	"That's what I get for marrying a brute of a man, a great, big, hulking physical specimen of a———" "I hate that word hulking," objected Tom crossly, "even in kidding." "Hulking," insisted Daisy (1.70–72).
	Some time toward midnight Tom Buchanan and Mrs. Wilson stood face to face discussing in impassioned voices whether Mrs. Wilson had any right to mention Daisy's name. "Daisy! Daisy! Daisy!" shouted Mrs. Wilson. "I'll say it whenever I want to! Daisy! Dai———" Making a short deft movement, Tom Buchanan broke her nose with his open hand (2.125–127).
	I called up Daisy half an hour after we found [Gatsby], called her instinctively and without hesitation. But she and Tom had gone away early that afternoon, and taken baggage with them (9.4).
	They were careless people, Tom and Daisy—they smashed up things and creatures and then retreated back into their money or their vast carelessness, or whatever it was that kept them together, and let other people clean up the mess they had made (9.145).
Even the strongest love cannot cross the divides of social class.	But with every word she was drawing further and further into herself, so he gave that up, and only the dead dream fought on as the afternoon slipped away, trying to touch what was no longer tangible, struggling unhappily, undespairingly, toward that lost voice across the room (7.291).
	They were careless people, Tom and Daisy—they smashed up things and creatures and then retreated back into their money or their vast carelessness, or whatever it was that kept them together, and let other people clean up the mess they had made (9.145).
	And as I sat there, brooding on the old, unknown world, I thought of Gatsby's wonder when he first picked out the green light at the end of Daisy's dock. He had come a long way to this blue lawn, and his dream must have seemed so close that he could hardly fail to grasp it. He did not know that it was already behind him, somewhere back in that vast obscurity beyond the city, where the dark fields of the republic rolled on under the night (9.150).
The idea and pursuit of a goal can be more rewarding than its actual attainment.	Her husband, among various physical accomplishments, had been one of the most powerful ends that ever played football at New Haven—a national figure in a way, one of those men who reach such an acute limited excellence at twenty-one that everything afterward savors of anticlimax (1.16).
	Possibly it had occurred to [Gatsby] that the colossal significance of that [green] light had now vanished forever. Compared to the great distance that had separated him from Daisy it had seemed very near to her, almost touching her. It had seemed as close as a star to the moon. Now it was again a green light on a dock. His count of enchanted objects had diminished by one (5.122).
	"Oh, you want too much!" [Daisy] cried to Gatsby. "I love you now—isn't that enough? I can't help what's past." She began to sob helplessly. "I did love him once—but I loved you too." Gatsby's eyes opened and closed. "You loved me *too*?" he repeated (7.263–265).

Continued on next page →

Gatsby is a good person—perhaps even a hero.	Gatsby turned out all right at the end; it was what preyed on Gatsby, what foul dust floated in the wake of his dreams that temporarily closed out my interest in the abortive sorrows and short-winded elations of men (1.4).
	[Gatsby] smiled understandingly—much more than understandingly. It was one of those rare smiles with a quality of eternal reassurance in it, that you may come across four or five times in life. It faced—or seemed to face—the whole external world for an instant, and then concentrated on *you* with an irresistible prejudice in your favor (3.76).
Try as we might to escape the world and realities into which we were born, we cannot escape our own pasts.	I see now that this has been a story of the West, after all—Tom and Gatsby, Daisy and Jordan and I, were all Westerners, and perhaps we possessed some deficiency in common which made us subtly unadaptable to Eastern life (9.124).
	So we beat on, boats against the current, borne back ceaselessly into the past (9.152).

Student Bingo Board for Text Evidence Bingo

B	I	N	G	O
		FREE SPACE		

8 Rhetoric Memory

For middle school and high school students

In Rhetoric Memory, which is based on the classic game Memory, students identify two expressions of the same concept (which have different connotations) and match them together. The student with the most matched pairs at the end of the game wins. Here's the catch: in order to keep a match, a student must explain the connotations of both expressions.

Setup

To play, middle school students must understand the terms *connotation* and *denotation* and be able to identify various connotations of words with similar definitions. Additionally, high school students must understand how to evaluate persuasive rhetoric.

Create a set of cards for each group of students. Cards must be printed as double-sided copies and then cut apart. When created properly, one side of the card will show a term with a connotative meaning and the other side will show the definition for the term. To illustrate, figure 8.1 (page 162) shows the front and back sides of a matching pair.

As seen in figure 8.1, each card has a connotative term on the front, face-up side and a definition (which is identical to the definition on its matching card) on the back, face-down side. Students collect pairs by matching two words with similar denotations but different connotations, such as *request* and *beg*. A student confirms his or her match by turning the cards over to see the

Argumentation Skills

- Distinguishing connotation from denotation
- Evaluating persuasive rhetoric
- Perspective taking

Materials

- Set of memory cards for each group of students (five to fifteen pairs per set; see reproducible sets on **marzanoresearch.com /activitiesandgames**)
- Stopwatch or timer (optional)

definitions (which will match if they are correct) and collects the match by explaining the connotative meanings of the two words on the front of the cards.

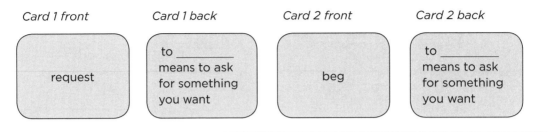

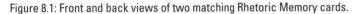

Figure 8.1: Front and back views of two matching Rhetoric Memory cards.

As a resource for this game, we provide twelve sets of paired terms (three sets for grades 5–6, three sets for grades 7–8, three sets for grades 9–10, and three sets for grades 11–12). At the end of this chapter, we list the matching words in each set along with each pair's shared denotation. For reproducibles of the fronts and backs of each set of cards, visit **marzanoresearch.com/activitiesandgames**. These can be printed as double-sided copies, cut apart, and used by students to play the game.

When teaching connotation and denotation to students, frame the distinction as a persuasive technique. Pose questions to students in the context of a debate or argument. For example, a teacher might say, "If I am trying to get permission from my parents to see a PG-13 movie by myself, would it be better for me to use the word *outrageous* or the word *fascinating* to describe the film?"

We provide multiple sets at various grade levels to allow for variety in content as well as flexibility in game play. Student groups can play a quick round using identical sets, or teachers can devote an entire class period to the game by giving each group a different set and playing in rotating stations. The upper-level cards can be rather challenging, so consider playing with lower-level cards at first—even with high school students—to introduce them to the basic concept of the game.

Take care not to mix different sets of cards together. Pairs have been purposefully included in specific sets to prevent confusion among students. For example, level 1—set A contains a match between *cheap* and *thrifty*, while level 2—set B contains a match between *economical* and *stingy*. If these words were in the same set, students might confuse them. Mixing these pairs together in the same set can overcomplicate the game and spur disputes within student groups. Keep them separate by reproducing multiple copies of each set, slicing them with a paper cutter, and storing them in separate plastic sandwich bags. Label each bag with a permanent marker. You can make the distinctions even clearer by making copies on different colored paper for each set.

Finally, divide the class into pairs or small groups, with no more than four students to a group. Give each group a set of cards. Students shuffle the cards, spread them on the floor or desk (wherever their group is playing), and position them in rows. Remind students that definitions should be face down and terms with connotative meanings should be face up. A properly dealt set of cards should look like the example in figure 8.2.

Figure 8.2: Set of properly dealt Rhetoric Memory cards.

Play

The object of the game is to match two terms that share a meaning but differ in their rhetorical expressions of that meaning. For example, consider the terms *pro-life* and *anti-choice*. Both terms describe the belief that abortion should be against the law, but each term implicitly expresses a different opinion about this belief. One student starts by choosing any two cards and flipping them over in place. The student reads the definition for each one. If they do not match, the student turns the cards back over and the next player gets a turn. Turns proceed in a clockwise fashion. Remind students to give their group mates enough time to read the definitions on the cards before flipping them back over. During other players' turns, as well as during their own, students should pay close attention, trying to remember what is on each card and where it is located. This makes everyone more likely to pick up a match.

If the two cards are a match, such as *request* and *beg*, the student must explain the connotation of each term in order to collect and keep the match. A logical response to any one of the following questions constitutes an explanation:

1. **Connotation question**—Does it sound good (positive) or bad (negative) when said this way? What makes it sound good/bad?

2. **Compare/contrast question**—How are the meanings of these words similar? How are they different?

3. **Intent question**—Why would someone say it this way?

4. **Target audience question**—To whom would someone say it this way?

Keep in mind that some of the vocabulary used on cards can make this game difficult for students, particularly English learners (ELs). To scaffold game play for your ELs, provide dictionaries for each group and allow students to look up words that they do not recognize.

Display this list of questions using a projector or distribute a copy of it to each group at the beginning of the game. Explanations can be short and uncomplicated. For example, a middle school student matching *purr* with *growl* might use connotations to explain the answer, pointing out that the former implies a nice-sounding noise, while the latter implies a scary-sounding noise. A high school student matching *ethnic cleansing* with *genocide* might use a combination of intent and target audience to explain his or her answer: The Nazi Party might have used a phrase like *ethnic cleansing* to persuade people that the mass murder of certain groups of people was good for humanity.

If the student can sufficiently explain the match, he or she keeps both cards and takes another turn, flipping two new cards. If the student cannot explain the match, he or she turns the cards back over and the next student takes a turn. The game ends when all of the cards have been matched. The player with the most matches is the winner.

Challenges

Students may be able to match two items correctly but unable to explain why the match makes sense. If this happens, another student in the group can *challenge* the explanation. When a student makes a challenge, either the defending student can agree that his explanation was insufficient and end his turn (he returns the cards face down to their original positions), or if he thinks his explanation was satisfactory, he can defend against the challenge. If he chooses to defend his answer, then the student who made the challenge raises her hand to alert the teacher. Each of the two students briefly makes a case to the teacher, who

Prepare in advance for responding to challenges by proactively presenting your expectations for game behavior. Say that you will give each student—the one declaring a challenge and the one defending against it—a fair chance to make a case, but in the end, you are the referee. Once you make your final call, students must stop arguing and comply with your verdict. Students who cannot adhere to these expectations should not be allowed to participate.

ultimately determines the results of the challenge. If the teacher agrees that the original explanation was not strong enough, the student who challenged has a chance to provide a better explanation and steal the match. However, if the teacher finds that the defending student's original explanation was good enough, then the defending student keeps the match and the challenging student must discard one of her previously earned matches (if she does not yet have a match, she discards the first match she earns and no player can earn points for it). If neither the original nor the "steal" explanation is strong enough, the cards are returned face down to their original positions and play continues.

Match Sets for Rhetoric Memory

The sets of cards for Rhetoric Memory are organized into four levels, each of which corresponds to a grade-level range. Level 1 pairs are suitable for grades 5–6, level 2 pairs for grades 7–8, level 3 pairs for grades 9–10, and level 4 pairs for grades 11–12. Each level contains three unique sets of word pairs. This allows teachers to divide a class into multiple groups, each with its own set, and have the groups rotate between sets to play multiple games. Keep in mind that these groupings are intended as a guide only; teachers should feel free to modify the grade-level specifications or the words themselves to suit the abilities of their students.

For reproducible copies of the fronts and backs of each set of cards (which can be printed double-sided and cut apart to make cards for game play), visit **marzanoresearch.com/activitiesandgames**. When printing and cutting apart sets of cards, pay careful attention to print the front and back of the same set of cards onto one sheet of paper. The front of level 1—set A should be printed on one side of a sheet of paper; the back of level 1—set A should be printed on the other side of the same sheet of paper. The sheet can then be cut along the lines to create accurate, double-sided cards that are ready for game play.

Level 1 (Grades 5–6)

Level 1—Set A		
request	beg	to _____ means to ask for something you want
shy	unfriendly	someone who is _____ does not always like to talk to people
odor	scent	a(n) _____ is a smell
cheap	thrifty	someone who is _____ does not want to spend much money
smart	nerdy	someone who is _____ knows lots of things
shack	cabin	a _____ is a small building where people live
brave	reckless	someone who is _____ will do something he or she is afraid of
slender	skinny	someone who is _____ has a thin-shaped body
swarming	gathering	when people are _____, it means they are coming together into one group
doctor	physician	a _____ is someone who takes care of sick people
foolish	unwise	someone who is _____ did not make a good decision
fascinating	outrageous	something that is _____ is so interesting that it surprises you

Level 1—Set B		
cop	police officer	a _____ is someone who makes sure people obey the law
energetic	wild	a child who is _____ has tons of energy
dirt	soil	_____ is loose earth that people use to plant seeds
old	antique	something that is _____ has been around for a very long time
music	noise	_____ is a sound or a bunch of sounds put together

Continued on next page →

refreshing	chilly	something that is _____ makes you feel cool, cold, or crisp
purr	growl	to _____ means to make a soft, low sound deep in the throat
house	home	a _____ is a place where you live
unusual	strange	something that is _____ surprises you because you have never seen anything like it before
leader	show-off	a _____ is a person who shows you how to do something
slow	unhurried	someone who is _____ takes his or her time and does not rush
filthy	messy	something that is _____ is dirty

Level 1—Set C		
demand	plead	to _____ means to ask for something
beast	pet	a _____ is an animal
gloomy	shady	a place that is _____ does not have very much light
genius	geek	a _____ is someone who is extremely smart or creative
chef	cook	a _____ is someone who makes food for other people
student	scholar	a _____ is someone who goes to school to learn
stretch the truth	lie	to _____ means to say something that you know is not true
stubborn	determined	someone who is _____ does not give up
gaudy	eye-catching	something that is _____ gets your attention right away
clever	sly	someone who is _____ comes up with new ideas very quickly
sloppy	casual	someone who is _____ does not worry about looking neat
flimsy	delicate	something that is _____ can easily break

Level 2 (Grades 7–8)

Level 2—Set A		
difficult	**challenging**	something that is _____ is hard to do
smile	**smirk**	a _____ happens when the corners of your mouth turn up
wealthy	**rich**	someone who is _____ has a lot of money
obsessive	**passionate**	someone who is _____ has a strong interest in something
stench	**aroma**	a(n) _____ is a smell
hut	**cottage**	a _____ is a building where people live
foolhardy	**courageous**	someone who is _____ will do something he or she is afraid of
bald	**experiencing hair loss**	someone who is _____ does not have as much hair as he or she used to
sneaky	**cunning**	someone who is _____ can easily trick other people
bossy	**assertive**	someone who is _____ always says what he or she is thinking
petite	**short**	someone who is _____ is not very tall
self-confident	**egotistical**	someone who is _____ is proud of himself or herself

Level 2—Set B		
snobby	**cultured**	someone who is _____ has very refined manners and taste
scrawny	**slim**	someone who is _____ has a thin-shaped body
old	**mature**	someone who is _____ has had many life experiences
economical	**stingy**	someone who is _____ does not like to spend money
curious	**nosy**	someone who is _____ wants to learn about new things
youthful	**immature**	someone who is _____ has not had very many life experiences yet
strong-willed	**bullheaded**	someone who is _____ does not give up and is persistent
judgmental	**critical**	someone who is _____ decides quickly whether he or she likes something or someone
weird	**unique**	someone who is _____ acts or looks different than other people
uneasy	**frightened**	someone who is feeling _____ feels nervous or afraid
giggle	**cackle**	to _____ means to laugh
imitate	**mock**	to _____ someone means to act just like him or her

Level 2—Set C		
nitpicky	meticulous	someone who is _____ looks for tiny mistakes and tries to fix them
blackened	burned	a hamburger that is _____ was cooked quickly at a high temperature
gift	bribe	a _____ is something you give someone because you know he or she will like it
conversational	chatty	someone who is _____ loves to talk to other people
headstrong	persistent	someone who is _____ never gives up
cocky	confident	someone who is _____ is very sure of himself or herself
cozy	cramped	a house that is _____ is very small and snug
plan	scheme	a _____ is an idea of something you are about to do
old	elderly	someone who is _____ has lived for a very long time
strict	firm	someone who is _____ does not back down or let people get away with things
blunt	honest	someone who is _____ always tells the truth
used book	recycled book	a _____ has been owned and read by more than one person

Level 3 (Grades 9–10)

Level 3—Set A		
thoughtful	calculating	acting in a carefully planned way
leisurely	lazily	doing something in a relaxed, unhurried way
photographers	paparazzi	people who use cameras to take pictures of celebrities
chore	duty	something you have to do whether you want to or not; a task
rally	riot	a large crowd of people protesting something
fur coat	proof of animal cruelty	clothing made from an animal's pelt
Columbus Day	Explorer's Day	a holiday celebrating the discovery of new worlds
factory	manufacturing plant	a building in which people produce items or put them together
death penalty	capital punishment	the execution of someone who was convicted of a serious crime
debate	argue	to discuss a topic with someone with whom you disagree
pro-life	anti-choice	the opinion that abortion should not be legal in the United States
broken home	single-parent family	a family in which one person instead of two people raises a child or children

Level 3—Set B

bum	homeless person	a person who cannot afford a place to live
the "lame-stream" media	mainstream media	a group made up of the largest and most popular news outlets, such as the *New York Times*, CNN, and Fox News
whistleblower	traitor, defector	someone who reveals government wrongdoing to the public, even when the information is confidential
affirmative action	reverse racism	the practice of offering special opportunities to marginalized groups of people to counteract discrimination (based on race, gender, and so on)
family values	socially conservative values	a set of beliefs centered on the idea that society functions best when families are made up of a husband, a wife, and children
fancy	extravagant	elaborate; lavish
simple	plain	ordinary; unsophisticated
corporate takeover	corporate acquisition	when one company purchases another company
energy exploration	drilling for oil	the process of mining oil from underground and using it to create energy
gun control legislation	gun safety legislation	laws that put restrictions on gun ownership (such as the types of guns people can own and how they can use them)
feminist	man-hater	someone who wants to end sexism (oppression based on a person's sex or gender)
brainwash	persuade	to convince someone to believe something

Level 3—Set C

enhanced interrogation techniques	methods of torture	painful procedures performed on prisoners to force them to reveal information
economic collapse	economic downturn	bad financial conditions in a society (such as depression or high rates of unemployment and bankruptcy)
gender wage gap	gender wage difference	the fact that men are generally paid more money at work than women
wife/husband	spouse or partner	someone in a marriage or partnership with at least one other person
exploit	leverage	to use something—or someone—to your advantage
eccentric	bizarre	strange or unusual (describes a person's behavior)
poor	underprivileged	not making enough money to live comfortably or easily in society
environmentalist	tree hugger	someone who advocates for protecting the Earth
job	career	an occupation; what someone does to earn money
selective	picky	very particular about small details
lady	chick	a woman
deviant	nonconformist	someone whose behavior is not considered "normal" by society's standards

Level 4 (Grades 11–12)

Level 4—Set A		
world policing	making the world safe for democracy	when a country uses military force or negotiation to spread its own values to other countries
forward-thinking progressive	bleeding-heart socialist	someone who believes it is the government's job to protect civil rights and solve social problems
advocate of freedom and morality	narrow-minded extremist	someone who believes the government should let people solve their own issues
racial profiling	identifying likely criminals	when an authority figure (like a police officer or an airport security agent) stops, searches, questions, or arrests someone because of his or her race
illegal alien	undocumented immigrant	someone who migrates to the United States and lives there without filling out the proper paperwork
terrorist	enemy insurgent	someone who uses violence, fear, and intimidation to reach a political or ideological goal
global warming hoax	clean energy campaign	movement to limit the effects of climate change by creating environmentally sustainable options
social safety nets	welfare handouts	when the government gives money to people with extremely low incomes
providing a path to citizenship	giving amnesty—a criminal pardon—to illegals	offering undocumented immigrants legal status, work permits, and—eventually—citizenship
government relief program	government bailout	when the government loans money to companies to prevent them from going bankrupt
prisoner	detainee	someone who is confined or held in custody
gambling	investing	to risk a certain sum of money in the hopes of earning more than you started with

Level 4—Set B		
correctional facility	prison	a building that holds people serving out a sentence for committing a crime
irresponsible	carefree	lacking anxiety or concern for duties
private	reclusive	appreciative of being alone and secluded from people
assertive	domineering	confident; forceful
the War on Women	the pro-life movement	describes legislation restricting reproductive options (such as abortion and birth control)
anti-traditional marriage	pro-marriage equality	the view that LGBT (lesbian, gay, bisexual, and transgender) couples should be legally allowed to marry

raising taxes on the rich	stealing money from job creators	when the government requires the wealthiest class to pay higher income taxes than the middle and lower classes
the rich or the "1 percent"	the successful or hard workers	the top-earning segment of the population; the people who make the most money
playing the race card	speaking out for civil rights	when someone labels a behavior, action, or belief as racist
the final solution	the Holocaust	the mass murder of Jews by the Nazi party between the years of 1941 and 1945
gaze	stare	to look intently at someone or something
competitive	cutthroat	someone who considers it very important to win

Level 4—Set C		
ethnic cleansing	genocide	an attempt to murder every member of a large group of people in order to destroy the entire race or ethnicity
propaganda	political campaign	a campaign to spread information that promotes a certain political view through slogans and images
freedom fighter	guerilla	a mobile, informal soldier who uses the element of surprise to fight against a larger, traditional army
waging a war on Christmas	separating church and state	deciding not to celebrate Christmas in places that are meant to be separate from religion (such as state buildings and public schools)
regulating the economy	suffocating the free market	when the government puts restrictions on a capitalist economy
physician-assisted suicide	euthanasia	when a doctor prescribes medication or performs procedures to help a person end his or her own life
returning to the Jewish homeland	denying Palestinian rights	the movement to create a Jewish national state in Palestine, an area now occupied by Jewish and Palestinian people
squander	spend	to exchange money or time for something else
spin doctor	political advisor	someone who uses the media to make a politician look good
captain	ringleader	the person in charge of a group or activity
protecting free speech	allowing hate speech	when the First Amendment safeguards speech that offends or threatens a group of people (based on race, sexual orientation, and so on)
substance abuser	junkie	a person who is so dependent on a substance that it is extremely difficult to quit

9 Claim Capers

For middle school and high school students

Claim Capers is a game designed to teach middle and high school students to use their powers of observation and close-reading skills to find and present evidence. The idea to use picture mysteries to teach students to support claims with evidence comes from a book by George Hillocks Jr. (2011) called *Teaching Argument Writing, Grades 6–12*. In the book, Hillocks outlines a detailed process for drawing conclusions, identifying evidence, and explaining how the evidence supports the claim. In this game, small groups of students inspect the scene of a crime and use their observations to decide what happened, why, and who is responsible. When the students come together to discuss their conclusions, the group with the most evidence to support its case wins!

Setup

The most important item that teachers must prepare for Claim Capers is a picture mystery, such as the one in figure 9.1 (page 174). The picture mystery depicted in figure 9.1 comes from Lawrence Treat's (1982) *Crime and Puzzlement 2: More Solve-Them-Yourself Picture Mysteries*. Treat is a renowned mystery writer who has worked with various illustrators to create entire volumes of picture mysteries, including the *Crime and Puzzlement* (1981, 1982) series and the children's book *You're the Detective!* (2010), which contains nonviolent crime puzzles for the younger set. His picture mysteries always include (1) an image of the scene, as shown in figure 9.1, (2) a short description of how the investigators came upon the scene, as well as any suspects that may be involved and other information not included in the

Argumentation Skills

- Making inductive inferences
- Citing textual evidence
- Presenting and supporting claims
- Explaining the relationship between claims, grounds, and backing

Materials

- Student-friendly picture mystery (such as figure 9.1 on page 174) or short, text-based "minute mystery"
- Detective's evidence organizer for each student (see reproducible on page 183)
- Interactive whiteboard, document camera, or projector

picture, and (3) a set of questions that illuminate various pieces of evidence and guide the reader through solving the mystery. Unlike many other quick-solve crime puzzles, which often hinge on one crucial piece of evidence (such as a minute detail in a suspect's story that reveals he or she is lying), Treat's picture mysteries usually include several different clues that the reader adds together to solve the case. Because the object of this game is to produce as much supporting evidence as possible, Treat's evidence-heavy mysteries work splendidly.

Figure 9.1: "The Custer Dinette" picture mystery.

From Crime and Puzzlement 2: More Solve-Them-Yourself Picture Mysteries *by Lawrence Treat, Illustrations by Kathleen Borowik Copyright © 1982 by Lawrence Treat, Illustrations by Kathleen Borowik*

If you want students to practice more with close reading and citing textual evidence, you might use text-based mystery stories (short vignettes ranging from a paragraph to a few pages in length) instead of pictures. The game works the same way: students carefully search for clues hidden in the narrative of each mystery, annotate them, and list them as evidence. You might even ask them to sketch out a crime scene based on the narrative to help them focus on seemingly tiny details. The following resources contain text-based mysteries for kids to read and solve:

- *Two-Minute Mysteries* by Donald J. Sobol (1967)—This classic compilation of short mysteries was written by the creator of *Encyclopedia Brown*. Each one is quite short—about a page and a half in length.

- *Kids' Whodunits: Catch the Clues!* and *Kids' Whodunits 2: Crack the Cases!* by Hy Conrad (2007, 2009)—Both books feature twelve-year-old Jonah Bixby, a sleuth whose mother is a detective with the local police department. The mysteries are each about three pages long and work great for younger students, particularly those in middle school. Author Hy Conrad has published many other quick-solve mystery titles for kids, including *Historical Whodunits* (2005), *Solve-It-Yourself Mysteries* (Conrad & Peterson, 1997), and *Almost Perfect Crimes: Mini-Mysteries for You to Solve* (1995).

◆ *Five-Minute Mini-Mysteries* by Stan Smith (2003)—Mathematics teachers will appreciate these thirty whodunit mysteries, as they incorporate logic puzzles and sometimes even math. Each mystery is about three pages long and includes an illustration.

◆ *Clue Mysteries: 15 Whodunits to Solve in Minutes* by Vicki Cameron (2003)—This book contains fifteen mysteries that feature characters from Hasbro's classic whodunit board game CLUE. These mysteries are a bit lengthier than the others on the list and so might be best reserved for older students.

Plan for student groups with three to five members each. Students begin the game working individually and then move into their groups; creating groups in advance allows teachers to ensure heterogeneous membership in terms of argumentation skills. Make enough copies of the detective's evidence organizer (see reproducible on page 183) for each student to have his or her own.

Finally, depending on the complexity of the mystery image you use, you may also choose to distribute a copy of the mystery to each group or to each individual student. This allows all students to inspect the crime scenes more closely, as well as annotate their own copies of the picture as they hunt for evidence.

Play

Game play occurs in three basic segments: (1) individual analysis, (2) small-group analysis, and (3) whole-class analysis. If you are very short on time, you might leave out the first segment; however, research shows that students benefit from think time (also called wait time) before they are expected to share their thoughts with others (Atwood & Wilen, 1991; Rowe, 1987; Tobin, 1987). Decide what format is best for your class, particularly when first introducing the game.

We strongly recommend solving a few picture mysteries as a whole class before sending students off to play the game independently or in small groups (this will take several class periods). Outline explicitly how students' detective's

The low-prep aspect of Claim Capers makes it a great warm-up or sponge activity (Hunter, 2004) for students to begin as soon as they enter class. Have them pick up a copy of the mystery—be it image or text based—on their way into the classroom, or display the picture using an interactive whiteboard or document camera. Either way, students immediately sit at their desks and start reading over the mystery and searching for evidence before class even begins. Only begin the game as a sponge activity like this if the class has played the game before and will know what to do without much explanation.

evidence organizers (see figure 9.2 on page 176) should look when completed (Must students write in complete sentences? Is there a minimum number of observations they must list to fulfill your expectations?). Then model your own method of solving a mystery and supporting a claim. Display the picture and your detective's evidence organizer using a document camera or overhead projector and talk through your thought process as you consider the scene. Demonstrate what kind of evidence to look for and complete the organizer together as a class, providing a gradual release as you and the students slowly fill in the columns. Make a few observations yourself and then ask students to offer their own. Ask them to explain the connection between observations and inferences and offer appraisals of their reasoning. Encourage them to critique your reasoning, as well: respond to the fallacies they identify in your own inferences and write them in the qualifiers column of the organizer.

Observations (I see _____)	Inferences (Which means _____)	Explanations (I know this because _____)	Qualifiers (But still _____)
Caleb Custer is lying face down on the floor beside the table.	Clara (his wife) did not turn him over to try to help him.	When an injured person is lying face down, someone who wants to help would probably turn that person over.	Maybe Clara was just too afraid to touch Caleb after he fell.
~~Caleb's chair has tipped over.~~			
There is a newspaper on the floor beside Caleb.	He was not paying attention to his wife during dinner.	One cannot read and have a conversation at the same time.	The newspaper could have just been lying in his lap or something—he may not have been reading it, necessarily.
A piece of broken plate is in the trash can.	Someone (not Caleb) threw it away. Maybe Clara? We already suspect she didn't try to help Caleb when he fell....	How else could the plate have made it into the wastebasket? Maybe Clara is a neat-freak, so she cleaned it up?	If it was Clara, wouldn't she throw away all the pieces of the plate?
~~There is a cookie jar on the counter.~~			
There is a plate half-filled with food across the table from him.	Clara had no appetite (maybe she was preoccupied?).	Sometimes people do not eat when they are too nervous.	Weak evidence—maybe Clara had a second helping or a big lunch. Plus her chair is pushed in—maybe she never even sat down.
Aside from the broken dishes, the apartment is very tidy.	One (or both) of the Custers is very neat.	A slob would not have such a tidy apartment.	(Probably.)
Clara said, "My husband—he took poison!" to the doctor.	Clara knew there was poison in Caleb's drink—and that it was the cause of his death—before the doctor saw or inspected him.	One would first assume death by natural causes (heart attack, seizure, choking, etc.) before jumping to poison.	(Most likely.)

Prosecution Claim: _Caleb's wife Clara Nettie poisoned him, possibly because he did not pay enough attention to her._

Figure 9.2: Completed student organizer for "The Custer Dinette" picture mystery.

Individual Analysis

First, individual students silently read the description of the scene and consider the picture independently. As they read, reread, and inspect, they look for textual evidence (from the description) and visual evidence (from the picture) that seems suspicious or might be important to solving the case. For example, consider "The Custer Dinette" picture mystery (see figure 9.1, page 174) from Lawrence Treat's (1982) *Crime and Puzzlement 2*. The accompanying description is as follows:

> It is axiomatic that the best poisons are delicious, otherwise who would take them? And the question was whether Caleb C. Custer poured this one by accident, by intention, or whether someone done him in. In any case, his wife, Clara Nettie, rushed into Dr. Minton's next door apartment at dinner time and screamed out hysterically, "My husband—he took poison—help him—quick!" Dr. Minton entered the Custer dinette at once and found what you see. Three people had had the opportunity of planting the poison in the carafe from which Caleb always poured out a dollop of his *eau-de-vie*. They were Clara Nettie, Caleb's brother Toby, and his business partner Allan Dale. The police immediately arrested Clara Nettie for the best of all reasons—she was there. Do you think they were justified? (p. 49)

The student looks carefully at the picture and identifies items in the crime scene that he thinks may be important (such as the newspaper, the broken plate, Clara's place setting, and so on). After closely reading the description and searching through the picture, he lists as many observations as possible in the *observations* column of his detective's evidence organizer. For example, a student might jot down the following clues:

- ◆ Caleb Custer is lying face down on the floor beside the table.
- ◆ Caleb's chair has tipped over.
- ◆ There is a newspaper on the floor beside Caleb.
- ◆ A piece of broken plate is in the trash can.
- ◆ There is a cookie jar on the counter.
- ◆ There is a plate half-filled with food across the table from him.
- ◆ Aside from the broken dishes, the apartment is very tidy.
- ◆ Clara said, "My husband—he took poison!" to the doctor.

Notice that the student has listed specific items from the picture in figure 9.1 ("There is a newspaper on the floor beside Caleb"), as well as some general notes about the scene (". . . the apartment is very tidy") and textual evidence from the description ("Clara said, 'My husband—he took poison!' to the doctor"). Some of these observations will reveal themselves to be crucial; others will turn out to be irrelevant. At this point, it doesn't matter. Students might try to focus on clues they believe will be useful in the end, but the list should be exhaustive rather than exclusive. In other words, the goal of this stage is jot down all observations before trying to separate useful evidence from useless evidence or determine what the clues mean. This listing process helps students pay close attention to the tiniest details of the picture, as well as perform a careful close reading of the description text. Tell them to write down everything they see and the critical details from what they read.

Give students no more than five minutes to read, observe, and create their lists. At this time, they may also try to add notes to other columns in the organizer, but assure them that they need not solve the mystery on their own in those five minutes. They will have plenty of time to work through it later in their small groups.

Small-Group Analysis

Next, students meet in their groups and act as members of a prosecution team. They share their observations and discuss the implications of each one, as well as any preliminary theories they may have about what happened in the case. Teachers may want to assign group roles, such as a discussion leader (someone who steers the group away from unrelated tangents) or a devil's advocate (a skeptic who constantly questions and critiques the group's reasoning).

 As previously mentioned, Treat's (1981, 1982) picture mysteries usually come with a set of questions that prompt readers to think on the right track to cracking the case. It is always possible to solve the mysteries without the questions, but they can be very helpful. You might choose to withhold the questions, give them to all students, or give them only to those who request a hint—it is up to you. Ultimately, though, the point of the activity is to teach students to give evidence, not to solve mysteries. Keep this in mind when considering whether or not to use the questions.

During this period, students must work together to fill in the remaining columns of their detective's evidence organizer and solve the case. Figure 9.2 (page 176) illustrates one group's completed detective's evidence organizer.

As shown in figure 9.2, students must make inferences about their observations, explain their reasoning, and agree on a solution. The organizer in figure 9.2 contains observations that the student generated independently. For most of the observations, the student has worked with his group to generate an *inference*, or a reasonable guess based on an observation. The student has then provided an *explanation* that clarifies each inference, including its connection to an observation. For example, the student has observed that Caleb is lying face down on the floor in the picture. From this, the student inferred that "Clara (his wife) did not turn him over to try to help him," explaining that "when an injured person is lying face down, someone who wants to help would probably turn that person over." Finally, the student adds a *qualifier* to the inference—"Maybe Clara was just too afraid to touch Caleb"—in which the student points out that Caleb's position does not necessarily prove that Clara killed him; there can still be reasonable doubt. Together, an inference supported by an observation and explanation (and perhaps containing a qualifier) makes one complete piece of evidence.

Once students have examined all of their observations in their small groups—and eliminated those that prove to be fruitless—they must organize the evidence and create an argument for their solution. As explained in the introduction to this book, there are four different elements of an effective argument: a claim (an assertion), grounds (support for the claim), backing (facts, expert opinions, or research-based evidence for the grounds), and qualifiers (exceptions or caveats). To form an argument, students structure these elements as shown in figure 9.3.

 As students fill in the areas of their organizer, their work will likely get messier. They may erase, rewrite, and refine inferences; add qualifiers; or scratch out observations that no longer seem to matter. This is part of the process.

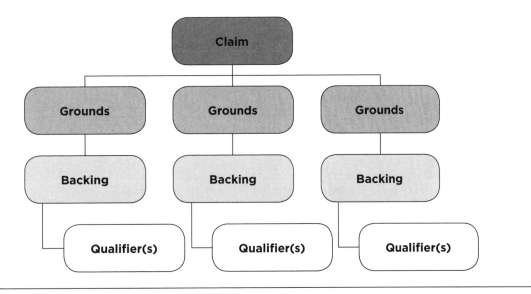

Figure 9.3: The organization of an effective argument.

Students make a claim, then support it with reasons why it is sound (grounds), as well as evidence for the reasons they give (backing). Any of these elements may also have qualifiers, as shown in figure 9.3.

Students use this format to organize their own arguments about the solution of the case, which they will present to the class at the end of the game. Figure 9.4 shows how students can use this structure to present the information on their organizers and create their arguments.

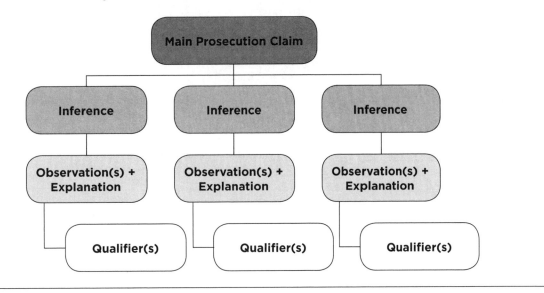

Figure 9.4: Organization of an argument in Claim Capers.

In a way, the structure of a group's argument in this game mirrors the structure presented in figure 9.3. The claim becomes the *main prosecution claim*, which is the group's primary assertion about what happened in the case and who is responsible. Prosecution claims must respond to the question posed in the description (in this case, "Do you think the police were justified in arresting Clara Nettie?"). Students may include additional information in these prosecution claims (such as a motive), but only if they have sufficient evidence to justify doing so. Ultimately, the small group's goal is to walk away from the discussion with a prosecution claim. In this example, the group uses the information in the organizer (figure 9.2, page 176) to claim that Caleb's wife Clara Nettie poisoned him.

The students in this group then use the inferences they generated as grounds for their claim. For example, they might point out that because Clara did not try to help Caleb, she was not concerned that he was hurt and probably killed him. Their observation that Caleb is lying face down in the picture serves as backing for the grounds that Clara did not try to help him—if she had, he would be lying face up. The group's entire argument is shown in figure 9.5.

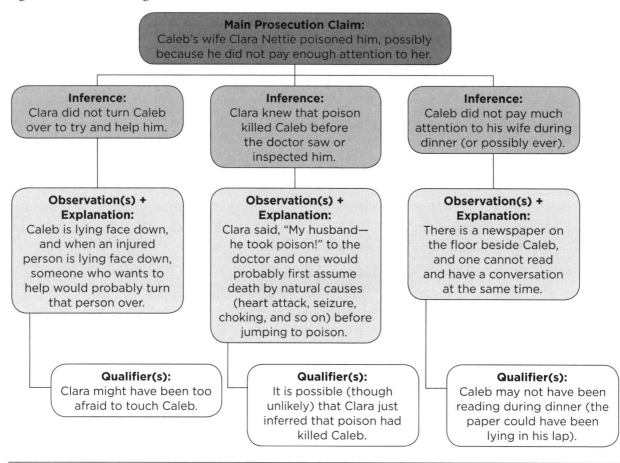

Figure 9.5: Organization of a group's Claim Capers argument with three complete pieces of evidence.

In the end, each group must (1) agree on a prosecution claim and (2) generate as many inferences—supported by observations and explanations—as possible to support it. Give groups a set amount of time to complete this activity. Students will probably need somewhere in the range of fifteen to thirty minutes to complete this activity; however, various factors may influence this number, including the age of your students, how skilled they are with the concept of argumentation, and how familiar they are with playing Claim Capers. When time runs out and the whole class meets, the prosecution team that has the highest number of complete pieces of evidence (an inference supported with an observation and explanation) wins.

Whole-Class Analysis

After small-group analysis, the teacher pulls the whole class back together to analyze the mystery as a class and award points to teams. Start by writing each team's name (you may simply use numbers or letters to designate each team) on the board. You will be tallying points beside each one of these names, so make sure the names do not consume too much space. Then, using an interactive whiteboard or document camera, display (1) the picture mystery and (2) the textual description large enough for the whole class to see.

Invite one group to share its main prosecution claim—its solution—to the mystery. Write this claim on the board. Then ask, "Did anyone make a different prosecution claim?" If so, write this claim on the board, as well. Do not read the solution from the book or share it with the class at this time. Accept as many different solutions to the mystery as your class has generated (it is, of course, possible that all groups will have arrived at the same solution—this is fine).

When all solutions to the mystery have been listed, return to the first solution in the list. Ask the group(s) who made that prosecution claim to give their evidence items (each of which should include an observation, inference, and explanation). As groups present different pieces of evidence, circle the observations on the picture or annotate them in the textual description, adding notes about the inferences, as shown in figure 9.6 (page 182).

 Students will likely disagree with one another during the whole-class discussion of evidence. Feel free to curb the debate or allow it to go on as long as you like; however, keep in mind that the ultimate goal of the game is not to teach students to solve mysteries, but to help them distinguish useful, relevant evidence from a red herring or a reasoning error. It may be that some of the most fruitful lessons about supporting a claim emerge from these concluding debates between student detectives.

Discuss each piece of evidence one by one as a class, allowing teams to dispute evidence they feel is inaccurate or erroneous. This can be as simple as saying, "Okay, the students in team 3 observe that half the broken plate is in the trash can, and from this they infer that someone—probably Clara—has taken the time to throw it away instead of rushing for help. Does anyone dispute this evidence?" When the majority of the class approves a piece of evidence, every team that has cited that same evidence earns a point. Keep track using tally marks on the board. If the class generally considers a piece of evidence to be irrelevant or fallacious, the teacher crosses it out on the board and informs the teams that have cited it that they cannot earn a point for it.

Move through each proposed prosecution claim. Allow the students to discuss all of the evidence they have for each one and award groups one point for each strong piece of evidence they cited during their small-group discussion. When all claims and evidence have been discussed, share the book's solution of the picture mystery with the class. If you like, you may also award one final point to each team whose prosecution claim matched the solution in the book. Regardless of the solution itself, the team with the most evidence for its solution is declared the winner.

The apartment is very neat and tidy.

Clara did not try to help Caleb after he fell.

Clara did not eat much of her food—too nervous?

Someone (probably Clara) took the time to throw part of this plate away.

Caleb was reading this newspaper during dinner (instead of talking to Clara)—motive?

Figure 9.6: An exemplar whole-class annotation of "The Custer Dinette" picture mystery.

From Crime and Puzzlement 2: More Solve-Them-Yourself Picture Mysteries *by Lawrence Treat, Illustrations by Kathleen Borowik Copyright © 1982 by Lawrence Treat, Illustrations by Kathleen Borowik*

Detective's Evidence Organizer

Observations (I see _____)	Inferences (Which means _____)	Explanations (I know this because _____)	Qualifiers (But still _____)

Prosecution Claim: _____

Teaching Argumentation: Activities and Games for the Classroom © 2015 Marzano Research • marzanoresearch.com

Visit **marzanoresearch.com/activitiesandgames** to download this page.

10 Convince the Crowd
For high school students

Convince the Crowd is a competitive debate game in which the teacher proposes a motion and two panels of students discuss it. Before a single speech is made, an audience of classmates votes either in favor of the motion or against it. The audience casts their votes on the same motion a second time after the debate takes place, allowing everyone to see which side has persuaded the most audience members to change their vote. The side that has the highest percentage difference between *before* votes and *after* votes is declared the winner.

This game is recommended for high school students who have had lots of practice with research and argumentation. It works especially well in language arts, science, and social studies classes. The game is modeled after Intelligence Squared (stylized as *intelligence²* or *IQ²*) debates (www.intelligencesquared.com). Motions in past Intelligence Squared debates cover a broad spectrum of topics, from politics ("The rich are taxed enough") to environmental issues ("The natural gas boom is doing more harm than good") to entertainment ("Ban college football"). We highly recommend showing one of these debates to students so they can get an overall picture of what a debate looks like and an idea of what form their classroom debates should take.

Setup

Like many styles of formal debate, Convince the Crowd can be an academically rich and personally rewarding experience for students, so long as it is properly introduced, explained, and prepared. Provided that

Argumentation Skills

- Presenting and supporting claims
- Organizing an argument
- Distinguishing a claim from alternate or opposing claims
- Identifying insufficient or irrelevant evidence
- Communicating responsibly
- Identifying errors in reasoning
- Evaluating persuasive rhetoric
- Perspective taking

Materials

- Stopwatch or timer
- Voting system (clickers, student mobile devices, slips of paper for *before* and *after* votes and buckets or hats to collect them in, or a similar system)
- One motion for each student group (see appendix B on page 215)

it is done well, the game will likely take you and your students several days of in-class preparation. For this reason, Convince the Crowd works well as a culminating unit activity (for instance, the game could be combined with a persuasive essay assignment).

Setup for Convince the Crowd can be divided into the following four stages: (1) forming teams and assigning motions, (2) brainstorming, researching, and planning, (3) writing and rehearsing opening statements, and (4) preparing the classroom for debate.

Forming Teams and Assigning Motions

To begin, use a roster to divide your class into groups of six. If need be, you can have one group of five, but do not exceed six. Keep a record of these groupings. No one knows the dynamic of your classroom better than you do, so the method by which you divide students is completely your choice. Regardless, we do recommend assigning groups yourself—randomly or otherwise—rather than allowing students to select their own group members, so as to encourage the development of collaborative skills and to discourage cliques from compromising the objective structure of the game.

 Beware of creating motions that are impossible to defend. Remember—the idea is to challenge both sides equally by giving students an opportunity to generate multiple pieces of evidence to support their claim. To illustrate, note the difference between the following motions: (1) "Cigarette smoking is bad for human health" versus (2) "Cigarette smoking should be banned in the United States." Claims like the one expressed in motion 1 are difficult to dispute because they are already widely accepted or commonly regarded as factual. Claims like the one expressed in motion 2 are advantageous because they are more unsettled, are still contentious, and therefore allow students to generate myriad grounds to support the initial claim. The motion that cigarettes do not have detrimental health consequences is practically indefensible. Students would have a very difficult time generating evidence for cigarette smoking's favorable impact on health. On the other hand, the motion that cigarettes should be federally illegal because they are unhealthy is debatable. Students can argue against a cigarette ban without trying to prove that cigarettes are perfectly healthy. Instead, they could argue that a ban on cigarettes would damage the livelihood of tobacco farmers, trample civil liberties, or incite a rise in crime.

Next, create a list of sharply framed claims, or *motions*, which relate to your content area (see appendix B on page 215 for a list of claims from a variety of content areas). You will need one motion for each group of six. It is important to note the difference between a motion (or claim) and a question. A *question* expresses a controversial issue with the sort of syntax that warrants a *yes* or *no* answer (for example, "Should the U.S. military be permitted to recruit at high schools?" or "Do violent video games lead to violent behavior?"). A *motion*, on the other hand, is essentially a claim in that it directly takes a position on a controversial issue (for example, "The U.S. military should be permitted to recruit at high schools" or "Violent video games do not lead to violent behavior"). Rather than answer yes or no, as with questions, the student audience will respond to motions with *agree*, *disagree*, or *undecided*. A science teacher, for example, might create motions such as "Genetically modified crops should not be grown," "Invasive species should be completely eradicated," "The auto racing industry should use biofuel instead of gasoline," or "Human cloning is wrong." A social studies teacher might devise motions such as "The government should have a say in our diets," "Social media companies should not regulate what users post on their sites," or "Rehabilitation should be the primary objective of the prison system." If you are an English language arts (ELA) teacher, the topics may relate to language and literature, but because argumentation itself is classified as an ELA standard in the Common Core State Standards, the topics could also be about almost anything you want (for example, "The Internet is hindering students from learning to read and write," "Performance-enhancing drug use should be permitted in sports," or "Fashion is valuable"). See appendix B for sample motions.

Once you have generated a list of motions or selected appropriate ones from appendix B, assign one motion to each group of six. Divide each group in half to form two teams of three, with one team arguing in favor of the motion and the other team arguing against the motion (see figure 10.1).

The process of forming teams and assigning positions on the motions is most easily and efficiently completed out of class during lesson planning. This also helps steer students' focus toward supporting claims and away from irrelevant distractions (such as whose team they are on, which motion or position they are being assigned to argue, and so on).

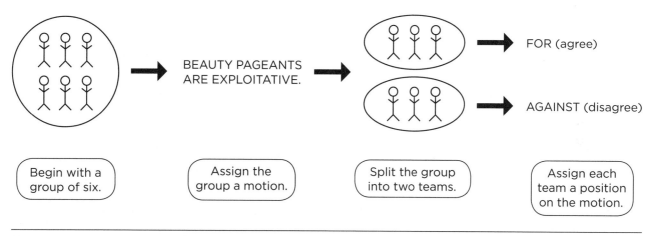

Figure 10.1: Process of forming teams and assigning motions.

Finally, let each team know when they will be debating their motion. Table 10.1 shows one way to plan out a schedule for debates.

Table 10.1: Sample Debate Schedule

	Monday, April 2	**Tuesday, April 3**	**Wednesday, April 4**	**Thursday, April 5**	**Friday, April 6**
Motion	Censorship is sometimes justified.	Whistle-blowing organizations like WikiLeaks are good for society.	Citizens should be required by law to vote.	The death penalty is a necessary evil.	Financial aid for education should be based solely on merit.
Arguing For	Marion, Tyra, Coby	Kashan, Jack, Grace	Allie, Todd, De'Ajanae	Sergio, Tori, Scarlett	Ricardo, Christina, Melissa
Arguing Against	Max, Danielle, Angela	Jalen, Molly, Valentina	Charlie, Tayanna, Dalton	Quentin, Jenny, Maya	James, Rafael, America

Each motion will take a full class period to debate, so designate each motion to a different day. With a class of twenty-four students, you will need to devote four days to game play; with a class of thirty students, you will need five days; and so on.

Brainstorming, Researching, and Planning

Throughout the brainstorming, researching, and planning process, students identify evidence that supports and does not support their claim, organize supporting evidence into grounds and backing, and use nonsupporting evidence to address and rebut potential arguments the other side may use during the debate. They also designate specific grounds to individual team members to ensure that each opening statement will present a unique argument in favor of or in opposition to the motion.

We recommend at least one full class period of planning and research time, but depending on the length of your class periods, this amount of time may be insufficient. Two to three days are ideal. At maximum, we recommend devoting no more than three to four class periods to preparation and research. It is also perfectly acceptable to require students to continue their research and practice the delivery of their speeches outside of class as homework, if necessary. However, begin the process in class to allow yourself to give direct instruction about research methods, provide feedback, and facilitate a gradual release.

To start the research process, students individually collect information related to their claim and then meet in their teams of three to classify the information collected as either supporting or nonsupporting information. For example, a team arguing in favor of the motion "Cigarette smoking should be banned in the United States" might have compiled the following evidence:

Throughout either the planning or the debate process, your students may point out flaws in the way you initially expressed the motion. Let's say, for instance, that your motion is "It is wrong for corporations to market to children." A student might point out that the word *wrong* is subjective and dependent on an individual's own definition of morality. Another student might add that even if the class could agree on a unanimous code of morality or even on a universal definition of the word *wrong*, it is hard to know what the motion is really proposing. If a student votes in favor of the motion, is she voting for an extension of federal restrictions on corporate marketing? If a student votes against the motion, is he condoning a tobacco company's teen advertising campaign? You want your students to address these qualifiers and ambiguities. Does the motion raise an issue of free speech? Is it an issue of the free market? Is it an issue of protecting children's rights? What is the best way to spin it to win the vote of the audience? In college and career settings, students will be barraged with controversies, many of which are not clearly defined, quantified, or operationalized. When students can draw attention to qualifiers and ambiguities, you have taught them to think deeply and critically. Recognize that leveraging the vagueness of a claim to work to one's advantage is a high-order persuasive skill, and encourage students to explicitly address and tackle these gray areas during the debate.

- A study of 2,537 postal workers published in the *American Journal of Public Health* found the work absence rate for smokers to be 33 percent higher than for nonsmokers (Ryan, Zwerling, & Orav, 1992).

- According to a Surgeon General's report, nine out of ten smokers start smoking at or before age eighteen (Centers for Disease Control and Prevention [CDC], 2012).

- *USA Today* reported that smokers cost their employers about 25 percent more in healthcare ("Employers Charging Smokers Extra," 2006).

- The Centers for Disease Control and Prevention (2005) estimated the amount lost to productivity and healthcare because of smoking to be $92 billion and $75.5 billion, respectively.

◆ About 86 percent of youth smokers (aged twelve to seventeen) choose Marlboro, Newport, or Camel, the three most heavily advertised brands (CDC, 2012).

◆ Only 58 percent of smokers over twenty-six choose Marlboro, Newport, or Camel, the three most heavily advertised brands (CDC, 2012).

◆ Cigarette advertising is more likely to influence teens to smoke than peer pressure (Evans, Farkas, Gilpin, Berry, & Pierce, 1995).

◆ In 2010, the combined profits of the six leading tobacco companies were $35.1 billion (World Lung Foundation, 2012).

◆ Sixty-seven percent of Americans drink alcohol (Gallup, 2010), but only about 20 percent smoke cigarettes (American Cancer Society, 2013).

◆ More than three out of four smokers want to quit, but feel addicted, according to a Gallup poll (Jones, 2005).

◆ Health insurance quote company Allied Quotes (2007) said, "For every pack of cigarettes smoked, that smoker costs the nation $7.18."

Students might also use time in their groups to brainstorm questions and other ideas related to the motion. If groups choose to brainstorm, remind them that brainstorming is a highly collaborative and informal process. No question, idea, or piece of evidence should be ruled out at this stage. Designate one teammate as the recorder—this person writes down absolutely everything—and encourage all members of the team to contribute freely and spontaneously. Figure 10.2 depicts the product of a brainstorming session by the team arguing in favor of the motion "Cigarette smoking should be banned in the United States."

FOR Banning Cigarettes—Brainstorm
- Cigarettes are bad for you
- Cigarettes kill people
- Cigarettes kill nonsmokers too (secondhand smoke, etc.)
- Cigarettes are expensive
- Are cigarettes protected in the Constitution?
- Why did Prohibition fail for alcohol?
- Kids can get addicted to cigarettes
- Advertising
- What about taxes? Is cigarette tax money essential?
- Cigarettes are drugs too, and we criminalized ecstasy and marijuana, so why not cigarettes?

Figure 10.2: Sample brainstorming list for debate preparation.

Notice that the students have recorded questions related to the motion (such as "Why did Prohibition fail for alcohol?"), suggested potential grounds to be researched more thoroughly (such as "Cigarettes are bad for you"), and identified opponent arguments that they may need to rebut during the debate (such as "Are cigarettes protected in the Constitution?" and "What about taxes? Is the money essential?").

Next, students sort the evidence they have collected and information from their brainstorming session into supporting and nonsupporting information for their claim. Table 10.2 shows how the team arguing for banning cigarettes might do this.

Table 10.2: Sorting Information Related to the Claim "Cigarette Smoking Should Be Banned in the United States"

Supporting	Nonsupporting
A study of 2,537 postal workers published in the *American Journal of Public Health* found the absentee rate for smokers to be 33 percent higher than for nonsmokers (Ryan et al., 1992).	Only 58 percent of smokers over twenty-six choose Marlboro, Newport, or Camel, the three most heavily advertised brands (CDC, 2012).
According to a Surgeon General's report, nine out of ten smokers start smoking at or before age eighteen (CDC, 2012).	In 2010, the combined profits of the six leading tobacco companies were $35.1 billion (World Lung Foundation, 2012).
USA Today reported that smokers cost their employers about 25 percent more in healthcare ("Employers Charging Smokers Extra," 2006).	Sixty-seven percent of Americans drink alcohol (Gallup, 2010), but only about 20 percent smoke cigarettes (American Cancer Society, 2013).
The Centers for Disease Control and Prevention (2005) estimated the amount lost to productivity and healthcare because of smoking to be $92 billion and $75.5 billion, respectively.	Are cigarettes protected in the Constitution?
About 86 percent of youth smokers (aged twelve to seventeen) choose Marlboro, Newport, or Camel, the three most heavily advertised brands (CDC, 2012).	Why did Prohibition fail for alcohol?
Cigarette advertising is more likely to influence teens to smoke than peer pressure (Evans et al., 1995).	What about taxes? Is cigarette tax money essential?
More than three out of four smokers want to quit, but feel addicted, according to a Gallup poll (Jones, 2005).	
Health insurance quote company Allied Quotes (2007) said, "For every pack of cigarettes smoked, that smoker costs the nation $7.18."	
Cigarettes are bad for you and can kill people, including nonsmokers (secondhand smoke).	
Cigarettes are expensive.	
Advertising is pervasive.	
Kids can get addicted to cigarettes.	
Cigarettes are drugs, too, and we criminalized ecstasy and marijuana, so why not cigarettes?	

Once students have sorted their evidence, information, and ideas, they should focus on organizing supporting information and ideas into categories, with the ultimate goal of creating three well-supported, well-reasoned grounds. Table 10.3 shows how the team has sorted their evidence and ideas. Notice that they have eliminated some ideas that provided weak evidence or contained errors in reasoning.

Table 10.3: Supporting Information Organized Into Grounds

Grounds	Supporting Information
Cigarette smoking harms the U.S. economy.	*USA Today* reported that smokers cost their employers about 25 percent more in healthcare ("Employers Charging Smokers Extra," 2006).
	The Centers for Disease Control and Prevention (2005) estimated the amount lost to productivity and healthcare because of smoking to be $92 billion and $75.5 billion, respectively.
	Health insurance quote company Allied Quotes (2007) said, "For every pack of cigarettes smoked, that smoker costs the nation $7.18."
	A study of 2,537 postal workers published in the *American Journal of Public Health* found the absentee rate for smokers to be 33 percent higher than for nonsmokers (Ryan et al., 1992).
Cigarettes impair the health of the whole population, even nonsmokers.	Cigarettes kill nonsmokers, too (secondhand smoke).
Children are susceptible to cigarette advertising and addiction.	According to a Surgeon General's report, nine out of ten smokers start smoking at or before age eighteen (CDC, 2012).
	About 86 percent of youth smokers (aged twelve to seventeen) choose Marlboro, Newport, or Camel, the three most heavily advertised brands (CDC, 2012).
	Cigarette advertising is more likely to influence teens to smoke than peer pressure (Evans at al., 1995).

Each of the three students takes one grounds and does more research individually to develop backing for it more fully. Students will present these grounds and backing during the debate. As illustrated in figure 10.3 (page 192), Janasia has elected to do further research on how cigarette smoking harms the U.S. economy. She has organized her backing into three categories (loss of worker productivity, rise in healthcare premiums, and how the cost of cigarettes outweighs profit gained). Teachers can use the reproducible provided on pages 206–207 at the end of this chapter and shown here in figure 10.3 to help students sort the grounds among the teammates and provide space for individual teammates to organize at least three pieces of backing for their grounds.

Once each student has done further research to more fully develop his or her grounds, groups can meet back together to address information they collected that does not support their claim. This information can be useful in preparing rebuttals to potential grounds the opposing team may present during the debate. Figure 10.4 (page 193) illustrates how the team from the previous example might do this.

| Name: Janasia A. | Circle One: | ⟨FOR the motion⟩ |
| | | AGAINST the motion |

Motion:

Cigarette smoking should be banned in the United States.

Teammate Names	Grounds
Janasia A.	Cigarettes harm the U.S. economy.
Liz R.	Cigarettes impair the health of the whole population, even that of nonsmokers.
Omar I.	Children are susceptible to cigarette advertising and addiction.

My Grounds	My Backing	
Cigarettes harm the U.S. economy.	1.	Productivity: Smoking leads to a less productive workforce because smokers are more likely to develop illnesses like asthma and cancer. Therefore, smokers are more likely to miss a large number of workdays. A study of 2,537 postal workers published in the *American Journal of Public Health* found the absentee rate for smokers to be 33 percent higher than for nonsmokers (Ryan et al., 1992).
	2.	Healthcare: Smokers are more expensive to insure because they are more prone to illness. *USA Today* reported that smokers cost their employers about 25 percent more in healthcare ("Employers Charging Smokers Extra," 2006). When smokers increase healthcare costs for insurance companies, they are sometimes forced to charge higher premiums to everyone, even nonsmokers.
	3.	Profit gained: The economic cost of smoking far outweighs the profit gained. The Centers for Disease Control and Prevention (CDC) estimates the amount lost to productivity and healthcare to be $92 billion and $75.5 billion, respectively. In 2010, the combined profits of the six leading tobacco companies were a mere $35.1 billion in comparison (World Lung Foundation, 2012). Health insurance quote company Allied Quotes (2007) said, "For every pack of cigarettes smoked, that smoker costs the nation $7.18."

Figure 10.3: Example organization template for a student panelist.

As illustrated in figure 10.4, students have preplanned evidence and reasons they can use to refute the arguments of their opponents, as well as detailed, research-based backing for these refutations.

Potential Opponent Grounds	Our Rebuttal
People have the right to choose whether or not to smoke. It is a violation of the U.S. Constitution to prevent them from doing so.	1. There is no such thing as a constitutional right to smoke. The Constitution lays out civil rights of specially protected groups. Smokers are not a protected group, and neither the Due Process Clause nor the Equal Protection Clause grants smokers a right to smoke. 2. The right to privacy does not apply to smoking. Because there is no specially protected right to smoke, state laws that stand in the way of tobacco control can be repealed/amended. 3. We recognize in our society that addiction is not a "choice," so it is not fair to consider smoking to be a rational decision.
Prohibition did not work for alcohol, so there is no way it will work for cigarettes.	Sixty-seven percent of Americans drink alcohol (Gallup, 2010), but only about 20 percent smoke cigarettes (American Cancer Society, 2013). Furthermore, more than three out of four smokers want to quit, but feel addicted, according to a Gallup poll (Jones, 2005). Since there are more people who drink than smoke, and since most of those who do smoke would like to quit, it seems that cigarette smoking today is not parallel to alcohol consumption in the Prohibition era.
Banning smoking will hurt the U.S. economy because the government depends on the cigarette tax.	The government does make money from cigarette taxation, but this profit does not outweigh the burden of cigarettes on our economy. The CDC estimates that productivity and healthcare drain nearly $167 billion as a result of cigarettes. On the other hand, the total profits of the six leading tobacco companies are only $35 billion. The taxes that the government deducts from this profit will total an even smaller number. Therefore, the taxes that come from the profits of cigarettes do not offset the money that cigarettes cost the U.S. in healthcare.

Figure 10.4: Example organization template for rebuttals to opponent grounds.

Writing and Rehearsing Opening Statements

Once students have finished collecting backing and conferred about rebuttals with their teammates, they can use their research to craft their opening statements. While your high school students may be well practiced in persuasive writing, do not expect them to necessarily know how to write a persuasive speech. The following list can be used to guide your instruction about the elements of a strong opening statement.

Composition/Writing

♦ Your grounds are the common thread that should be woven through all of the backing you provide in your opening statement. Clarify how each piece of backing supports the grounds you are presenting for your team's claim.

♦ Remember to write for the ear rather than the eye. The audience will never read your opening statement; you will be speaking it aloud.

♦ Use declarative sentences in the active voice. Active voice shows that the subject of the sentence is performing the action or causing something to happen, which confers agency to the subject. Consider the claim "Global warming should be a priority of the U.S. government." To phrase this claim in active voice, make *the U.S. government* the subject, make *prioritize* the verb, and make *global warming* the direct object ("The U.S. government should prioritize global warming").

Rehearsal/Revision

♦ Edit your opening statement. Read it aloud yourself to hear how it flows. Pare it down to two minutes by eliminating filler and focusing on actual evidence.

♦ Rehearse your delivery. Practice at least three times using a mirror or video camera. Watch and listen to your presentation and pay attention to your tempo, timing, and volume. Convey passion and enthusiasm about your message.

♦ Use a stopwatch to time yourself so you can get an idea of your pacing. Try to end your statement just before the moderator tells you your time has expired.

Presentation

♦ Do not read your opening statement verbatim to the audience. There is no need to try to memorize it word for word, but referring occasionally to a 3 × 5 note card is much more effective than simply reading the statement aloud.

♦ Use natural hand gestures, keeping your hands away from your sides where the audience can see them. Try to make eye contact with every single audience member.

♦ Generate anticipation in the minds of the audience members by foreshadowing—or briefly referencing—the grounds a teammate will address later in the debate. You can do this with a parenthetical statement; for example, you might say, "Another important aspect of the debate, of course, is _____. My teammate Ethan will be discussing this issue further in his opening statement."

♦ Dress to impress. Wear clean, comfortable, professional clothing that you can avoid fiddling with, lest the audience be too distracted by your fidgeting to hear your argument.

An exemplary opening statement is shown in the following excerpt from an Intelligence Squared debate, in which Pulitzer Prize–winning journalist Buzz Bissinger passionately argues in favor of banning college football on the grounds that it compromises the integrity of the university. Audio, video, and a full transcript of Bissinger's delivery can be found on the Intelligence Squared U.S. website (http://intelligencesquaredus.org /debates/past-debates/item/589-ban-college-football).

> One of the things that we are looking at and must look at which makes this debate pertinent is the role of the university. It is pivotal . . . A recent book by two sociologists, Richard Arum and Josipa Roksa says that basically undergraduates embrace college life, and it is shaped and oriented to nonacademic endeavors. The amount of study time has gone—and this was by two labor economists. Study time in colleges has gone from over 40 hours in the 1960s to 20 hours in the 1980s to currently 13 hours of study time. And I believe that at the top of what has become the university distraction, the distracted university is football, is football. It sucks all the air out of the room. The amount of money that coaches make is insulting. It is insulting when a coach is making five to 10 to 15 times more than a college president. What does it say? What does it say about the priorities of a university? It says that the head coach runs the school. . . . A few facts in what they call the football bowl subdivision, the big 125 schools. Spending per student in those schools, $13,471. Spending per athlete, $91,053. 6.8 times as much for a student athlete. In the famed SEC, 11.6 times as much. . . . And that's not from me, that's from Andrew Zimbalist who is considered the leading sports economic professor in the country . . . From USA Today June 16, 2011, more than $470 million, more than $470 million, most of it in student fees by students who do not play sports went into subsidized college athletic programs, in particular in football. . . . Salaries of coaches, I mentioned it, average salary for a football coach, $1.47 million. That's up 55 percent in six seasons. A professor, 1986 to 2007, his salary went up 30 percent. The college president, 100 percent. The football coach, 500 percent. 500 percent. (Intelligence Squared U.S., 2012, pp. 11–12)

As shown in the transcript, Bissinger's opening statement exemplifies many characteristics of a strong speech. First, he used direct, declarative sentences without "I" statements to make his case. Rather than say, for instance, "I feel that it is wrong for a coach to make so much money," he phrased his opinion as someone might present a fact: "The amount of money that coaches make is insulting." Secondly, Bissinger's opening statement is very well organized. He begins by clearly asserting his position and his grounds (that college football should be banned because it compromises the role of the university). He then proceeds to outline each piece of backing (study time in colleges has decreased, coaches have inflated salaries, and some colleges devote more money to student athletes than to students who are not athletes), referencing specific studies and citing statistics that support each of these points. Table 10.4 (page 196) depicts how Bissinger's process of prewriting for his opening statement might look had he used the reproducible graphic organizer on pages 206–207.

Table 10.4: Sample Prewriting Organization for Buzz Bissinger's Opening Statement

My Grounds	My Backing
College football compromises the role of the university.	1. Study time in colleges has decreased: Undergraduates embrace college life when it is oriented to nonacademic endeavors (Arum & Roksa, 2011). Study time has gone down from forty to twenty to thirteen hours of study (Babcock & Marks, 2011).
	2. Coaches have inflated salaries: The average salary for a football coach is $1.47 million ("*USA Today* College Football Coach," 2011). Salary for coaches has risen by 55 percent in six seasons ("*USA Today* College Football Coach," 2011).
	3. Colleges devote more money to student athletes than to students who are not athletes: Spending per student in the biggest 125 schools is $13,471, while spending per athlete is $91,053 (that is 6.8 times as much). In the SEC (Southeastern Conference), it is 11.6 times as much. Over $470 million (most in student fees by students who do not play sports) went into subsidized college athletic programs, particularly football (Berkowitz & Upton, 2011).

Watch videos or read transcripts of debates and opening statements with your class to incite a discussion about the strengths and weaknesses of the debaters. This will help your students learn or review the differences between speechwriting and formal writing; concrete evidence and anecdotal evidence; persuasive writing and other forms of writing. Use the following list of links to guide you in selecting sources to view or listen to with your students, keeping in mind that teachers should screen any clip that will be used in class to ensure it is appropriate:

- CNN's (2012) "Make or Break Debate Moments" from famous presidential debates (www .youtube.com/watch?v=4Y8SZDH3B_4)

- Al Sharpton and Christopher Hitchens (n.d.) debate religion (www.learnoutloud.com/Free -Audio-Video/Religion-and-Spirituality /Christianity/Al-Sharpton-and-Christopher -Hitchens-Debate/26418)

- The "Past Debates Archive" on the Intelligence Squared website includes full video, audio, and transcripts of past debates on a variety of motions from many content areas (http:// intelligencesquaredus.org/debates/past -debates)

Third, Bissinger wrote for the ear. He composed his statements in such a way that made them sound compelling to the audience. While the speech may not seem very eloquent in writing, Bissinger's statement is captivating when spoken. He did not always use complete sentences or shy away from rhetorical questions, as one should in formal writing. He repeated certain words and phrases to emphasize important points (for example, the word *insulting* and the phrase *more than $470 million*), yet he stayed on message throughout the speech without using fluffy or flowery language.

Preparing the Classroom for Debate

Finally, attend to the physical layout of your classroom. Depending on the length of class periods at your school, one round of Convince the Crowd may take up an entire period. To optimize the time you have in class with your students, it may be useful to arrange the furniture in the classroom before class begins. Position enough desks or tables at the front of the room to accommodate six student panelists. Divide these in half, with one on each side of the room, to separate the *for* panelists from the *against* panelists, as shown in figure 10.5.

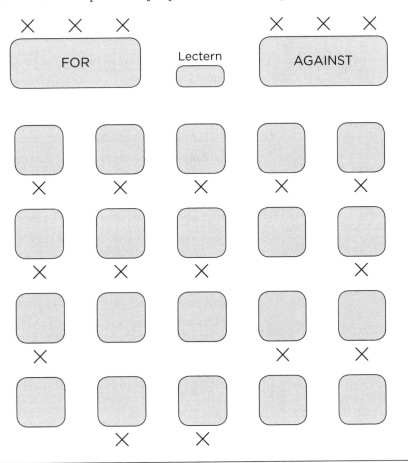

Figure 10.5: Physical layout of the classroom for Convince the Crowd.

If you teach different subjects throughout the day and want to avoid devoting planning and passing periods to moving desks and tables back and forth, you can also just use six chairs at the front of the room.

Small touches to your classroom's appearance also make a big difference in setting the scene to build excitement for the game, even with high school students. Post signs that read *FOR* and *AGAINST* visibly at each of the two debating tables or sides of the room. If you usually speak at a podium or lectern, you may decide to temporarily designate it for student panelists to use during the game. If you have a band, orchestra, or chorus teacher at your school, you might ask to borrow one or two music stands for a few days while your class plays Convince the Crowd.

Play

Game play is likely to take an entire class period for each debate, depending on the length of your class periods. Table 10.5 depicts the structure of Convince the Crowd when used in a class period that is forty-five minutes in length. This structure can be modified to suit the length of your class periods (for instance, if your school has hour-long class periods, you can expand the time allotted for audience questioning or give your students four to five minutes each for opening statements instead of two). You can also opt to use the forty-five-minute structure to play the game and then use the remaining class time to debrief about the debate.

 Perform some quick checks for understanding with your students to ensure that they have heard and understood the rules and behavioral expectations. There are a number of easy ways to do this, including choral response (you ask a question such as "When a student is speaking, your mouths should be . . ." and all students respond with the answer "Closed!"), cold calling (you ask a question and randomly choose one student to answer it), or finger voting (you ask a question, you present three possible answers, and on your signal, students hold up one, two, or three fingers, depending on the answer they think is the correct one).

Begin by inviting the two teams scheduled to debate the motion to sit at their respective tables at the front of the room. Encourage the rest of the class, the audience, to applaud. Next, briefly outline the motion for debate, your expectations for civil conduct, and the structure of the game. You might say something like, "Ladies and gentlemen, welcome to our first Convince the Crowd debate. I will be moderating the six debaters at two tables that you see sharing the stage here with me. These two teams will be debating the following motion, three against three: 'Cigarette smoking should be banned in the United States.' I would like to remind you that while this debate is a contest, I expect respectful conduct from each of you."

At this point, present clear, explicit expectations for civil conduct. Your role as the moderator is to regulate and incentivize courteous discussion throughout the debate. Before you begin, it is crucial that you directly convey the rules of proper debate decorum. Make sure to point out that these expectations apply to audience members and debaters alike. Your list may include the following:

- Calm demeanor

- Applause after opening statements and closing remarks

- Silence while others are speaking (particularly during opening statements, rebuttals, answers to questions, and closing remarks)

- Reasonable volume and tone of voice

- Disciplined and respectful word choice

- No personal attacks against opponents

- Attentive body language

Present a brief overview of the structure of the game. Remind the class that there will be two rounds of voting: one at the beginning of the debate, and a second at the end of the debate. These votes will be used to determine the winning team. The team with the greatest difference between their initial percentage of audience votes and the end percentage will win. Outline the three rounds. Round 1 is for opening statements from each

Table 10.5: Convince the Crowd Debate Format (Designed for a Forty-Five-Minute Class Period)

Activity		Time
Moderator Introduction	Moderator (teacher) briefly outlines the motion for debate and briefly reviews the rules of the game.	Three to four minutes
Preliminary Voting	Students (excluding the debate panelists) use clickers or pieces of scrap paper to cast their "before" votes about the motion. Students can vote either (1) *for* the motion, (2) *against* the motion, or (3) *undecided*. Votes submitted on scrap paper must be collected at this time by an audience member and placed into the "before" receptacle (hat, shoebox, crate, container, or something similar).	Thirty seconds
Round 1	Panelist 1 gives an opening statement arguing *for* the motion.	Two minutes
	Panelist 2 gives an opening statement arguing *against* the motion.	Two minutes
	Panelist 3 gives an opening statement arguing *for* the motion.	Two minutes
	Panelist 4 gives an opening statement arguing *against* the motion.	Two minutes
	Panelist 5 gives an opening statement arguing *for* the motion.	Two minutes
	Panelist 6 gives an opening statement arguing *against* the motion.	Two minutes
Round 2	Panelists respond to two or three questions from the teacher and as many questions from students in the audience as time permits. Audience members raise their hands to ask questions. When the moderator calls on a student, he or she directs the question to a specific panelist, who has thirty seconds to respond. After these thirty seconds are up, the teacher gives each panelist a chance to respond to the same question (panelists may decline to answer questions if they so desire).	Fifteen minutes
Round 3	Each of the panelists makes closing remarks.	One minute each (six minutes total)
Final Voting	Students (excluding the debate panelists) use clickers or pieces of scrap paper to cast their "after" votes about the motion. Students can vote either (1) *for* the motion or (2) *against* the motion; they are no longer permitted to vote *undecided*. Votes submitted on scrap paper must be collected at this time by an audience member and placed into the "after" receptacle.	Thirty seconds

of the panelists, round 2 is for audience questions and debater rebuttals, and round 3 is for closing remarks. After debaters present their closing remarks, the audience will vote for the second time to decide the victor.

Next, display the motion and three voting options (agree, disagree, or undecided) on the chalkboard, whiteboard, or projector. If you are not using clickers, distribute two slips of scrap paper to each student. Give them about thirty seconds to silently read the motion for debate and write *agree, disagree*, or *undecided* on one of the slips of paper. They will save the second slip of paper at their desks to use at the end of the debate. After thirty seconds have passed, collect the votes and place them in a receptacle clearly labeled with the word *before*.

If you are using electronic voting, you have options. You can either use clickers (these typically come with software that can be installed on your computer or interactive whiteboard) or a free electronic polling system, such as Poll Everywhere (www.polleverywhere.com), in which students use their own mobile devices (cell phones, laptops, tablets, and so on) to vote. Figure 10.6 presents a screenshot of the Poll Everywhere interface.

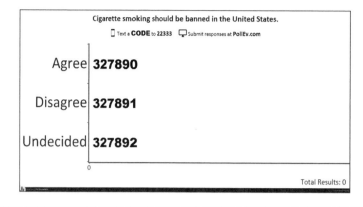

Figure 10.6: Screenshot of the Poll Everywhere interface.

Source: Copyright © 2013 by Poll Everywhere. Reprinted with permission.

Poll Everywhere allows you to enter your own motion and options to create polls in seconds without registering or paying for anything. Type the motion for debate into the Poll Question bar, and write *agree*, *disagree*, and *undecided* for your multiple-choice options. The full-screen feature allows you to fill your web browser with a bar graph to display on your projector or interactive whiteboard. The site recognizes when a student texts in a vote more than once from the same phone number, so you do not have to worry about students virtually stacking the ballot box by sending multiple texts for the same motion.

If you typically do bell work at the beginning of each class (some teachers call this a "do now" or a "warm-up"), you can also have students vote as they enter the classroom to save time and maintain a lively pace—just be sure to establish the procedure in advance so students are aware of your expectations for entering the classroom on game day. Place a tray filled with slips of scrap paper near the entrance of the classroom. As students walk into the classroom, they each pick up two slips of scrap paper. They read the motion for debate, which you will have already displayed somewhere in the classroom. On the first slip of paper, students record their opinion (agree, disagree, or undecided) and place their vote in the receptacle at the front of the room labeled *before*. They save the second slip of scrap paper on their desks to use at the end of the debate. However, be aware that this method can compromise the privacy and objectivity of your students' votes (they could converse with other students about the motion, misunderstand the directions, or refrain from voting without you noticing). If you do not have strict procedures about entering the room and beginning bell work, you may want to wait for the bell to ring before voting. This will give you time to give explicit directions to your students about the procedure for voting.

One of the benefits of clickers or Poll Everywhere is that they allow you to display the results of a poll instantly for your class to see. As students vote, the results will be displayed on the screen in real time in the form of a bar graph. Take advantage of this opportunity to build excitement for your class by showing the results from the first round of polling before the debate begins. Give students about thirty seconds to vote and then close the poll. If you sign up for an account with Poll Everywhere, you can save the poll; if not, you can just keep the window open to save the results of the first round of voting. Just in case, though, you may want to jot down the results of the first round of voting somewhere. Remind students that the results from the first round of voting do not reveal any information about who is winning or losing. To reiterate, it doesn't matter which team garners the *highest* percentage of votes by the end of the match; instead, the winning team is the one that convinces the greatest percentage of voters to change their minds. It will not be clear which team wins until the difference between the first and second round of votes has been calculated.

 While you may prefer to mandate silence during speeches to demonstrate respect, some teachers permit students to use quiet hand gestures while students are speaking, such as snaps or jazz fingers. Let's say, for instance, that a student wants an appropriate way to congratulate a debater on making a good point or an audience member for articulating an excellent question. To avoid loud, distracting noises like hooting, hollering, or applauding, he might snap his fingers. If a student would like to show her agreement with a debater, she might use jazz fingers, outstretching her arms and waggling her fingers at the student who made the point. Be sure to set the tone, establish norms, and practice procedures for these gestures beforehand.

After you have completed the first round of voting, round 1 can begin. Introduce the panelists and remind them that they have exactly two minutes to deliver their opening statements. Use the stopwatch to gauge the time. You may choose to give debaters time signals, such as holding up an index finger for one minute remaining, a hooked index finger for thirty seconds remaining, an index finger pointing to the side for fifteen seconds remaining, and counting down the last five seconds on all five fingers, curling fingers one by one into a balled fist, which indicates that time is up. If debaters have their own stopwatches (on mobile devices or watches, for instance) or if you have extras, you could also permit them to keep track of their own time during their opening statement. If they exceed this time limit, then you, the moderator, will cut them off. Introduce the first panelist arguing *in favor* of the motion. On your cue, that panelist begins her opening statement. After the statement has ended, the audience claps, you introduce the first panelist arguing *against* the motion, and that panelist begins his opening statement. The presentation of opening statements continues in this back-and-forth fashion until every panelist has delivered his or her statement.

During opening statements, audience members and debaters must demonstrate active listening (sitting up in their chairs, making eye contact, and so on). Allow debaters to write notes and compose rebuttals during the speeches of other speakers, so long as they do so silently and without consulting their teammates. Do not permit physical indicators of exasperation or disrespect during speeches (such as eye rolling, loud sighs, head shaking, incredulous facial expressions, and so on). Justify this rule by explaining that body language is still a form of communication, no matter how "silent" it may seem.

After students have completed their opening statements, inform the debaters and the audience that round 1 is over and round 2 is about to begin. Explain that during round 2, panelists respond to questions from the audience and offer quick-draw rebuttals directly to one another. Before you turn the questions over to the student audience, you ask one to three questions first as the moderator. This gives you a chance to do three things: (1) model effective questioning for the audience, (2) briefly summarize the premises established or arguments made by each side, and (3) address ambiguities and contradictions in the arguments as soon as possible.

 If your students are struggling to exhibit respectful decorum during the debate, start providing in-game consequences for disrespectful conduct and rewards for respectful conduct. The easiest and most effective way to do this is to add or detract argument time from the panelists. Do not detract time from the opening statements, as these are direct reflections of your students' hard work during the research and preparation process. Instead, add to or deduct seconds from rebuttals and answers to questions during round 2 or from closing remarks during round 3.

The first reason to ask questions on your own is to model the format of an effective audience question. Questions should be addressed to one specific panelist (for example, "This question is for Tara . . .") or to one specific side ("This question is for the 'against' side. . ."). The questions should be as direct and focused as possible.

A second reason for the moderator to ask a question or two first is to briefly summarize the premises or arguments established in the opening statements. Intelligence Squared moderator John Donvan usually opens his first question in round 2 with a short summary of the arguments, as shown in the following excerpt from the "ban college football" debate:

> They [gesturing to the side in favor of the motion] make two kinds of arguments, one, the medical argument that it abuses the players, hurts them physically, literally is rattling the brains in their heads, and a financial argument that college football twists universities' priorities so that these schools are less in the education business than they are in the football business, that in these—on those campuses, football becomes a distraction. The team arguing against the motion . . . they both played in college, and they are arguing that football is a great unifier for the players and for schools. . . . I want to go to the side arguing against the motion. Your opponents are making a very broad philosophical argument that college football, as it stands now has no place on university campuses because it makes the schools more about football than it does about education, that this actually causes harm. . . . And they broke this down to a very specific question: Why should these coaches be making millions of dollars and millions of dollars more than the president of universities? (Intelligence Squared U.S., 2012, pp. 16–17)

Notice that Donvan gives his brief synopsis of opening statements and ends with a direct question, targeted at a specific side.

The third benefit of the moderator opening round 2 with his or her own question is to clarify any vagueness in the arguments so far. You may try to push panelists to yield certain points to the opposing team, to elucidate their specific position on the issue, or to broach issues that have as yet gone unaddressed. Donvan, for example, asks questions such as this:

> I want to put a question to this side because there's something about your argument that I realize I'm not clear on. Do you believe that athletics have a place, a formal place, in education, period? In the same way, for example, that music, painting, performance may? (Intelligence Squared U.S., 2012, p. 33)

As the moderator, you might also point out loopholes, allowances, and contradictions in the arguments (but give the opposing side a chance to address them first). In the following example, the panelists arguing against a ban on college football concede that the issues their opponents are raising are valid:

> **[Panelist] Jason Whitlock:** The coaches are earning too much. They should share some with the players. They should have less padded practices and less contact—they should walk things back until we figure it out. You don't just jump to banning. . . .
>
> **John Donvan:** You're actually yielding a lot of their points, that there's a real problem there, so you do yield—
>
> **[Panelist] Jason Whitlock:** No one denies there's a problem.

> **[Panelist] Tim Green:** There was a problem back in 1976—
>
> **John Donvan:** So [you do yield that] the head injuries are real and the money problem is real. (Intelligence Squared U.S., 2012, pp. 27–28)

The panelist responding to the question has thirty seconds to respond. Hold the panelists to this thirty-second time limit. Use your stopwatch if necessary. After thirty seconds have passed, offer the other panelists on both sides a chance to respond to the same question. Panelists may decline to answer questions if they wish, but if they choose to answer them, the responses may not exceed thirty seconds.

After you have asked one or two questions to get the ball rolling, turn the questions over to the students in the audience. Audience members must raise their hands to ask questions. When you—the moderator—call on an audience member, that student should also address his or her question to one specific panelist. If you need to clarify a student question, do so at your discretion. The following excerpt from the "ban college football" debate on Intelligence Squared shows the moderator clarifying and reframing a question from an audience member:

> **[Audience Member]:** My question is, it's [the discussion has] been kind of black and white, either ban or not ban. But what—what would you suggest as ways or not suggest as ways to encourage—to—
>
> **John Donvan:** Well, can I twist your question just a tad because—
>
> **[Audience Member]:** Sure.
>
> **John Donvan:** I've been wondering the same thing. If it go—would you be okay with putting it this way? . . . Is there a reformable version of college football that you guys [the against side] would accept? Because they actually are talking about [just making] some changes. (Intelligence Squared U.S., 2012, pp. 40–41)

Of all the rounds in the game, round 2 is the most challenging for the teacher because it can become heated, confrontational, and emotional. Because of this, it is crucial that you reiterate your expectations for communicating responsibly (see page 42) before beginning the round. It is also vital that you be a fair, assertive moderator, because even after giving explicit directions, you will likely still need to engage in some firm moderation during the debate. One of the key roles of the moderator is to control the adherence to the rules and integrity of the debate so that the students do not feel tempted to do so. When student audience members or debaters begin policing other students because you have not, it can spell disaster. Put out the following fires right away to avoid trouble later in the game:

◆ When a panelist dodges a question or refuses to answer it directly, say something like "Let me interrupt you just for a moment, because I'm not sure what you're saying really gets to the core of what the question was asking." Call the person out to prevent him or her from using the question to bring up a different point.

◆ Panelists should be permitted to interact directly with one another during round 2, but if two panelists start talking over one another, address them by name to indicate whose turn it is to speak. For example, say, "It's Carina. Jeremy, we'll come back to you." Then be consistent and follow through. If you tell Jeremy you are going to let him speak when Carina has finished, make sure you do.

◆ If one or two students begin to dominate the conversation, ask them to pause. You might say, "One moment, Melissa. I'd like to hear Hiyab's perspective on this question, actually, because I think it is relevant to the arguments he made in his opening statement." Offer the other panelists a chance to provide their points of view, as well.

◆ Students may try to interrupt one another to contest a fact or dispute a point. Prevent this by simply telling the student to let the other finish speaking ("Dominic, let her finish").

◆ Do not permit audience members to argue with the debaters. They may only ask questions. Audience members may try—consciously or otherwise—to sneak their own arguments and opinions into the debate when they are called on to ask a question. Donvan does a good job of moderating this, as well:

> **[Audience Member]:** If you're going to ban football, then you'd better start banning basketball and all of the other sports because they just have the same problems as football. This country isn't about banning. This is about building and it's—

> **John Donvan:** Can you turn this to a question? [Audience member agrees, but then continues to argue.] Wait, wait, wait, wait, okay, I have to set you down because we've only got four seats up here [for panelists], but thank you. (Intelligence Squared U.S., 2012, pp. 43–45)

When fifteen minutes have elapsed, announce the end of round 2 and the beginning of round 3. Give each panelist about one minute to present closing remarks to the audience. Panelists may choose to prepare closing remarks in advance, but let them know that it may be useful to wait to outline closing remarks until they have heard the arguments from the opposing side. Panelists may jot down notes throughout the debate and use those notes to guide closing remarks. As with opening statements, delivery of closing remarks should alternate between teams. Expectations for closing remarks are the same as for opening statements (see page 201).

After each panelist has given closing remarks, begin the second and final vote to determine the winner. Remind audience members of the motion one more time and explain that their votes should indicate which side they believe has made the best argument. If you are using Poll Everywhere, make sure you set up a second poll in a new tab or window so as not to lose the results from the first poll. Do not include an "undecided" option in the final vote.

The team that has swayed the most audience members between the two votes is the winner. As previously mentioned, the team with the greatest percentage of votes may not actually be the winner of the game. Rather, the winning team is the one that makes the best argument and persuades the highest percentage of voters to change their minds, producing the greatest difference. Figure 10.7 displays a situation in which the team with the highest percentage of votes at the end of the debate is not the winning team.

RESULTS

Before the debate:
For the motion: 20 percent
Against the motion: 50 percent
Undecided: 30 percent

After the debate:
For the motion: 48 percent
Against the motion: 52 percent

Figure 10.7: Sample set of results before and after the debate.

As shown in figure 10.7, the team arguing against the motion had the highest percentage of votes after the debate (52 percent). To determine the winner of Convince the Crowd, subtract the team's percentage before the debate from the team's percentage after the debate. Taking the results displayed in figure 10.7, for example, the team arguing in favor of the motion would subtract 20 percent from 48 percent to get 28 percent. The team arguing against the motion would subtract 50 from 52 to get 2 percent. Therefore, the team arguing in favor of the motion had the greatest change in percentage between the first and second rounds of voting. The percentage of audience members voting in favor of the motion grew from 20 percent to 48 percent (a 28 percent gain), whereas the percentage of audience members voting against the motion rose only from 50 percent to 52 percent (a 2 percent gain). Therefore, the team arguing in favor of the motion won by a landslide (28 percent), despite the fact that most audience members still voted *against* the motion.

When the winner has been determined, congratulate all of the panelists on a spirited debate and give them a round of applause. Encourage opposing panelists to shake hands.

Student Panelist Organizer for Convince the Crowd

Name:	Circle One:	FOR the Motion
		AGAINST the Motion

Motion:	
Teammate Name	**Grounds**

My Grounds	My Backing
	1.
	2.
	3.

Potential Opponent Grounds	Our Rebuttal

Appendix A
Facts and Opinions

Organized by level of difficulty

This appendix can be used for:

◆ I Think, I Like, I Believe

◆ Fishing for Facts

◆ Rapid Fire

The following tables contain lists of facts and opinions to use in elementary classrooms. Middle school teachers may also decide to consult these lists for review with sixth- or seventh-grade students. The statements presented in these lists are generally designed to require little to no background knowledge to distinguish them as facts or opinions.

The facts and opinions are organized by difficulty into three tables: easy, medium, and challenging. Each table contains a set of seventy facts and opinions to use with students. Groupings are based on the complexity of the vocabulary used and the amount of content knowledge a student needs to recognize facts. Use preassessments and your judgment as a teacher to determine which list to use with your students. To illustrate, consider the following fact from the *challenging* list: "The eight planets in the solar system are Mercury, Venus, Earth, Mars, Jupiter, Saturn, Uranus, and Neptune." A first grader may or may not be familiar with the eight planets, but a fifth grader almost certainly will. Similarly, an *easy* fact, such as "One plus one equals two," while appropriate for early elementary students, will not challenge students in upper elementary.

Easy

Facts	Opinions
The sky is blue.	I think homework is boring.
There are books in the library.	My favorite color is blue.
Vegetables are good for you.	Dr. Seuss is the best author ever.

Continued on next page →

Facts	Opinions
Horses have four legs.	Cats are the best kind of pet.
There are seven days in a week.	I love going to the library.
Elephants have trunks.	Carrots are disgusting.
Animals need food and water to survive.	Summer is my favorite time of year.
One plus one equals two.	I like to go fishing.
That T-shirt is pink.	Spicy foods don't taste good.
Fish have scales and gills.	The weather is beautiful today!
Dr. Seuss books usually rhyme.	Math is harder than reading.
Dentists take care of your teeth.	I want to eat pizza tonight.
Most flowers bloom in the spring.	I like green apples better than red apples.
Some playgrounds have big slides.	Selena Gomez is an awesome singer.
When there is sun and rain at the same time, it often makes a rainbow.	I hate it when spiders get inside the house.
It is night when the sun sets.	Paint is more fun than crayons.
Most birds can fly.	Babies are cuter than puppies.
Leaves change colors in the autumn.	Glow-in-the-dark ceiling stars are the best bedroom decoration.
Monday comes before Tuesday in the week.	Watching TV is the best activity.
Some farmers grow pumpkins.	I love playing on the swings at recess.
People use cameras to take pictures.	I do not like seeing the doctor.
Z is the last letter of the English alphabet.	I like Hot Cheetos as a snack.
A soccer ball is round.	I believe recess is the best part of school.
Most turtles have hard shells.	I think everyone should play video games.
A raincoat can help keep you dry in a storm.	I love swimming.
Spiders have eight legs.	I think Jake stole my lunch.
Ice cream melts if you leave it in the sun.	Rats are bad pets.
Butter and cheese are made from milk.	This has been the worst day ever.
Ladybugs are insects.	Yellow is the best color for a car.
Chrysanthemum is a book about a mouse who dislikes her name.	Jumping rope is not fun.
Giraffes have longer necks than zebras do.	Friday is the best day of the week.
Broccoli is a very healthy vegetable.	Macaroni and cheese tastes better than broccoli.
Rhinos are bigger than kittens.	*Chrysanthemum* is my favorite book.
It is not safe to run with scissors.	I wish dragons were real.
Tuesday and Thursday are weekdays.	Balloons are fun to pop!

Medium

Facts	Opinions
A healthy diet includes fruits and vegetables.	Sleeping outside in a sleeping bag is the best part of camping.
Mercury, Venus, and Mars are all planets.	Hot dogs taste better than hamburgers.
George Washington was the first president.	It is okay to lie if you don't want to get into trouble.
Our school has a library.	Students should go to sleep by 8 p.m. every night.
Your body weighs less on the Moon than it does on Earth.	Sometimes it is so hard to be left-handed!
The mailman delivers mail every day except Sunday and holidays.	Nosy neighbors are annoying.
The Earth orbits the Sun.	Popcorn tastes better with lots of butter.
Most people are right-handed.	Lois Lowry is an excellent writer.
Dalmatians have black spots on a white coat.	Field trips are the best part of school.
My teacher makes jokes during class.	My teacher is hilarious.
Koala bears are usually gray.	Science class is very interesting.
People used to read by candlelight before there was electricity.	Panda bear cubs are the cutest baby animal.
Exercise is good for your health.	Mikayla is the best singer in the class.
There is no school on Sundays.	The comics are the best part of reading the newspaper.
People grow plants, flowers, and vegetables in their gardens.	My neighbor's garden is very beautiful.
There are many species of insects on the planet.	Halloween is too scary for small children.
Lizards eat crickets and other bugs.	Egg sandwiches are disgusting.
People have many different hair colors, like brown, blond, red, black, and white.	It feels too hot when the sun is out.
Rabbits are mammals.	We should play more football in gym class.
Children are younger than adults.	It is harder to subtract numbers than to add them.
Rollerblading is one way to exercise.	Playing a sport is the best way to exercise.
Smoking cigarettes can give you lung cancer.	Red is the prettiest color for hair.
There are many different kinds of soda, such as Mountain Dew, Pepsi, and Dr. Pepper.	Mountain Dew is a much better soda than Pepsi or Dr. Pepper.
The dinosaurs were reptiles.	That's not a good TV show.
Some people like vanilla ice cream better than chocolate.	I think George Washington was a great leader.
Jasmine, Belle, and Sleeping Beauty are all Disney princesses.	Basketball is no fun to watch—it is only fun to play.
A triceratops is a dinosaur with three horns on top of its head.	Like most vegetables, green beans do not taste good.
The Nile River in Africa is one of the longest rivers in the world.	Clownfish have gorgeous scales.

Continued on next page →

Facts	Opinions
The Nintendo Wii is newer than the Nintendo 64.	It is sometimes okay for people to litter, even though it is bad for the Earth.
Washington, DC, is the capital of the United States.	Sharks are terrifying creatures.
Beverly Cleary wrote the book *Ramona Quimby, Age 8*.	Hummingbirds are cool animals to see while birdwatching!
Many bats are *nocturnal*, which means they hunt at night.	The inventors of sidewalk chalk should create a kind that does not wash off in the rain.
An orca is a kind of dolphin.	Marshmallows taste better when they have been burnt in a campfire.
Giraffes have long tongues.	The best toppings to put on a pizza are pepperoni and lots of cheese.

Challenging

Facts	Opinions
There are many different whale species, including blue whales, humpbacks, belugas, and narwhals.	Flying in an airplane is way too scary to do all on your own.
J. K. Rowling wrote the best-selling *Harry Potter* series.	J. K. Rowling should have written more *Harry Potter* books!
Barack Obama has made many speeches to the nation during his time as president.	Stores should be closed on Sundays.
Some frogs are poisonous.	Laser tag is the best activity to do for your birthday!
The Green Bay Packers won the Super Bowl for the fourth time in 2010.	The Green Bay Packers are the best team in the NFL.
Some people do not like to drink coffee.	The spelling test was easy.
The Declaration of Independence was signed in 1776.	Everyone should read the news every day.
Blue whales use baleen to filter water and catch krill to eat.	The *Hunger Games* movie was not as good as the book.
Sometimes the grocery store gives free samples.	Everyone should learn how to swim.
You get a point for scoring a goal in soccer.	Jaya has the best shot on the basketball team.
December is spelled D-E-C-E-M-B-E-R.	Learning to type is the best way to learn to write.
LEGO sets are popular toys at Christmas.	Thanksgiving is not complete without pumpkin pie.
The Empire State Building is in New York City.	There are beautiful sunsets over the lake.
Sarah, Plain and Tall was written by Patricia MacLachlan.	Golf is a boring game.
If you drop an egg on the floor, it will probably break.	All third graders should read *Sarah, Plain and Tall*.
The capital of Colorado is Denver.	The peacock is the most elegant kind of bird.

Facts	Opinions
There is a big Lantern Festival during the Chinese New Year.	Students should be allowed to use calculators on math tests.
Reading the news is one way to learn about what is going on in the world.	I think there is too much pollution in big cities.
Paris is the capital city of France.	Middle school students are too old for trick-or-treating!
Hanukkah is a Jewish holiday.	Paris is the best city to visit in France.
There are five Great Lakes: Superior, Michigan, Huron, Erie, and Ontario.	Teachers have the easiest jobs.
Chocolate chip cookies were invented in Massachusetts.	If you care about this country, you should vote.
Owls cannot digest their prey whole, so they cough up pellets made of fur, feather, and bones.	Michael Jordan is the best basketball player in history.
Thailand sends more rice to other countries than any other country in the world.	Eating meat is cruel and unkind.
Jackie Robinson was the first African American to play baseball in the major leagues.	Recycling aluminum cans, plastic bottles, and glass containers is easy and smart.
The Taj Mahal, a gigantic white tomb in India, took more than twenty years to build.	Pokémon is a great video game, but the TV show is awful.
The eight planets in the solar system are Mercury, Venus, Earth, Mars, Jupiter, Saturn, Uranus, and Neptune.	Astronauts are brave for going up into space to explore.
People in Japan eat mostly rice, noodles, and fish, along with dishes like miso soup.	The most relaxing way to read a book is inside of a fort made of blankets and chairs.
Eating too much red meat is unhealthy and can lead to disease.	Abraham Lincoln was the greatest president the United States has ever had.
Americans declared independence from England on July 4, 1776.	Raking leaves into a pile and jumping in is one of the best things to do during autumn.
All of the dinosaurs are extinct, but scientists are not 100 percent sure why.	Even though they cannot fly, penguins are the cutest birds on the planet.
In order to grow, flowers need water, oxygen, sunlight, and a pollinator, such as a bumblebee.	The most useful superpower would be the ability to fly.
The official language of Egypt is Arabic.	Skateboarding is harder than jumping rope.
Orcas are sometimes called killer whales.	Kids should be allowed to stay up until midnight on December 31 to celebrate New Year's Eve.
Native American artists in the Hopi tribe carve and paint *kachina* dolls to represent spirits.	It is unfair that kids cannot watch any movie or television show they want.

Appendix B
Claims

Organized by grade level

This appendix can be used for:

◆ Argument Relay

◆ Convince the Crowd

The following tables contain lists of claims to use in the classroom. While the claims are meant to be used with the aforementioned games, they also make excellent topics for class discussion, prompts for essay-writing exercises, or subjects for research reports. Furthermore, the claims in each list pertain to an array of different content areas (including language arts, science, social studies, mathematics, foreign language studies, and the fine arts), which makes teaching argumentation relevant and achievable in a variety of classrooms.

The claims are organized by grade level, with one list each for elementary, middle, and high school students. Each of the three lists contains one hundred claims to use with students in that grade range; there are three hundred unique claims in total. Claims have been classified into grade levels based on subject matter, requisite background knowledge, and level of external research required, as well as by vocabulary and complexity of the claim itself. As with the facts and opinions listed in appendix A (page 209), teachers should feel free to use the claims that are most appropriate for their specific groups of students, even if we have placed them at a different level. For example, if a teacher gives context, leads a class discussion, and rewords it, a high school claim can become a middle school claim, a middle school claim can become an elementary claim, and so on. Elementary and middle school claims can also be made more complex to be used at the high school level. For example, the simple elementary school claim "All kids should learn karate" might be adapted for high school students as "Women in college should be required to take self-defense courses," which encompasses a wider range of issues at a much higher level of complexity.

Elementary

The best movie ever is _____.	Movies are better in 3-D.
The best television show ever is _____.	It's not about winning; it's how you play the game.
The best song ever is _____.	Kids should not have to do chores at home.
The best book ever is _____.	It is better to ride your bike than to ride in a car.
If you find money at school, you should turn it in to a teacher.	Even kids can help to protect the environment and save the planet.
TV is not good for you.	Hats should not be allowed in school.
Our school should get rid of its playground to keep kids from getting hurt.	iPads are better than books.
If you see teasing or bullying at school, you should tell a teacher.	Kids deserve longer recesses.
It is wrong to keep animals in zoos.	Robots cannot replace humans.
Soccer is the best sport.	Humans should not dump trash into outer space.
It is not okay to keep wild animals as pets.	All-girl or all-boy classrooms are better for kids than mixed classrooms.
It's bad when an animal goes extinct.	Kids should be paid for going to school.
Video games are better than board games.	Students should not have to wear uniforms to school.
Kids need more holidays from school.	It is better for a president to be really smart but also mean than less smart but also kind.
Inside beauty is better than outside beauty.	Countries should not be ruled by kings and queens.
Dogs make better pets than cats.	All students should have to take Spanish class.
Kids should be allowed to vote for president.	Homework should be banned.
All kids should play sports.	Schools should ban peanut butter because some kids have allergies.
It is never okay to lie.	Snowball fights should be banned at recess.
We should not have school on Saturdays.	Kickball is better than dodgeball.
Movies are better than books.	Fifth grade should be a part of middle school.
Playing inside is better than playing outside.	Fireworks and sparklers are safe for kids.
If you see someone cheating, you should tell a teacher.	It is important to learn to play an instrument (like the piano, drums, or the flute).
All kids should learn karate.	Kids should have more field trips at school.
Reading is important.	It is more important to be kind than to be popular.
Kids should get to choose their own bedtime.	Being a kid is more fun than being an adult.
Schools should offer fast food (like nachos or hamburgers) in lunchrooms.	Hunting should be banned.
Girls should be allowed to play football with boys.	Dodgeball and tackle football should never be played in gym class.

Kids should be allowed to use electronics (like cell phones, iPods, and tablets) during recess.	Kids should have to get good grades in order to play sports.
Earning an allowance is good for kids.	Violence is never okay.
Books are better than television.	Kids should get in trouble if they waste food at lunch.
Peer pressure is sometimes good for you.	Fur coats should be banned.
It is more important to be smart than it is to be good-looking.	Bullies should be kicked out of school.
Elementary schools should have their own sports teams (like middle and high schools).	Kids should always get to choose what to eat for dinner.
Living in the country is better than living in the big city.	Pets should be allowed at school.
It is important to learn history.	Kids under age thirteen should be allowed to watch PG-13 movies.
Our school should get rid of _____ [choose a sport or club] to save money.	Teachers should not use candy to reward students.
Our school should add _____ [choose a sport or club].	Parents should not take their kids out of school to travel or go on vacation.
Kids should not be required to go to school—it should be their choice.	Kids who are ten or older should be allowed to stay home by themselves.
All schools should teach the arts (like music, drawing, and theater) to students.	Professional athletes are paid too much money.
Rollerblading and skateboarding should not be allowed on the sidewalk.	It should be against the law to not recycle.
Students should be allowed to eat during class.	Summer is the best season of the whole year.
Summer vacation should be shorter.	Gym class is more exciting than art class.
All kids in kindergarten through high school should have to go to gym class.	Kids should not have to learn cursive in school.
All students should learn how to type on a keyboard before middle school.	Being kind is more important than making a lot of money.
Our city is a great place to live in.	Video games make you smarter.
Kids should be allowed to sell things they make (like cookies or yarn bracelets) to other kids at recess.	Kids should be allowed to spend as much time as they want with their friends.
Kids should be allowed to bring games and toys to school to play at recess.	Walt Disney was the most creative person who has ever lived.
Cheerleading is a sport.	Students should not be allowed to drink soft drinks at school.
People should not keep animals in cages.	The Olympics are too expensive.
Students should be allowed to chew gum in school.	There should be more wild animal sanctuaries in the world.
It is important for kids to travel and learn about other cultures.	The United States should try to send more astronauts to the Moon.
Kids should only be allowed to watch television a few times per week.	Computers will replace teachers someday.

Continued on next page →

Schools should serve breakfast.	Books are better than television.
It is wrong to eat meat.	It is better to be smart than beautiful.
Kids should vote on the foods the cafeteria offers for lunch.	Flying on airplanes should be less expensive.
There should be at least one school dance every year.	Kids should have a say in making the school rules.
Parents should pay their kids to behave.	Kids shouldn't have boyfriends or girlfriends until they are in middle school.

Middle School

Parents should be punished if their kids break the law.	Seat belts should be mandatory by law.
The death penalty is a necessary evil and should not be banned.	Women should not be allowed to fight in the military.
Skateboarding should be allowed on public streets.	School should begin later in the morning and end around dinnertime.
Students should not be forced to stand during the Pledge of Allegiance.	Cigarette smoking should be banned in the United States.
Schools should be single gendered.	It should be illegal to ride a bike without a helmet.
Scientists should not test medicines and vaccines on animals.	Teachers and students should be allowed to pray in school.
Students should be allowed to wear headphones during standardized tests.	The United States should lower the voting age to fourteen.
Parents should not control what their kids see on TV and the Internet.	Kids should not be allowed to date before they get to high school.
Violence on television is bad for kids.	The government should not put a high tax on soda.
Year-round school would not help kids learn more.	People should not care about what celebrities do in their private lives.
Schools should replace textbooks with iPads.	The government should give money to religious charities.
The driving age should be lowered to fourteen.	Companies should be allowed to put advertisements on school lockers and buses.
Homeschooling is better for kids than public schooling.	Sending emails and text messages is not harmful to students' learning.
Schools should not ban cell phones.	Newspapers and magazines should stop focusing on celebrity gossip.
Students should have to take cooking classes in school.	U.S. citizens should be required to serve in the military when they reach a certain age.
The FIFA World Cup is a waste of money.	The United States should change its national anthem to a dance hit.
_____ [athlete] is the best player in _____ [sport].	Field trips should always be educational in some way.
Standardized tests are not good for students.	War is sometimes necessary.

Teachers and principals should be allowed to censor what students write in a school newspaper.	Principals have the right to do random locker searches in their schools.
Sea animal amusement parks like SeaWorld are cruel and should be shut down.	Hollywood movies have a trend of being sexist.
Middle school should be combined with high school.	The Internet builds relationships more than it harms them.
The government should allow students to enter the "real world" of work after graduating from middle school.	Immortality (living forever) would be a curse, not a blessing.
Class sizes are too big.	The United States should stop spending money on space exploration.
All food served in the cafeteria should be healthier.	Metal detectors are necessary in some schools to protect the students.
Rap music does not deserve a bad reputation.	School cafeterias should be required to provide vegan or vegetarian lunch options.
Professional athletes are not always good role models.	Schools must take steps to stop bullying.
Facebook should not allow users under the age of eighteen.	Single-gender classrooms are better for middle school students than co-gender classrooms.
The government should ban animal dissection in public schools.	Violent video games do not lead to violent behavior.
The public's right to know is more important than the privacy of celebrities, politicians, and athletes.	People younger than eighteen should not be allowed to get piercings and tattoos.
Passing periods between classes should be longer.	Sports, arts, and after-school clubs are just as important for kids as classes in school.
Companies should not be allowed to sell toy weapons to children.	Schools should ban makeup.
Students should be allowed to grade their teachers.	Schools should get rid of letter grades.
The United States should not ban any guns, including assault weapons, handguns, and hunting rifles.	The United States should amend the Constitution to ban flag burning.
The United States should have a draft for serving in the military.	The United States should switch to the metric system.
Students who participate in extracurricular activities (such as sports, clubs, and so on) should be randomly drug tested.	The United States should get rid of the penny.
Our state should raise the minimum wage.	Plastic bags in grocery stores should be banned.
The United States should pay reparations (give money, goods, or land) to people whose ancestors were slaves.	Prisoners should be allowed to vote.
Our state should allow undocumented immigrants to get driver's licenses.	Video games should be considered works of art, just like literature, music, painting, dance, photography, and film.
The United States should require high school students to pass a national exit exam before they can graduate.	Scientists should rule the world.

Continued on next page →

Violent sports like mixed martial arts (MMA) and boxing should be banned.	Social media websites like Facebook should stop people from posting hate speech.
People under the age of eighteen should be charged as adults in murder cases.	It should be illegal to text while driving.
Middle school students deserve to have their own lockers.	Volunteer work should be a school requirement.
Americans who were born outside the United States and then became citizens should be allowed to run for president.	Humans have become too dependent on computers and technology.
Gambling should be illegal everywhere in the United States.	Citizens should be required by law to vote.
The United States should ban music, movies, or video games that contain violence against women.	Professional athletes who use performance-enhancing drugs should be left out of the Hall of Fame.
Downloading music from the Internet is just the same as stealing it.	Human cloning is wrong.
Middle schools should allow restaurants or vendors (such as McDonald's or Pepsi-Cola) to set up in schools and sell lunch to students.	Middle schools should spend more time on reading and math and cut back on electives (such as art, technology, and music classes).
Middle school students should not be allowed at shopping malls or movie theaters without an adult.	Middle school students should be able to choose what subjects they study in school.
People should lose their jobs if their work or business harms the environment.	Beauty pageants are exploitative.
Reading fiction is just as important as reading informational texts.	Google is making people dumber.

High School

All high school students should be required to read Shakespeare.	Antibiotics should not be given to livestock.
Professional and college sports teams should eliminate American Indian references from their mascots.	Invasive species should be completely eradicated.
France should allow Muslim women to wear a *niqab* (a full-face veil) in public places.	People who live in apartment buildings should not be allowed to have large dogs.
Cities with too much traffic should ban the use of personal cars.	Professional auto racers should be required to use biofuel (which usually comes from plants) instead of gasoline.
Addictive drugs should be illegal.	Workplaces should allow new fathers to take paid paternity leave.
Teenagers should not be allowed to use tanning salons.	The government should raise taxes on junk food to promote healthy eating.
Every state should pass the DREAM Act, which allows certain undocumented immigrants to live in the United States (kids who are brought to the United States by their parents, teens who graduate from U.S. high schools, or people who serve in the military).	Social media companies should not regulate free speech, even if users post hateful or threatening messages.

Racial profiling is sometimes justified in the interest of national security.	Rehabilitation should be the primary objective of the prison system.
The U.S. military should be allowed to recruit at high schools.	People should not consider what politicians do in their private lives when deciding whether to vote for them.
The U.S. government should honor human rights activist Harvey Milk with a national holiday.	The Internet is hindering students from learning to read and write.
Hollywood movie studios should stop using the Motion Picture Association of America's (MPAA) rating system for movies (such as G, PG, PG-13, R, and NC-17).	Performance-enhancing drug use should be allowed in sports.
Reality shows are the worst form of television.	Whale hunting (whaling) should be banned internationally.
Fashion is valuable.	The United States should give undocumented immigrants legal status.
Censorship is sometimes justified.	Affirmative action for jobs, college applications, and so on should be abolished.
Whistle-blowing organizations like WikiLeaks are good for society.	Restricting individual freedoms and privacy is a necessary price for national security.
U.S. high schools should not block the video-sharing website YouTube on school computers.	People are essentially good.
Animal cloning is not a good idea.	Income taxes should be higher for people who earn more money instead of equal for all.
All high school students should be required to take courses in the arts (such as music, theater, film, and so on).	It is unfair to make elderly people retake their driver's tests.
Detention facilities like Guantánamo Bay and Abu Ghraib are inhumane and should be closed.	The driving age should be raised to age eighteen.
Colleges and universities should get rid of early-admission programs for prospective students.	Taking a year off before college is a good idea.
Assault weapons like AK-47s should be banned in the United States.	Colleges rely too much on standardized test scores (like the ACT and SAT).
The NBA should drop its minimum-age requirement for players and allow high school athletes to be included in the draft.	Standardized test scores are not always a good indication of how well a school is doing.
The U.S. government should reverse its amendment to Title IX and ban single-sex education (all boys or all girls).	New parents should be required by law to take a course on parenting.
The United States should not make English its official language.	Drunk drivers should be imprisoned on the first offense.
College athletes should be paid.	Financial incentives should be offered to high school students who perform well on standardized tests.
Financial aid for education should be based solely on merit.	Security cameras violate the privacy rights of U.S. citizens.
The U.S. government should prioritize global warming.	Public schools should offer comprehensive sex education to prevent teen pregnancy and disease.

Continued on next page →

Fast food and soft drink companies should not be allowed to sponsor the Olympics.	The United States should do more to control the cost of college.
Government and military personnel deserve the right to a labor strike.	The United States should send a manned spacecraft to Mars.
College athletes should be exempt from regular class attendance policies.	Genetically modified crops should never be grown or sold.
Homeschooled students should be allowed to participate in public school activities.	Scientists should be worried about the shortage of honeybees.
Torture is sometimes necessary.	Dolphin captivity is never acceptable.
The U.S. election process is unfair.	Feminism is sexist toward men.
Hate speech should not be protected under the First Amendment.	The United States should invest in geothermal energy.
Government-mandated curfews help keep teenagers safe and out of trouble.	The United States needs more national parks and wildlife sanctuaries.
Americans should not be allowed to adopt non-American infants and children.	Corporations should be allowed to patent genes.
All forms of government welfare should be abolished.	U.S. public schools must include global climate change in the curriculum.
Students should have to declare majors in high school.	Science can explain romantic love.
Religion leads to war.	The United States should drill for oil in Alaska.
Only certain citizens should be allowed to carry concealed weapons.	Physician-assisted suicide (euthanasia) is not ethical for doctors to perform.
The pharmaceutical industry is corrupt.	U.S. citizens should be required to provide the government with DNA samples.
The U.S. government has too much power during wartime.	It is worth the environmental drawbacks of fracking to obtain the benefits of shale gas.
Science in the United States is going downhill.	Scientists have a responsibility to be activists.
The United States should adopt voter ID cards to prevent voter fraud.	The Internet is good for a democracy.
Scientists should not pursue immortality.	Social inequality leads to more crime.
The United States should ban genetic engineering of infants.	The United States should elect presidents using popular vote only.
Capitalism is better than socialism.	Vaccination should be mandatory for all U.S. citizens.
Cosmetic surgery should be banned in the United States.	Marriage is an outdated, unnecessary institution.
Gay and lesbian couples should be able to adopt children.	Prostitution is wrong and should never be legal in any circumstance.
Corporal (physical) punishment should be allowed in schools.	Print newspapers are obsolete.

References and Resources

Academy of Nutrition and Dietetics. (2013). *Eating right during pregnancy.* Accessed at www.eatright.org/Public/content .aspx?id=6808 on March 28, 2014.

ACT. (2009). *ACT national curriculum survey 2009.* Iowa City, IA: Author.

Adams, R. (2013, January 28). It takes planning, caution to avoid being "it." *The Wall Street Journal.* Accessed at http:// online.wsj.com/article/SB10001424127887323375204578269991660836834.html on July 15, 2013.

Alexander, K. L., Entwisle, D. R., & Olson, L. S. (2007). Lasting consequences of the summer learning gap. *American Sociological Review, 72*(4), 167–180.

Allied Quotes. (2007). *How the effects of smoking are driving up costs.* Accessed at www.alliedquotes.com/Resources /Health-Insurance-Rates.html on December 20, 2013.

American Cancer Society. (2013). *Cancer facts & figures 2013.* Atlanta, GA: Author. Accessed at www.cancer.org/acs /groups/content/@epidemiologysurveilance/documents/document/acspc-036845.pdf on July 12, 2013.

American Civil Liberties Union. (n.d.). *Close Guantánamo.* Accessed at www.aclu.org/close-guantanamo on December 20, 2013.

American Civil Liberties Union. (2013). *Teach kids, not stereotypes.* Accessed at www.aclu.org/womens-rights/teach-kids -not-stereotypes on December 20, 2013.

American Dental Association. (2013). *Chewing gum.* Accessed at www.ada.org/1315.aspx on November 7, 2013.

American Psychological Association. (2009). *Stress in America.* Accessed at www.apa.org/news/press/releases/stress/2009 /stress-exec-summary.pdf on July 24, 2013.

Anair, D., & Mahmassani, A. (2012). *State of charge: Electric vehicles' global warming emissions and fuel-cost savings across the United States.* Cambridge, MA: Union of Concerned Scientists. Accessed at www.ucsusa.org/assets/documents /clean_vehicles/electric-car-global-warming-emissions-exec-summary.pdf on December 4, 2013.

Anatomy of a stump speech. (2012, January 3). *The New York Times.* Accessed at www.nytimes.com/interactive/2012/01/03 /us/politics/gop-stump-speeches.html#romney on December 12, 2013.

Anderson, A. A., Brossard, D., Scheufele, D. A., Xenos, M. A., & Ladwig, P. (2013). The "nasty effect": Online incivility and risk perceptions of emerging technologies. *Journal of Computer-Mediated Communication.* Accessed at http:// onlinelibrary.wiley.com/doi/10.1111/jcc4.12009/pdf on October 18, 2013.

Arum, R., & Roksa, J. (2011). *Academically adrift: Limited learning on college campuses.* Chicago: University of Chicago Press.

Asch, S. E. (1956). Studies of independence and conformity: A minority of one against a unanimous majority. *Psychological Monographs: General and Applied, 70*(9), 1–70.

Atwood, V. A., & Wilen, W. W. (1991). Wait time and effective social studies instruction: What can research in science education tell us? *Social Education, 55*(3), 179–181.

Babcock, P. S., & Marks, M. (2011). The falling time cost of college: Evidence from half a century of time use data. *The Review of Economics and Statistics, 93*(2), 468–478.

Beinecke, F., & Gerard, J. M. (2010, September). Should the U.S. halt offshore drilling? *The New York Times Upfront, 143.* Accessed at http://teacher.scholastic.com/scholasticnews/indepth/upfront/debate/index.asp?article=d090610 on July 12, 2013.

Berkowitz, S., & Upton, J. (2011). Athletic departments see surge financially in down economy. *USA Today.* Accessed at http://usatoday30.usatoday.com/sports/college/2011-06-15-athletic-departments-increase-money_n.htm on December 20, 2013.

Bishop, B. (2008). *The big sort: Why the clustering of like-minded America is tearing us apart.* New York: Houghton Mifflin.

Bon Jovi, J. (2010, December 9). *CNN Larry King Live: Interview with Jon Bon Jovi* [Transcript]. Accessed at http://transcripts.cnn.com/TRANSCRIPTS/1012/09/lkl.01.html on July 25, 2013.

Brett, J. (1989). *The mitten.* New York: Putnam.

Brunsma, D. (2004). *The school uniform movement and what it tells us about American education: A symbolic crusade.* Lanham, MD: Rowman & Littlefield.

Cahill, L., Gorski, L., & Le, K. (2003). Enhanced human memory consolidation with post-learning stress: Interactions with the degree of arousal at encoding. *Learning and Memory, 10*(4), 270–274.

Cameron, V. (2003). *Clue mysteries: 15 whodunits to solve in minutes.* Philadelphia: Running Press.

Campbell, D. E. (2008). Voice in the classroom: How an open classroom climate fosters political engagement among adolescents. *Political Behavior, 30,* 427–454.

Carleton, L., & Marzano, R. J. (2010). *Vocabulary games for the classroom.* Bloomington, IN: Marzano Research.

Centers for Disease Control and Prevention. (2005, June 30). Smoking deaths cost nation $92 billion in lost productivity annually [Press release]. Accessed at www.cdc.gov/media/pressrel/r050630.htm on December 20, 2013.

Centers for Disease Control and Prevention. (2006). *Heat-related deaths—United States, 1999–2003.* Accessed at www.cdc.gov/mmwr/preview/mmwrhtml/mm5529a2.htm on December 20, 2013.

Centers for Disease Control and Prevention. (2011, May). Asthma in the US: Growing every year. *CDC Vital Signs.* Accessed at www.cdc.gov/vitalsigns/pdf/2011-05-vitalsigns.pdf on December 20, 2013.

Centers for Disease Control and Prevention. (2012). *Preventing tobacco use among youth and young adults* (A report of the Surgeon General). Accessed at www.cdc.gov/tobacco/data_statistics/sgr/2012/consumer_booklet/pdfs/consumer.pdf on December 20, 2013.

Chappell, B. (2013, May 14). Experts say prize-winning photo of Gaza funeral is authentic. *NPR News.* Accessed at www.npr.org/blogs/thetwo-way/2013/05/14/183983184/photographer-defends-prize-winning-photo-of-gaza-funeral on July 24, 2013.

Christina H. (2012, June 26). 8 stupid arguments that Internet debates always devolve into [Web log post]. Accessed at www.cracked.com/blog/8-stupid-arguments-that-internet-debates-always-devolve-into/ on March 28, 2014.

CMT Insider Interview: Dolly Parton. (2009, March 20). Accessed at www.cmt.com/news/country-music/1607426 /cmt-insider-interview-dolly-parton.jhtml on July 25, 2013.

CNN. (2012, September 28). *Best moments from presidential debates* [Video file]. Accessed at www.youtube.com /watch?v=4Y8SZDH3B_4 on March 6, 2014.

Congressional Budget Office. (2010, December 2). *S. 3392: Development, relief, and education for Alien Minors act of 2010.* Accessed at www.cbo.gov/sites/default/files/cbofiles/ftpdocs/119xx/doc11991/s3992.pdf on December 20, 2013.

Conrad, H. (1995). *Almost perfect crimes: Mini-mysteries for you to solve.* New York: Sterling.

Conrad, H. (2005). *Historical whodunits.* New York: Sterling.

Conrad, H. (2007). *Kids' whodunits: Catch the clues!* New York: Sterling.

Conrad, H. (2009). *Kids' whodunits 2: Crack the cases!* New York: Sterling.

Conrad, H., & Peterson, B. (1997). *Solve-it-yourself mysteries.* New York: Sterling.

Cooper, H., Valentine, J. C., Charlton, K., & Melson, A. (2003). The effects of modified school calendars on student achievement and on school and community attitudes. *Review of Educational Research, 73*(1), 1–52.

Copen, C. E., Daniels, K., Vespa, J., & Mosher, W. D. (2012, March 22). *First marriage in the United States: Data from the 2006–2010 National Survey of Family Growth* (Report No. 49). Accessed at www.cdc.gov/nchs/data/nhsr /nhsr049.pdf on December 20, 2013.

Correa, T., & Jeong, S. H. (2010). Race and online content creation: Why minorities are actively participating in the Web. *Information, Communication and Society, 14*(5), 638–659.

Cowan, P., & Maitles, H. (2012). Preface and framework. In P. Cowan & H. Maitles (Eds.), *Teaching controversial issues in the classroom: Key issues and debates* (pp. 1–9). New York: Continuum International.

Cracked.com. (2010). *Internet argument techniques.* Accessed at www.cracked.com/funny-3809-internet-argument -techniques/ on March 28, 2014.

Cummings, M. (2012). *Effective debriefing tools and techniques: Learn to play to learn.* Accessed at http://campkesem .org/wp-content/uploads/2012/09/Effective-Debriefing.pdf on September 17, 2013.

DaimlerChrysler. (2007). *360 degrees: FACTS of sustainability 2007.* Accessed at http://sustainability.daimler.com /daimler/annual/2013/nb/English/pdf/1688161_daimler_sust_2007_reports_sustainabilityreport2007facts_en.pdf on July 15, 2013.

Daneshvary, N., & Clauretie, T. M. (2001). Efficiency and costs in education: Year-round versus traditional schedules. *Economics of Education Review, 20,* 279–287.

Davies, A. (2013, March 20). Elon Musk explains why a big argument against electric cars is totally wrong. *Business Insider.* Accessed at www.businessinsider.com/elon-musks-ted-talk-on-tesla-spacex-and-solarcity-2013-3 on December 4, 2013.

Death Penalty Information Center. (2014). *Innocence and the death penalty.* Accessed at www.deathpenaltyinfo.org /innocence-and-death-penalty on March 28, 2014.

Del Vecho, P., Lasseter, J. (Producers), Buck, C., & Lee, J. (Directors). (2013). *Frozen* [Motion picture]. United States: Walt Disney Studios.

de Maupassant, G. (1992). The necklace. In *The necklace and other short stories* (pp. 31–37). New York: Dover Thrift Editions. (Original work published 1885)

DeNavas-Walt, C., Proctor, B. D., & Smith, J. C. (2012). *Income, poverty, and health insurance coverage in the United States: 2011* (Report No. P60–243). Accessed at www.census.gov/prod/2012pubs/p60-243.pdf on July 5, 2013.

Dickinson, E. (1960). *The complete poems of Emily Dickinson*. Boston: Little, Brown. (Original work published 1890)

Dossett, D., & Munoz, M. (2000). *Year-round education in a reform environment: The impact on student achievement and cost-effectiveness analysis*. Louisville, KY: University of Louisville.

Dr. Seuss. (1985). *The cat in the hat*. New York: Random House. (Original work published 1957)

Duggan, M., & Smith, A. (2013). *6% of online adults are Reddit users*. Washington, DC: Pew Research Center. Accessed at http://pewinternet.org/Reports/2013/reddit.aspx on July 11, 2013.

Ebert, R. (1998). *Citizen Kane* [Film review]. Accessed at www.rogerebert.com/reviews/great-movie-citizen-kane-1941 on July 12, 2013.

Employers charging smokers extra for health insurance. (2006). *USA Today*. Accessed at http://usatoday30.usatoday .com/money/workplace/2006-02-16-smokers-cost-more_x.htm on December 20, 2013.

Entertainment Software Association. (2013a). *2013 sales, demographic and usage data: Essential facts about the computer and video game industry*. Accessed at www.theesa.com/facts/pdfs/ESA_EF_2013.pdf on November 8, 2013.

Entertainment Software Association. (2013b). *Games & violence*. Accessed at www.theesa.com/facts/violence.asp on December 20, 2013.

Epstein, J. A., & Harackiewicz, J. (1992). Winning is not enough: The effects of competition and achievement orientation on intrinsic interest. *Personality and Social Psychology Bulletin, 18*(2), 128–138.

Evans, N. A., Farkas, E., Gilpin, E., Berry, C., & Pierce, J. P. (1995). Influence of tobacco marketing and exposure to smokers on adolescent susceptibility to smoking. *Journal of the National Cancer Institute, 87*, 1538–1545.

Fairclough, P. (2009). *Soccer strategies: Attacking, defending, goalkeeping*. Buffalo, NY: Firefly Books.

Federal Bureau of Investigation. (2012). *Crime in the United States, 2011: Violent crime* (Uniform Crime Report). Accessed at www.fbi.gov/about-us/cjis/ucr/crime-in-the-u.s/2011/crime-in-the-u.s.-2011/violent-crime/violentcrimemain _final.pdf on July 24, 2013.

Feltz, D. L., & Weiss, M. R. (1984). The impact of girls' interscholastic sport participation on academic orientation. *Research Quarterly for Exercise and Sport, 55*(4), 332–339.

Fischbeck, P. S., Gengler, B., Gerard, D., & Weinberg, R. S. (2007). An interactive tool to compare and communicate traffic safety risks: TrafficSTATS. *Journal of the Transportation Research Forum, 46*(3), 87–102. Accessed at http:// journals.oregondigital.org/trforum/article/view/671/576 on July 12, 2013.

Fischer, G. H. (1968). *Ambiguous > animals > swan and squirrel*. Accessed at www.planetperplex.com/en/item/swan -and-squirrel/ on December 18, 2013.

Fisher, D., Frey, N., & Rothenberg, C. (2008). *Content-area conversations: How to plan discussion-based lessons for diverse language learners*. Alexandria, VA: Association for Supervision and Curriculum Development.

Fitzsimmons, W. (2007, November). Should colleges end early admissions? *The New York Times Upfront, 143*. Accessed at http://teacher.scholastic.com/scholasticnews/indepth/upfront/debate/index.asp?article=d111907 on July 12, 2013.

Follman, M., Aronsen, G., & Pan, D. (2012, July). A guide to mass shootings in America. *Mother Jones*. Accessed at www.motherjones.com/politics/2012/07/mass-shootings-map on July 12, 2013.

Gales, N., Leaper, R., & Papastavrou, V. (2008). Is Japan's whaling humane? *Marine Policy, 32*(3), 408–412.

Gallup. (2010). U.S. drinking rate edges up slightly to 25-year high. *Gallup*. Accessed at www.gallup.com/poll/141656 /Drinking-Rate-Edges-Slightly-Year-High.aspx on March 27, 2014.

Garber, A. K., & Lustig, R. H. (2011). Is fast food addictive? *Current Drug Abuse Reviews, 4*(3), 146–162.

Gil de Zúñiga, H., & Valenzuela, S. (2011). The mediating path to a stronger citizenship: Online and offline networks, weak ties, and civic engagement. *Communication Research, 38*, 397–421.

Gillen-O'Neel, C., Huynh, V. W., & Fuligni, A. J. (2013). To study or to sleep? The academic costs of extra studying at the expense of sleep. *Child Development, 84*(1), 133–142.

Good, T. L., & Brophy, J. E. (2003). *Looking in classrooms* (9th ed.). Boston: Allyn & Bacon.

Good, T. L., & Findley, M. J. (1985). Sex role expectations and achievement. In J. B. Dusek (Ed.), *Teacher expectancies* (pp. 271–294). Hillsdale, NJ: Erlbaum.

Graff, G. (2004). *Clueless in academe: How schooling obscures the life of the mind.* New Haven, CT: Yale University Press.

Greene, J. P., Kisida, B., & Bowen, D. H. (2014). The educational value of field trips: Taking students to an art museum improves critical thinking skills, and more. *Education Next, 14*(1). Accessed at http://educationnext.org/the-educational -value-of-field-trips/ on November 7, 2013.

Grøntved, A., & Hu, F. B. (2011). Television viewing and risk of type 2 diabetes, cardiovascular disease, and all-cause mortality: A meta-analysis. *Journal of the American Medical Association, 305*(23), 2448–2455.

Guitar Center. (2001). *Smashing basses with Mike Dirnt of Green Day.* Accessed at http://gc.guitarcenter.com/interview /greenday/ on July 24, 2013.

Hahn, C. L. (1991). Controversial issues in social studies. In J. Shaver (Ed.), *Handbook of research on social studies teaching and learning* (pp. 470–480). New York: Macmillan.

Hahn, C. L. (1998). *Becoming political: Comparative perspectives on citizenship education.* Albany: State University of New York Press.

Halpern, D. F., Eliot, L., Bigler, R. S., Fabes, R. A., Hanish, L. D., Hyde, J., et al. (2011). The pseudoscience of single-sex schooling. *Science, 333*(6050), 1706–1707. Accessed at www.educ.ethz.ch/halpern-09-23-11_1_.pdf on November 8, 2013.

Haystead, M. W., & Marzano, R. J. (2009). *Meta-analytic synthesis of studies conducted at Marzano Research on instructional strategies.* Englewood, CO: Marzano Research.

Hazelwood School District et al. v. Kuhlmeier et al., 484 U.S. (1988).

Henn, S. (2013, April 3). Facebook's online speech rules keep users on a tight leash [Web log post]. Accessed at www.npr.org/blogs/alltechconsidered/2013/04/03/176147408/facebooks-online-speech-rules-keep-users-on-a -tight-leash on July 13, 2013.

Hepburn, L., & Hemenway, D. (2004). Firearm availability and homicide: A review of the literature. *Aggression and Violent Behavior: A Review Journal, 9*(4), 417–440.

Hess, D. E. (2002). Discussing controversial public issues in secondary social studies classrooms: Learning from skilled teachers. *Theory and Research in Social Education, 30*(1), 10–41.

Hess, D. (2011). Discussions that drive democracy. *Educational Leadership, 69*(1), 69–73.

Hillocks, G., Jr. (2011). *Teaching argument writing, grades 6–12: Supporting claims with relevant evidence and clear reasoning.* Portsmouth, NH: Heinemann.

Hlavach, L., & Freivogel, W. H. (2011). Ethical implications of anonymous comments posted to online news stories. *Journal of Mass Media Ethics, 26*(1), 21–37.

Hof, P. R., & Van der Gucht, E. (2007). Structure of the cerebral cortex of the humpback whale, Megaptera novaeangliae (Cetacea, Mysticeti, Balaenopteridae). *The Anatomical Record, 290*(1), 1–31.

Huckfeldt, R., & Sprague, J. (1995). *Citizens, politics, and social communication: Information and influence in an election campaign.* Cambridge, England: Cambridge University Press.

Hughes, T. P., Baird, A. H., Bellwood, D. R., Card, M., Connolly, S. R., Folke, C., et al. (2003). Climate change, human impacts, and the resilience of coral reefs. *Science, 301*(5635), 929–933. Accessed at www.sciencemag.org/content/301/5635/929.abstract?sid=2ac9402f-4140–4ac1–8997-e07d73bb706c on July 24, 2013.

Humes, W. (2012). Democracy, trust and respect. In P. Cowan & H. Maitles (Eds.), *Teaching controversial issues in the classroom: Key issues and debates* (pp. 13–23). New York: Continuum.

Hunter, R. (2004). *Madeline Hunter's mastery teaching: Increasing instructional effectiveness in elementary and secondary schools.* Thousand Oaks, CA: Corwin Press.

Intelligence Squared U.S. (Producer). (n.d.). *Past debate archives* [Video file]. Accessed at http://intelligencesquaredus.org/debates/past-debates on March 6, 2014.

Intelligence Squared U.S. (Producer). (2011, June 9). *Freedom of the press does not extend to state secrets* [Debate transcript]. Accessed at http://intelligencesquaredus.org/images/debates/past/transcripts/free-press.pdf on July 11, 2013.

Intelligence Squared U.S. (Producer). (2012). *Ban college football* [Debate transcript]. Accessed at http://intelligencesquaredus.org/images/debates/past/transcripts/ban-college-football.pdf on April 4, 2014.

Intelligence Squared U.S. (Producer). (2013, April 4). *Abolish the minimum wage* [Debate transcript]. Accessed at http://intelligencesquaredus.org/images/debates/past/transcripts/040313%20minimum%20wage.pdf on July 11, 2013.

IOC chief Jacques Rogge admits "question mark" over McDonald's and Coca-Cola sponsoring Olympics. (2012, July 9). *The Telegraph.* Accessed at www.telegraph.co.uk/sport/olympics/news/9385751/IOC-chief-Jacques-Rogge-admits-question-mark-over-McDonalds-and-Coca-Cola-sponsoring-Olympics.html on July 12, 2013.

Israel, D. (2009). *Staying in school: Arts education and New York City high school graduation rates* (A report for the Center of Arts Education). New York: Center for Arts Education. Accessed at www.cae-nyc.org/sites/default/files/docs/CAE_Arts_and_Graduation_Report.pdf on November 8, 2013.

Ito, T. A., Larsen, J. T., Smith, N. K., & Cacioppo, J. T. (2002). Negative information weighs more heavily on the brain: The negativity bias in evaluative categorizations. In J. T. Cacioppo (Ed.), *Foundations in social neuroscience* (pp. 575–597). Cambridge, MA: MIT Press.

Johnson-Laird, P. N. (1983). *Mental models.* Cambridge, MA: Harvard University Press.

Johnson-Laird, P. N., & Byrne, R. M. J. (1991). *Deduction (Essays in cognitive psychology).* Hillsdale, NJ: Erlbaum.

Jones, J. (2005, August 15). Most smokers want to quit, but feel they are addicted. *Gallup.* Accessed at www.gallup.com/poll/17830/most-smokers-want-quit-feel-they-addicted.aspx on December 20, 2013.

Jones, M., & Wheatley, J. (1990). Gender differences in student-teacher interactions in science classrooms. *Journal of Research in Science Teaching, 27*(9), 861–874.

Jurkowitz, M., Hitlin, P., Mitchell, A., Santhanam, L., Adams, S., Anderson, M., et al. (2013). *The state of the news media 2013: The changing TV news landscape.* Washington, DC: Pew Research Center. Accessed at http://stateofthemedia.org/2013/the-changing-tv-news-landscape/ on July 12, 2013.

Kahne, J., Rodriguez, M., Smith, B., & Thiede, K. (2000). Developing citizens for democracy? Assessing opportunities to learn in Chicago's social studies classrooms. *Theory and Research in Social Education, 28*(3), 311–338.

Kaid, L. L., McKinney, M. S., & Tedesco, J. C. (2007). Introduction: Political information efficacy and young voters. *American Behavioral Scientist, 50*(9), 1093–1111.

Kasser, S. L. (1995). *Inclusive games: Movement fun for everyone!* Champaign, IL: Human Kinetics.

Kirby, D. (2013). *Death at SeaWorld: Shamu and the dark side of killer whales in captivity.* New York: St. Martin's Griffin.

Kling, R., Lee, Y.-C., Teich, A., & Frankel, M. S. (1999). Assessing anonymous communication on the Internet: Policy deliberations. *Information Society, 15*(2), 79–90.

LaBarre, S. (2013, September 24). Why we're shutting off our comments. *Popular Science.* Accessed at www.popsci.com /science/article/2013-09/why-were-shutting-our-comments on October 18, 2013.

Lauzen, M. M. (2012). It's a man's (celluloid) world: On-screen representations of female characters in the top 100 films of 2011. *Center for the Study of Women in Television and Film.* Accessed at http://womenintvfilm.sdsu.edu /files/2011_Its_a_Mans_World_Exec_Summ.pdf on November 6, 2013.

Lemov, D. (2010). *Teach like a champion: 49 techniques that put students on the path to college.* San Francisco: Jossey-Bass.

Leshner, A. I., Altevogt, B. M., Lee, A. F., McCoy, M. A., & Kelley, P. W. (2013). *Priorities for research to reduce the threat of firearm-related violence.* Washington, DC: National Academies Press.

Liu, Y. Y. (2013). *The third shift: Child care needs and access for working mothers in restaurants.* New York: Restaurant Opportunities Centers United. Accessed at http://rocunited.org/the-third-shift/ on July 24, 2013.

Lomborg, B. (2013, March 11). Bjorn Lomborg: Green cars have a dirty little secret. *Wall Street Journal.* Accessed at http://online.wsj.com/news/articles/SB10001424127887324128504578346913994914472 on December 9, 2013.

Lowen, C., Waitt, C. (Producers), & Hirsch, L. (Director & Producer). (2011). *Bully* [Motion picture]. United States: The Weinstein Company.

Lowry, N., & Johnson, D. W. (1981). Effects of controversy on epistemic curiosity, achievement, and attitudes. *The Journal of Social Psychology, 115*(1), 31–43.

Mankiw, N. G. (2010, June 5). Can a soda tax save us from ourselves? *The New York Times.* Accessed at www.nytimes .com/2010/06/06/business/06view.html on November 7, 2013.

Mann, M. E., & Selin, H. (2013). *Global warming.* Accessed at www.britannica.com/EBchecked/topic/235402/global -warming on July 3, 2013.

Marzano, R. J. (2007). *The art and science of teaching: A comprehensive framework for effective instruction.* Alexandria, VA: Association for Supervision and Curriculum Development.

Marzano, R. J., Brandt, R. S., Hughes, C. S., Jones, B. F., Presseisen, B. Z., Rankin, S. C., et al. (1988). *Dimensions of thinking: A framework for curriculum and instruction.* Alexandria, VA: Association for Supervision and Curriculum Development.

Marzano, R. J., Hagerty, P. J., Valencia, S. W., & DiStefano, P. P. (1987). *Reading diagnosis and instruction: Theory into practice.* Englewood Cliffs, NJ: Prentice Hall.

Marzano, R. J., & Heflebower, T. (2012). *Teaching & assessing 21st century skills.* Bloomington, IN: Marzano Research.

Marzano, R. J., & Pickering, D. J. (with Arredondo, D. E., Blackburn, G. J., Brandt, R. S., Moffett, C. A., Paynter, D. E., Pollock, J. E., et al.). (1997). *Dimensions of learning: Teacher's manual* (2nd ed.). Alexandria, VA: Association for Supervision and Curriculum Development.

Matsumura, L. C., Slater, S. C., & Crosson, A. (2008). Classroom climate, rigorous instruction and curriculum, and students' interactions in urban middle schools. *The Elementary School Journal, 108*(4), 293–312.

McCann, M. (2005). Arrested NBA players: Education, age, and experience [Web log post]. Accessed at http://sports-law .blogspot.com/2005/07/nba-players-that-get-in-trouble-with_20.html on July 12, 2013.

McCaughey, M., & Ayers, M. D. (2003). *Cyberactivism: Online activism in theory and practice.* New York: Routledge.

McGraw, C. (2013, August 25). School bus ads bring needed revenue to Colorado Springs-area districts. *The Colorado Springs Gazette*. Accessed at http://gazette.com/school-bus-ads-bring-needed-revenue-to-colorado-springs-area-districts/article/1505252 on November 7, 2013.

McWatt, J. (2012, July 11). McDonald's and Coca Cola should have no place in Olympics, says Wales' top doctor. *WalesOnline*. Accessed at www.walesonline.co.uk/news/wales-news/mcdonalds-coca-cola-should-no-2027266 on July 12, 2013.

Michaels, S., O'Connor, M. C., & Hall, M. W. (with Resnick, B.). (2010). *Accountable Talk® sourcebook: For classroom conversation that works*. Pittsburgh, PA: University of Pittsburgh. Accessed at http://2012-leadership-forum.iste.wikispaces.net/file/view/AT-Sourcebook.pdf on December 20, 2013.

Milewski, G. B., Johnson, D., Glazer, N., & Kubota, M. (2005). *A survey to evaluate the alignment of the new SAT Writing and Critical Reading sections to curricula and instructional practices* (College Board Research Report No. 2005–1/ETS RR-05–07). New York: College Entrance Examination Board.

Milgram, S. (1963). Behavioral study of obedience. *The Journal of Abnormal and Social Psychology, 67*(4), 371–378.

Miller, A. (2003). *The crucible*. New York: Penguin. (Original work published 1953)

Miller, R., & Pedro, J. (2006). Creating respectful classroom environments. *Early Childhood Education Journal, 33*(5), 293–299.

Milton, J. (1644). *Areopagitica; A speech of Mr. John Milton for the Liberty of Unlicenc'd Printing, to the Parlament of England* [Speech]. Accessed at www.dartmouth.edu/~milton/reading_room/areopagitica/ on October 14, 2013.

Moriarty, B., Douglas, G., Punch, K., & Hattie, J. (1995). The importance of self-efficacy as a mediating variable between learning environments and achievement. *British Journal of Educational Psychology, 65*(1), 73–84.

Mossberger, K., Tolbert, C. J., & McNeal, R. S. (2007). *Digital citizenship: The Internet, society and participation*. Cambridge, MA: MIT Press.

National Center for Education Statistics. (2010). *The nation's report card: Civics 2010—National Assessment of Educational Progress at grades 4, 8, and 12*. Accessed at http://nces.ed.gov/nationsreportcard/pdf/main2010/2011466.pdf on October 18, 2013.

National Center for Injury Prevention and Control. (2012). *Understanding school violence: Fact sheet*. Accessed at www.cdc.gov/violenceprevention/pdf/schoolviolence_factsheet-a.pdf on December 19, 2013.

National Congress of American Indians. (2013). *Anti-defamation & mascots*. Accessed at www.ncai.org/policy-issues/community-and-culture/anti-defamation-mascots on July 12, 2013.

National Governors Association Center for Best Practices & Council of Chief State School Officers. (2010a). *Common Core State Standards for English language arts & literacy in history/social studies, science, and technical subjects*. Washington, DC: Authors.

National Governors Association Center for Best Practices & Council of Chief State School Officers. (2010b). *Common Core State Standards for English language arts & literacy in history/social studies, science, and technical subjects—Appendix A: Research supporting key elements of the standards and glossary of key terms*. Washington, DC: Authors.

National Governors Association Center for Best Practices & Council of Chief State School Officers. (2010c). *Common Core State Standards for English language arts & literacy in history/social studies, science, and technical subjects—Appendix B: Key exemplars and sample performance tasks*. Washington, DC: Authors.

National Governors Association Center for Best Practices & Council of Chief State School Officers. (2010d). *Common Core State Standards for mathematics*. Washington, DC: Authors.

Nicks, S. (2010, April 29). The 2010 TIME 100: Taylor Swift. *TIME*. Accessed at www.time.com/time/specials/packages/article/0,28804,1984685_1984940_1985536,00.html on July 25, 2013.

Norwood, C. (1943). *Curriculum and examination in secondary schools*. London: HMSO.

Nystrand, M., Gamoran, A., & Carbonaro, W. (1998). *Towards an ecology of learning: The case of classroom discourse and its effects on writing in high school English and Social Studies* (CELA Research Report No. 11001). Accessed at www.albany.edu/cela/reports/nystrand/nystrandtowards11001.pdf on December 19, 2013.

Office of the U.S. Surgeon General. (2001). *Youth violence: A report of the Surgeon General*. Rockville, MD: Author. Accessed at www.ncbi.nlm.nih.gov/books/NBK44294/ on November 8, 2013.

Onyper, S. V., Carr, T. L., Farrar, J. S., & Floyd, B. R. (2011). Cognitive advantages of chewing gum: Now you see them, now you don't. *Appetite, 57*(2), 321–328.

Open Society Foundations. (2011). *Unveiling the truth: Why 32 Muslim women wear the full-face veil in France*. Accessed at www.opensocietyfoundations.org/sites/default/files/unveiling-factsheet-english-20110411.pdf on July 12, 2013.

Organisation for Economic Co-operation and Development. (2013). *Better life index*. Accessed at www.oecdbetterlifeindex.org/countries/australia/ on December 20, 2013.

Papacharissi, Z. (2004). Democracy on-line: Civility, politeness, and the democratic potential of on-line political discussion groups. *New Media and Society, 6*(2), 259–284.

Pew Research Center. (2009, October). *Mapping the global Muslim population: A report on the size and distribution of the world's Muslim population*. Accessed at www.pewforum.org/uploadedfiles/Topics/Demographics/Muslimpopulation.pdf on July 24, 2013.

Pew Research Center. (2013). *High school drop-out rate at record low: Hispanic high school graduates pass whites in rate of college enrollment*. Washington, DC: Author. Accessed at www.pewhispanic.org/files/2013/05/PHC_college_enrollment_2013-05.pdf on December 20, 2013.

Ponter, J. R. (1999). Academic achievement and the need for a comprehensive, developmental music curriculum. *NASSP Bulletin, 83*(604), 108–114.

Postman, N. (1997). *The end of education: Redefining the value of school*. New York: Knopf.

Radiolab. (2010, August 9). *Bonus video: Words* [Video file]. Accessed at www.radiolab.org/story/91974-bonus-video-words/ on April 4, 2014.

Rauscher, F. H., Shaw, G. L., & Ky, K. N. (1993). Music and spatial task performance. *Nature, 365*, 611.

Reader, B. (2012). Free press vs. free speech? The rhetoric of "civility" in regard to anonymous online comments. *Journalism and Mass Communication Quarterly, 89*(3), 495–513.

Reeve, J., & Deci, E. L. (1996). Elements of the competitive situation that affect intrinsic motivation. *Personality and Social Psychology Bulletin, 22*(1), 24–33.

Reno v. American Civil Liberties Union, 521 U.S. 844 (1997).

Reyes, M. R., Brackett, M. A., Rivers, S. E., White, M., & Salovey, P. (2012). Classroom emotional climate, student engagement, and academic achievement. *Journal of Educational Psychology, 104*(3), 700–712.

Roeper, R. (2012, April 4). Movie's MPAA should be rated I—for inconsistent. *Chicago Sun-Times*. Accessed at www.suntimes.com/news/roeper/11721589-452/movies-mpaa-should-be-rated-i-for-inconsistent.html on July 25, 2013.

Roozendaal, B. (2003). Systems mediating acute glucocorticoid effects on memory consolidation and retrieval. *Progress in Neuro-Psychopharmacology and Biological Psychiatry, 27*(8), 1213–1223.

Rowe, M. B. (1987). Wait time: Slowing down may be a way of speeding up. *American Educator, 11*(1), 38–43.

Ryan, J., Zwerling, C., & Orav, E. J. (1992). Occupational risks associated with cigarette smoking: A prospective study. *American Journal of Public Health, 82*(1), 29–32.

Sadker, M., & Sadker, D. (1995). *Failing at fairness: How our schools cheat girls.* New York: Touchstone Press.

Salen, K., & Zimmerman, E. (2004). *Rules of play: Game design fundamentals.* Cambridge, MA: MIT Press.

Sarafian, K., Stanton, A., Lasseter, J., Docter, P. (Producers), Andrews, M., & Chapman, B. (Directors). (2012). *Brave* [Motion picture]. United States: Walt Disney and Pixar.

Scruton, R., Ellis-Jones, A., & O'Keefe, D. (1985). *Education and indoctrination: An attempt at definition and a review of social and political implications.* Harrow, England: Education Research Centre.

Shah, D. V., Cho, J., Eveland, W. P., Jr., & Kwak, N. (2005). Information and expression in a digital age: Modeling Internet effects on civic participation. *Communication Research, 32*(5), 531–565.

Sharpton, A., & Hitchens, C. (n.d.). *Al Sharpton and Christopher Hitchens debate religion* [Video file]. Accessed at www.learnoutloud.com/Free-Audio-Video/Religion-and-Spirituality/Christianity/Al-Sharpton-and-Christopher-Hitchens-Debate/26418 on March 6, 2014.

Shaver, J., Davis, O. L., Jr., & Helburn, S. W. (1978). *An interpretative report on the status of precollege social studies education based on three NSF-funded studies* (Report to the National Science Foundation). Washington, DC: National Council for the Social Studies. Accessed at http://files.eric.ed.gov/fulltext/ED164363.pdf on March 31, 2014.

Shils, E. (1992). *Civility and civil society.* New York: Paragon House.

Shors, T. J., Weiss, C., & Thompson, R. F. (1992). Stress induced facilitation of classical conditioning. *Science, 257*(5069), 537–539.

Shulman, P. (2005, November 13). Harry who? *The New York Times.* Accessed at www.nytimes.com/2005/11/13/books/review/13shulman.html?pagewanted=all&_r=0 on April 4, 2014.

Sifferlin, A. (2012, November 19). What you should know about caffeine. *TIME Magazine.* Accessed at http://healthland.time.com/2012/11/19/what-you-should-know-about-caffeine/ on July 24, 2013.

Simmonds, M. P., Haraguchi, K., Endo, T., Cipriano, F., Palumbi, S. R., & Troisi, G. M. (2002). Human health significance of organochlorine and mercury contaminants in Japanese whale meat. *Journal of Toxicology and Environmental Health, 65*(17), 1211–1235.

Smith, A. (2012). *Cell Internet use 2012.* Washington, DC: Pew Research Center. Accessed at http://pewinternet.org/Reports/2012/Cell-Internet-Use-2012.aspx on July 11, 2013.

Smith, S. (2003). *Five-minute mini-mysteries.* New York: Sterling.

Sobol, D. J. (1967). *Two-minute mysteries.* New York: Scholastic.

Stromblad, C. (2011, June 24). *Neil Young gives props to Taylor Swift.* Accessed at http://theboot.com/neil-young-taylor-swift/ on July 25, 2013.

Swift, T., Martin, M., & Shellback. (2012a). I knew you were trouble [Recorded by Taylor Swift]. On *Red* [CD]. Nashville, TN: Big Machine Records.

Swift, T., Martin, M., & Shellback. (2012b). We are never ever getting back together [Recorded by Taylor Swift]. On *Red* [CD]. Nashville, TN: Big Machine Records.

Text of Obama's speech at the U.N. (2013, September 24). *The New York Times.* Accessed at www.nytimes.com/2013/09/25/us/politics/text-of-obamas-speech-at-the-un.html on December 12, 2013.

Thayer, E. L. (1888, June 3). Casey at the bat [Poem]. *The Daily Examiner.* Accessed at http://blogs.loc.gov/catbird/2013/06/the-first-publication-of-casey-at-the-bat/ on December 4, 2013.

Thompson, R. S., Rivara, F. P., & Thompson, D. C. (1989). A case-control study of the effectiveness of bicycle safety helmets. *The New England Journal of Medicine, 320*(21), 1361–1367.

TIME for Kids Staff. (2011, December 13). *Debate! Should dodge ball be banned in schools?* Accessed at www.timeforkids .com/news/debate/23691 on November 7, 2013.

TIME for Kids Staff. (2013, September 13). *Debate! Should computers grade student essays?* Accessed at www.timeforkids .com/news/debate/103106 on November 7, 2013.

Tobin, K. (1987). The role of wait time in higher cognitive level learning. *Review of Educational Research, 57*(1), 69–95.

Torney-Purta, J., Lehmann, R., Oswald, H., & Shulz, W. (2001). *Citizenship and education in twenty-eight countries: Civic knowledge and engagement at age fourteen.* Amsterdam, the Netherlands: International Association for the Evaluation of Educational Achievement.

Totten, S. (1999). Should there be Holocaust education for K–4 students? The answer is no. *Social Studies and the Young Learner, 12*(1), 36–39.

Toulmin, S. E. (2003). *The uses of argument* (Updated ed.). Cambridge, England: Cambridge University Press.

Toulmin, S. E., Rieke, R. D., & Janik, A. (1981). *An introduction to reasoning.* New York: Macmillan.

Treat, L. (1981). *Crime and puzzlement: 24 solve-them-yourself picture mysteries.* Jaffrey, NH: Godine.

Treat, L. (1982). *Crime and puzzlement 2: More solve-them-yourself picture mysteries.* Jaffrey, NH: Godine.

Treat, L. (2010). *You're the detective! 24 solve-them-yourself mysteries.* Jaffrey, NH: Godine.

U.S. Const. amend. II.

U.S. Consumer Product Safety Commission. (2008). *Spring shifts kids' sports into high gear, CPSC and Chicago White Sox encourage use of safety gear* (Release No. 08–252). Accessed at www.cpsc.gov/en/Newsroom/News-Releases/2008 /Spring-Shifts-Kids-Sports-Into-High-Gear-CPSC-and-Chicago-White-Sox-Encourage-Use-of-Safety-Gear/ on December 20, 2013.

U.S. Department of Agriculture. (2011, June 2). First lady, agriculture secretary launch My Plate icon as a new reminder to help consumers to make healthier food choices [Press release]. Accessed at www.cnpp.usda.gov/Publications/MyPlate /PressRelease.pdf on December 20, 2013.

U.S. Energy Information Administration. (2013, April). *Annual energy outlook 2013 with projections to 2040.* Washington, DC: Author. Accessed at www.eia.gov/forecasts/aeo/pdf/0383(2013).pdf on December 4, 2013.

USA Today college football coach salary database, 2006–2011. (2011). *USA Today.* Accessed at http://usatoday30 .usatoday.com/sports/college/football/story/2011-11-17/cover-college-football-coaches-salaries-rise/51242232 /1 on December 20, 2013.

Van Honk, J., Kessels, R. P. C., Putnam, P., Jager, G., Koppeschaar, H. P. F., & Postma, A. (2003). Attentionally modulated effects of cortisol and mood on memory for emotional faces in healthy young males. *Psychoneuroendocrinology, 28*(7), 941–948.

Viacom International. (2003). Adam Sandler, Mike Myers, Amanda Bynes, Frankie Muniz, Jennifer Love Hewitt, Jackie Chan, SpongeBob SquarePants, Tony Hawk, Michelle Kwan, B2K, Los Angeles Lakers and more score at Nickelodeon's 16th Annual Kids' Choice Awards [Press release]. Accessed at www.nickkcapress.com/2003KCA/ on July 15, 2013.

Viacom International. (2004). Jim Carrey, Amanda Bynes, Frankie Muniz, Outkast, Ellen Degeneres, Hilary Duff, Tony Hawk, "Harry Potter," Mia Hamm, "SpongeBob SquarePants," Nelly, Los Angeles Lakers and more capture top honors at Nickelodeon's 17th Annual Kids' Choice Awards [Press release]. Accessed at www.nickkcapress .com/2004KCA/ on July 15, 2013.

Viacom International. (2005). 2005 Kids' Choice Awards winners: Adam Sandler, Hilary Duff, Will Smith, Usher, Avril Lavigne, Romeo, Raven, "SpongeBob SquarePants," Tony Hawk, Green Day, "Lemony Snicket's A Series Of Unfortunate Events" and more grab top honors at Nickelodeon's 18th Annual Kids' Choice Awards [Press release]. Accessed at www.nickkcapress.com/2005KCA/winnersrelease.php on July 15, 2013.

Viacom International. (2006). Winners release: Will Smith, Lindsay Lohan, Chris Rock, Kelly Clarkson, Drake Bell, Jamie Lynn Spears, Lance Armstrong, Jesse McCartney, "SpongeBob SquarePants," "Harry Potter," Green Day and more score top honors at Nickelodeon's 19th Annual Kids' Choice Awards [Press release]. Accessed at www .nickkcapress.com/2006KCA/winnersrelease.php on July 15, 2013.

Viacom International. (2007). 2007 KCA winners release: Adam Sandler, Dakota Fanning, Beyoncé, Justin Timberlake, Queen Latifah, Ben Stiller, SpongeBob SquarePants, Harry Potter, American Idol, Happy Feet—and more—walk off with honors at Nickelodeon's slime-soaked, milestone 20th Annual Kids' Choice Awards [Press release]. Accessed at www.nickkcapress.com/2007KCA/winners.php on July 15, 2013.

Viacom International. (2009). 2009 winners release: Beyoncé, Will Smith, Vanessa Hudgens, Jack Black, iCarly, Selena Gomez, SpongeBob SquarePants, The Jonas Brothers, Jesse McCartney, Miley Cyrus, Madagascar: Escape 2 Africa, and more nab top honors at Nickelodeon's 22nd Annual Kids' Choice Awards [Press release]. Accessed at www .nickkcapress.com/2009KCA/winners.php on July 15, 2013.

Viacom International. (2010). Taylor Lautner, Miley Cyrus, iCarly, Jim Carrey, Taylor Swift, Black Eyed Peas, SpongeBob SquarePants, Ryan Sheckler, Jay-Z, Selena Gomez, Alvin and the Chipmunks: The Squeakquel, Misty May Treanor and more pick up coveted orange blimps at Nickelodeon's 23rd Annual Kids' Choice Awards [Press release]. Accessed at www.nickkcapress.com/2010KCA/releases/winners/ on July 15, 2013.

Viacom International. (2011). Johnny Depp, Justin Bieber, Selena Gomez, iCarly, The Black Eyed Peas, Miley Cyrus, Jennette McCurdy, SpongeBob SquarePants, Eddie Murphy, Despicable Me, Shaquille O'Neal and more win coveted orange blimps at Nickelodeon's 2011 Kids' Choice Awards [Press release]. Accessed at http://nickkcapress .com/2011KCA/release/winners on July 15, 2013.

Viacom International. (2012). Katy Perry, Tim Tebow, Taylor Lautner, Big Time Rush, Selena Gomez, Kristen Stewart, Victorious, LMFAO, SpongeBob SquarePants, Justin Bieber, Puss In Boots and more win coveted orange blimps at Nickelodeon's 25th Annual Kids' Choice Awards [Press release]. Accessed at http://nickkcapress.com/2012KCA /releases/winners1 on July 15, 2013.

Viacom International. (2013). Katy Perry, Selena Gomez, Justin Bieber, One Direction, Kristen Stewart, Dwayne Johnson, LeBron James, SpongeBob SquarePants, Johnny Depp, The Hunger Games and more win coveted orange blimps at Nickelodeon's 26th Annual Kids' Choice Awards [Press release]. Accessed at http://nickkcapress.com/2013KCA /release/winners2 on July 15, 2013.

Wagner, T. (2008). *The global achievement gap: Why even our best schools don't teach the new survival skills our children need—And what we can do about it*. New York: Basic Books.

Wang, W., Parker, K., & Taylor, P. (2013, May 29). *Breadwinner moms*. Washington, DC: Pew Research Center. Accessed at www.pewsocialtrends.org/files/2013/05/Breadwinner_moms_final.pdf on July 12, 2013.

Wilson, L. (2013, February). *Shades of green: Electric cars' carbon emissions around the globe*. Accessed at http:// shrinkthatfootprint.com/wp-content/uploads/2013/02/Shades-of-Green-Full-Report.pdf on December 4, 2013.

Wood, T. D. (2012). Backpacks: How to load. Accessed at www.rei.com/learn/expert-advice/loading-backpack.html on July 24, 2013.

World Lung Foundation. (2012). *New tobacco atlas estimates U.S. $35 billion tobacco industry profits and almost 6 million annual deaths*. Accessed at www.worldlungfoundation.org/ht/display/ReleaseDetails/i/20439/pid/6858 on December 20, 2013.

Wyatt, R. O., Katz, E., & Kim, J. (2000). Bridging the spheres: Political and personal conversation in public and private spaces. *Journal of Communication, 50*(1), 71–92.

xkcd.com. (2008a). *Duty calls* [Comic]. Accessed at http://xkcd.com/386/ on December 19, 2013.

xkcd.com. (2008b). *Internet argument* [Comic]. Accessed at http://xkcd.com/438/ on March 27, 2014.

Zehner, O. (2013, June 30). *Unclean at any speed: Electric cars don't solve the automobile's environmental problem*s. Accessed at http://spectrum.ieee.org/energy/renewables/unclean-at-any-speed on December 9, 2013.

Index

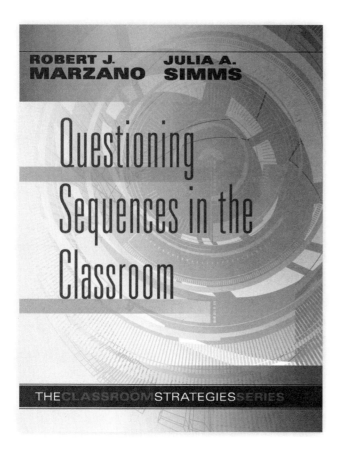

Enhance students'
argumentation skills

 Signature PD Service

Games and Activities for Teaching Argumentation Workshop

Based on an analysis of argumentation in the Common Core State Standards, this workshop presents 13 component skills critical for student success as they construct and support claims.

Learn concrete strategies and processes for directly teaching the 13 skills, along with a variety of classroom games and activities that students can engage in to practice and reinforce those skills. Appropriate for elementary, middle, and high school teachers, this workshop will give you the tools you need to help students understand and practice argumentation in the classroom.

Benefits

- Identify specific elements of the CCSS that relate to argumentation.
- Uncover component skills that students need to learn as they develop a deeper capacity to construct and support claims.
- Discover practical strategies and mini-lesson ideas for teaching argumentation skills in your classroom.
- Explore ways to incorporate games and activities into your lessons, from on-the-fly sponge activities to team-based games and end-of-unit extended projects.

Learn more!

marzanoresearch.com/OnsitePD
888.849.0851